Inside the Bubble

Inside the Bubble: Campaigns, Caucuses, and the Future of the Presidential Nomination Process is a behind-the-scenes look at the 2020 Democratic nomination process focusing on the Iowa caucuses and the campaign workers who located there. For decades, Iowa held the first contest in the presidential nomination process, and individuals interested in campaign work considered it a "holy grail." But in 2020, a record number of Democrats seeking to unseat President Trump – and the hundreds of young campaign workers who located to Iowa – created a political event unmatched in scope and scale. Those workers, embedded in the caucus bubble, focused for months on finding supporters for their candidate and ensuring they attended their precinct event – the first step in selecting delegates to the national convention. And then Caucus Day came, and with it a technology-driven fiasco that seemed to foreshadow a year of pandemic and protest. The lessons learned in 2020 underscored the importance of local staff who organize and mobilize supporters for a candidate in whom they believe. And those lessons are applicable to any race of any party in any state. For students of US politics as well as aspiring candidates, political journalists, and campaign professionals, this book captures the drama and human perspective of campaigns and elections in America.

Barbara Trish is Professor of Political Science at Grinnell College, Grinnell, Iowa. She directs the Rosenfield Program in Public Affairs, International Relations, and Human Rights.

Bill Menner is a consultant on rural development and rural health. He was a White House appointee within the US Department of Agriculture and previously worked as a public radio political reporter.

"I've covered 10 Iowa caucuses and made more than 60 trips to the state – and still I learned something on nearly every page. Memo to 2024 campaign reporters: Don't even think about flying into Des Moines or Cedar Rapids without a copy of this book in your baggage."

David Shribman, *Pulitzer winning political columnist*

"This book is an invaluable resource for political journalists trying to make sense of the Iowa caucuses. This account makes the caucuses, with all their arcane rules and quirky traditions, accessible and compelling, told from the vantage point of the staffers who make them happen."

Melanie Mason, *Political Reporter*, Los Angeles Times

"Through the window of the 2020 Iowa caucus, *Inside the Bubble* views the various players (candidates, surrogates, staffers, consultants, contractors, journalists, activists, voters, and technologies) and the politics of the 2020 presidential nomination campaign. Students of campaign politics, as well as their recent and aspiring participants, will benefit from this excellent in-depth examination of the 'nuts and bolts' of campaigns and its vignettes about the personal experiences of its players."

Paul A. Beck, *Ohio State University (Emeritus)*

"This really well-written book captures the drama and importance of the Iowa caucuses – and of US presidential campaigns more generally. It would be a great choice for classes on campaigns, political parties, and elections. My students love to hear about young people's experiences in politics and campaigns, which then open their minds to understanding American politics."

Marjorie R. Hershey, *Indiana University (Emerita)*

"*Inside the Bubble* explains the incredible complexities and nuance of the first presidential nominating contest, specifically the 2020 Caucus, in accessible and easy-to-understand terms. By heavily incorporating the voices of campaign staffers, this book presents a unique, engaging, and human perspective on the Iowa Caucus."

Jimmy Dahman, *Former Campaign Staffer, Biden for President, Pete for America*

Inside the Bubble
Campaigns, Caucuses, and the Future
of the Presidential Nomination Process

Barbara Trish and Bill Menner

NEW YORK AND LONDON

First published 2022
by Routledge
605 Third Avenue, New York, NY 10158

and by Routledge
2 Park Square, Milton Park, Abingdon, Oxon OX14 4RN

Routledge is an imprint of the Taylor & Francis Group, an informa business

© 2022 Taylor & Francis

The right of Barbara Trish and Bill Menner to be identified as authors of this work has been asserted by them in accordance with sections 77 and 78 of the Copyright, Designs and Patents Act 1988.

All rights reserved. No part of this book may be reprinted or reproduced or utilised in any form or by any electronic, mechanical, or other means, now known or hereafter invented, including photocopying and recording, or in any information storage or retrieval system, without permission in writing from the publishers.

Trademark notice: Product or corporate names may be trademarks or registered trademarks, and are used only for identification and explanation without intent to infringe.

Library of Congress Cataloging-in-Publication Data
Names: Trish, Barbara, 1961– author. | Menner, Bill, 1961– author.
Title: Inside the bubble : campaigns, caucuses, and the future of the presidential nomination process / Barbara Trish, Bill Menner.
Description: New York, N.Y.: Routledge, 2021. |
Includes bibliographical references and index.
Identifiers: LCCN 2021005250 (print) | LCCN 2021005251 (ebook) |
ISBN 9780367429782 (paperback) | ISBN 9781032039220 (hardback) |
ISBN 9781003189718 (ebook)
Subjects: LCSH: Presidents–United States–Nomination. |
Presidential campaigns–United States. | Primaries–United States. |
Political parties–United States.
Classification: LCC JK521 .T73 2021 (print) |
LCC JK521 (ebook) | DDC 324.2736–dc23
LC record available at https://lccn.loc.gov/2021005250
LC ebook record available at https://lccn.loc.gov/2021005251

ISBN: 978-1-032-03922-0 (hbk)
ISBN: 978-0-367-42978-2 (pbk)
ISBN: 978-1-003-18971-8 (ebk)

Typeset in Bembo
by Newgen Publishing UK

 Printed in the United Kingdom
by Henry Ling Limited

To D.A. Smith and John H. Kessel, friends and mentors.

Contents

Preface ix
List of Abbreviations x

1 One Year Out 1
2 The Promised Land 18
3 Setting Up Shop 33
4 Summertime 48
5 New Again 65
6 The Party Umbrella 79
7 Doubling Down 93
8 Engagement and Economics 113
9 The Final Stretch 127
10 Caucuses, Chaos, and Coronavirus 144
11 The Shadow of 2020 164

Index 168

Preface

Our deepest appreciation to the many individuals who responded to our requests for interviews or just visited with us, allowing us to become a part of their lives, even for a short while. We also owe much to the many people who helped in this project who aren't named or referenced in the book. In particular, Poweshiek County Democratic Party Co-Chair John Grennan provided invaluable insights, unfailingly. Grinnell College students David Gilbert and Leah Steding contributed deft research assistance. And each of our children – Jack, Robert, Ann, and Kate – supported the effort in tangible ways, often exactly when we needed their assistance.

One of our biggest challenges was to get approval from some of the campaigns to allow their staff to talk on the record. We are especially grateful to those campaigns that gave us access – and to the staff and others who spoke on the record. Campaign organizers are a particular focus in the book, and we protect their identities by using pseudonyms. For all others, with one exception, we rely on real names.

Over the years, we have provided supporter housing to campaign staffers. We've learned a lot from them and have enjoyed their company. We're appreciative of those who provided supporter housing – over a variety of campaigns – to our son Jack and to his wife, Jessica.

What good fortune to be able to work with Jennifer Knerr at Routledge and to get early, smart feedback from then-anonymous reviewers Peverill Squire, Laurie L. Rice, and Daniel Schlozman. Daniel Schlozman's "caucus bubble" metaphor helped us tremendously.

On one level, this is an account of a specific political cycle, the likes of which may never be seen again. But it is primarily an observation about the people in US party and campaign politics who do the heavy lifting of democracy. The staffers, activists, volunteers, voters, even candidates: Our hats are off to all of them.

Abbreviations

CCI	(Iowa) Citizens for Community Improvement
DCCC	Democratic Congressional Campaign Committee
DNC	Democratic National Committee
ED	Executive Director
FCC	Federal Communications Commission
FEC	Federal Elections Commission
GOTC	Get Out the Caucus
GOTV	Get Out the Vote
HQ	Headquarters
IBEW	International Brotherhood of Electrical Workers
IDP	Iowa Democratic Party
JJ	Jefferson-Jackson Dinner
LBJ	Lyndon Baines Johnson
LJ	Liberty and Justice Dinner
LUR	Lowest Unit Rate
NAMI	National Alliance on Mental Illness
NGP-VAN	Firm that provides VAN product
NSLVE	National Study of Learning, Voting and Engagement
PAC	Political Action Committee
P2P	Person to Person
PTO	Personal Time Off
RCV	Ranked-Choice Voting
RPI	Republican Party of Iowa
SDE	State Delegate Equivalent
UAW	United Auto Workers
UBI	Universal Basic Income
UFCW	The United Food and Commercial Workers Union
USPS	US Postal Service
VAN	Voter Activation Network

1 One Year Out

It was a Saturday morning in March 2019, raining steadily as Jacob Hamblin walked into the Malcom Auditorium, just a little late for the start of the county Democratic Party's odd-year caucus. He had arrived in Iowa one week earlier – from Ohio, his home state, where he'd handled outreach to colleges and universities for the Hillary Clinton campaign in 2016. This time around, he was working for New Jersey Senator Cory Booker. For Democrats in Iowa, odd-year caucuses – unlike *The Caucuses* – are obscure affairs – county party meetings during sleeper years when everyone's supposed to take a break from politics. Hardly anyone shows up, which makes sense given the time and location: 9 am on a weekend in the middle of winter in Malcom, IA. Population 272.[1]

The Malcom Auditorium isn't an auditorium by any conventional definition, and even "event space" seems way too ostentatious. The aging community center, featuring 60-year-old Malcom High School class photos, glass-enclosed historic basketballs, paneled walls and a foot-high raised stage, might as well have been a small church hall or a VFW bingo parlor circa 1965. There's no need for pretense since Malcom doesn't have many other places to gather, and no one in Iowa gets into politics because of aesthetics anyway. But for the 25 or so local Democrats who showed up – even though the caucuses were 11 months off – there was little time to fit in all the work that could make or break presidential hopefuls and the caucuses themselves.

Jacob was in Malcom on March 9, 2019, because that's what campaigns did. The room held some of the most eligible Democrats in the county – volunteers willing to show up, argue over platform positions, write checks, and knock on doors. Those folks are the currency of a successful caucus campaign, the raw material for any staffer who will need to persuade and mobilize Iowans to attend the caucuses. Good news for Jacob: the competition that day was light. Two John Delaney staffers were on hand with slick brochures, t-shirts, and bumper stickers. Delaney, the wealthy former congressman from Maryland, had freely spent his own money on his campaign since first arriving in the state 18 months earlier. Because of that, local Democrats in the room were accustomed to the Delaney presence. Staffers had been attending regular party meetings for months, reciting again that Saturday, more-or-less word-for-word, the Delaney bio most attendees had heard before.

The presence of a Cory Booker staffer, however, was something new, a sign that the 2020 Democratic nomination campaign to unseat President Donald Trump had begun in earnest. As of that Saturday in March, 11 hopefuls had officially declared their candidacy to seek the nomination of the Democratic Party, hoping to face off against the president in the general election, itself 20 months down the road. Democratic activists and elected office-holders in Iowa and nationwide had been waging their own campaigns of resistance to the president ever since his win over Hillary Clinton in November, 2016. This meeting was a concrete early step in the official process to pick the party's nominee. Booker, though certainly not a leading candidate, was credible, with experience and some degree of name recognition, though not yet making much of a dent in the polls.

The account you'll read in this book is, at one level, the story of a unique political contest: the 2020 Iowa caucuses. On another level, it represents any number of factors distinguishing modern campaign politics more broadly, with applicability well beyond this narrow case. There would be a similar cast of characters regardless of the setting: party and campaign activists, paid staff, new forms of allied organizations, and – of course – the media. The formal rules – the institutional structure – would matter in some fashion, maybe affecting the outcome but certainly helping to structure the decisions of the political actors and activities undertaken by them. Same for the norms of behavior and dynamics of politics unique to the political setting. While the uncertainty hanging over the caucuses in 2020 may have been more pronounced than that of many other political contests, uncertainty is a given in political life. The successes and failures of technology happen everywhere, not just in politics, and look closely enough and you'll see lingering in the technologies – and the rules, for that matter – the subtle and not-so-subtle messages about power.

This account about the Iowa caucuses is also a story about people – especially the paid staff, laboring in an industry marked by instability. Like wide swaths of the modern American workforce, they move from job to job, adjusting their career aspirations along the way to respond to opportunities in front of them. They find themselves living in circumstances they hadn't anticipated, needing to learn both the culture of the work and the place. And perhaps more than most, they have work and personal lives palpably entangled.

While this account of the Iowa caucuses starts in Malcom, versions of what transpired that day in March 2019 played out in other venues across Iowa and – to some extent – nationwide in the months preceding the formal February 2020 start of the nomination process. The details differ significantly by state for a variety of reasons: differences in rules and political culture, the shape of the field, and the competitive standing of the candidates, not to mention the candidates involved. Even the Republicans, whose re-nomination of Donald Trump was never much in question, went through something vaguely similar, though mostly under the radar.

The Democratic and Republican parties in the US each select their presidential nominees through complex, sequential processes. These differ from those processes used to select party nominees for other elective offices. They also depart from how presidential nominations worked in the past. But to understand the 2020 Democratic contest – especially as it transpired in Iowa, the first state in that formal process – it's important to turn the clock back. In fact, the reason that Jacob Hamblin, the Delaney staffers, and the smattering of local Democrats were at the Malcom Auditorium 18 months before the 2020 presidential election had something to do with 1968 and a few other years too.

The Shadow of the Past

1968 was a watershed year for presidential nomination politics, setting in motion fundamental changes in the way parties select their nominees (Ranney, 1975; Norrander, 2015; Kamarck, 2019). Nomination, like parties themselves, had evolved over the course of US history. But the changes after 1968 were distinctive, giving a real voice to average Democrats and Republicans. Before that, party insiders had a near monopoly on the power to pick their nominee, a situation that existed for more than 160 years.

The precise structure of insider control varied over time. Back in the early years of the republic – when political parties began to take shape – members of Congress selected the presidential nominees. That made sense because party presence was mostly confined to Congress. Soon parties evolved, and so did presidential nominations. In the first decades of the nineteenth century, electoral politics became more democratic, at least by the standards of the era. States extended the franchise to white males. They also gave voters a new role in presidential elections: allowing the voters – and not state legislators – to pick the states' electors in the Electoral College, which then, like now, elected the president (Aldrich, 1995).

New voters represent new opportunities, and US parties are skilled at adjusting to meet opportunities (Brewer & Maisel, 2018; Masket, 2016; Hershey, 2017; Reichley, 1992). Back in the early days of the republic they responded by building an organizational presence outside of Congress – committees, meetings, and rallies – to target those new voters. These early voter mobilization structures were largely at the local and state level, to be expected given that's where elections play out (Aldrich, 1995). Remember, the US federal system is populated by local and state elected officials. But soon the party organizational structure expanded to the national level. And in 1832, the Democratic Party – the offshoot of one of the two original parties – held a national convention to nominate its presidential nominee (Norrander, 2015). Placing nominations in the hands of a convention was a dramatic departure from having members of Congress pick the nominee.

Despite the change, party insiders still called the shots, and this insider control was reinforced by the way parties functioned in that era.

The mid-to-late nineteenth century was a golden age for US political parties because they were strong and essential for political life. The hook in many places was the spoils system, through which the party that controlled the government rewarded supporters with jobs and other things of value (Merton, 1957; Riordan, 1948; Hershey, 2017). The party "boss," typically an elected mayor or governor, presided over the patronage machine. Naturally, an exchange mechanism like this enhanced power and insulated those in office – and sometimes looked more like organized crime than democratic governance. It gave parties a stranglehold on political power.

Enter the Progressives. They were turn-of-the-twentieth-century reformers targeting political parties and pushing – successfully – a swath of reforms to limit party power: the civil service, the Australian ballot, and even voter registration. The large-scale adoption of the direct primary was particularly important because it built in a role for voters – voting in an election – in the selection of party nominees (Nardulli, 2013, pp. 239–242).[2] Parties had been experimenting with the direct primary for decades at the local level, and Wisconsin in 1903 was the first state to adopt legislation establishing statewide direct primaries (Ware, 2002). The use of state primaries for presidential nomination came a little later, beginning with Oregon in 1910. New Hampshire adopted the primary model in 1916, and starting in 1920 – and still in place in 2020 – held the first primary (Moore & Smith, 2015). It's important to note that presidential primaries are *indirect*, in the sense that voters cast ballots for delegates who will attend conventions, as opposed to directly selecting the nominee.

The early impact of the presidential primaries is tricky to judge. Something easy to overlook is that primaries subject parties to greater government control. Because they are essentially state-run elections, they inject government regulation into an activity that had previously been controlled by the parties themselves (Ware, 2002). In terms of effect on nomination outcomes, the impact may be less than imagined. When presidential primaries were first introduced and through much of the twentieth century, power still remained in the hands of party insiders – local party bosses and national party leaders who could interfere with the process if things weren't heading in a direction they supported (Kamarck, 2019). But the situation began to change dramatically in 1968 at the Democratic National Convention, where the challenge to insider control of presidential nomination became epic.

The 1968 Democratic nomination campaign occurred as the nation was mired in a bloody and unpopular war in Vietnam and, after April 1968, reeled from the assassination of civil rights leader Martin Luther King, Jr. The sitting president, Democrat Lyndon Johnson (LBJ), had opted not to seek re-nomination. And the final days of a three-way contest to lead the ticket were rocked by the assassination of Robert F. Kennedy, the front-runner and brother of the slain president John F. Kennedy.

When Democrats assembled for their national convention in Chicago in late August, the fault lines were already drawn: outsiders vs. insiders. Young anti-war protesters, aligned behind the candidacy of Minnesota Senator Eugene McCarthy, challenged the establishment, embodied by Chicago Mayor Richard J. Daley, the boss heading up one of the few remaining urban political machines and hosting the national convention. Prepared for violence and ready to agitate even before the convention started, Daley dispatched police to the streets, ostensibly to control the protesters. The result was intense and violent conflict, even permeating the floor of the convention (Farber, 1988). In the end, the Democrats nominated LBJ's vice-president, Hubert Humphrey, an establishment figure who had not competed in a single state delegate-selection contest and who carried the baggage of LBJ's unpopular escalation of the Vietnam War. Humphrey lost to Republican Richard Nixon in November in a campaign that focused in large part on law and order.

The image of Chicago in 1968 remains a symbol of the unrest of the 1960s. For the Democratic Party, it means even more. It's the point at which the party set in motion changes to its nomination procedures. Amid the turmoil of the convention and potential electoral ruin, and without a way to mend the internal divisions, the Democrats created a reform commission – the McGovern-Fraser Commission – to consider changes to the presidential nomination rules. By the start of the 1972 presidential cycle, the party had adopted many of the commission's proposals, including a complicated array of guidelines for state parties to follow in selecting delegates to the national nominating convention. These guidelines placed limits on the power of party insiders and structured open processes for delegate selection (Norrander, 2015), essentially mandating that the delegates selected through these processes would be the ones to select the nominee at the national convention. They also triggered what amounts to a continuous process of tweaking the rules that govern nomination, hoping to put in place a system that optimizes the likelihood of selecting a nominee who will win against the Republicans.

It's no stretch to say that contemporary presidential nomination politics is fundamentally about delegate selection. That's not always obvious, even to people who follow politics closely, since there's plenty of peripheral drama to capture attention. Even for campaign staff and volunteers, given the swirl of their day-to-day activities and everything necessary to run a credible campaign, it's easy to lose track of the endgame – winning states' delegates, the individuals who will go on to the national convention and formally select the presidential and vice-presidential nominees.

When a staffer like Jacob shows up in Iowa one year out, he's there to start laying the groundwork for the first step in Iowa's delegate-selection process, the precinct caucuses. Even though Democrats and Republicans in Iowa use a direct primary to nominate candidates for lower-level offices, for presidential nominations they have relied on a tiered system of meetings – caucuses and conventions – that extend over about a five-month period, starting with the precinct caucuses. At each step in the process, attendees selected delegates to the next stage. It all culminated with the selection of the state's delegates who would formally vote – at the party's national convention – for the presidential nominee. By March 2019, some Democratic candidates vying for the presidency had already begun to put staff in place in hopes of eventually winning national convention delegates in Iowa in a formal process to begin on February 3, 2020, the date of the Iowa caucuses.

The reality, though, is that Iowa is a small state, sending very few – just 41 in 2020 – delegates pledged to candidates to the national convention. Amounting to about 1% of the total number, their numerical impact likely would be insignificant. But the Iowa campaigns, as well as the results reported on caucus night, carry more weight than the number of delegates would suggest. That's because Iowa has held its caucuses before any other state's presidential nomination contest.

There's some history behind that too. 1972 is a good place to start.

In 1972, Iowa Democrats selected an early date for their caucuses, earlier than any other state's primary or caucuses. They didn't set out to be first, but were pushed into that position because of a combination of factors – custom, rules, and a bit of a fluke. But once the significance of going first became apparent, both parties in Iowa worked to protect the state's first-in-the-nation position.

The national Democratic Party in 1972 had opted for a July 9th national convention. Concerns about internal Democratic Party divisions at the 1968 Chicago convention clearly had some merit, and they probably contributed to Humphrey's general election loss to Nixon (Converse et al., 1969, fn 7). The choice of the national convention date followed the custom that the "out-party" – the party that doesn't control the presidency – goes first. This, in turn, triggered an early start for Iowa's delegate-section contest.

Iowa Democratic Party (IDP) rules required that meetings in that multi-stage caucus/convention sequence – starting with the precinct caucuses and ending with the state convention – be separated by at least 30 days (Squire, 1989). The rationale was that it took time for the party to process paper and distribute material for each meeting in the sequential process. In 1972, that time frame was not all that far-fetched, given that designing and printing materials back then was not as easy as it is now. So working back from that July 9 national convention date, the state convention could have been held as late as early June, which would allow for an early February date for the caucuses. But Iowa lore says the June date wouldn't work for a state convention because of a run on hotel rooms in Des Moines, the state capital and site of the state party convention. Bumping the state convention earlier meant everything else had to come early, and the first date that worked for the caucuses was January 24, 1972 (Klein, 2012).

In 1972, Iowa Democrats going first didn't seem too significant and the results not that remarkable. Front-runner, Edmund Muskie, senator from Maine, would come out on top in the Democratic caucuses, though lagging behind expectations. But South Dakota Senator George McGovern – the same McGovern whose commission had drafted the new national party rules – performed better than expected (Winebrenner & Goldford, 2010) and picked up some media buzz. Only in retrospect did Iowa seem important, a first notch in what would become McGovern's eventual path to nomination (Squire, 1989).[3] Both Democratic and Republican state parties, in light of the 1972 Democratic contest in Iowa, picked up on the potential for Iowa to make a splash with early caucuses, and both opted for the same early date – January 19 – for the 1976 contest. That year, the potential significance of being first was apparent from the outset.

As the 1976 cycle approached, Democrats perceived that Gerald Ford, the incumbent who became president when Richard Nixon resigned, was vulnerable.[4] Not surprisingly, there was a big field of Democratic hopefuls that year, including Jimmy Carter, the largely unknown former governor of Georgia, with advisers who understood the potential of Iowa (Kamarck, 2019). The Carter campaign set its sights on Iowa by doing quaint things – like showing up to celebrate an anniversary of a county official's service or giving interviews to small town newspapers. On a hunch that there might be a straw poll vote taken at an October 1975 Democratic dinner in Ames, Carter's team organized supporters to attend, bring friends and influence others to vote. He easily won the impromptu vote, and with it the *New York Times* headline "Carter Appears to Hold a Solid Lead in Iowa" (Kessel, 1984, p. 260).

Jimmy Carter's early work organizing and campaigning in Iowa also paid off on caucus night when he registered first among the candidates in the field, trailing only "uncommitted."[5] With this second-place "win," he gained credibility and attention – ultimately leading to the nomination and the presidency. The 1976 takeaway for candidates: retail politics, forging face-to-face relationships with Iowans, is the path to caucus success, and early success in Iowa can lead to later national success. The takeaway for parties in Iowa, both Democratic and Republican, was that their first-in-the-nation status had great value because it lured candidates and the media to the state. With them came other good things for the party organizations – like money and engaged activists.

Over the years, Iowa parties fought to secure the coveted first spot. For the most part, national parties and the incumbent presidents who led them lent their support.[6] For the 1980 contest, the DNC adopted a window rule – "Rule 10A" (Wekkin, 1984) – requiring that primaries and caucuses fall within a 13-week period beginning the second Tuesday in March, but it granted Iowa and New Hampshire exceptions, in part because of then-incumbent President Carter's sway over the party. He owed a debt of gratitude to Iowa for his 1976 win and imagined the state could help him with re-nomination in 1980. Maneuvering in advance of the 1984 contest actually prompted the Iowa general assembly to pass a law *requiring* that Iowa hold its caucuses at least eight days earlier than any other binding nominating event.[7]

None of this actually resolved the issue of caucus timing, and routinely each cycle the parties in Iowa would negotiate with their national counterparts to continue holding the caucuses first in the sequential array. Other states would also jockey for early position (Parshall, 2018; Hagen & Mayer, 2000). There's even been high drama, like in 1996, when the Republican field was wide open with nine candidates vying for the chance to go up against Democratic incumbent Bill Clinton. Just two months before the early February Iowa caucuses, Louisiana Republicans made a last-minute calendar change, scheduling their caucuses six days before Iowa's. Republicans in Iowa balked, appealing – unsuccessfully – to the US Department of Justice and to the federal courts. In the end, the state party chair got written pledges from most of the candidates running to not compete in Louisiana (Winebrenner & Goldford, 2010). But 1996 was the anomaly. In the years that followed, Iowa always went first, even if it meant scheduling the caucuses for an unusually early date, like January 3 in 2008.

That said, Iowa's first-in-the-nation position had never been assured, in no small part because of this persistent normative question: Why should *Iowa* go first? Should a state that's relatively old, white, and rural hold a privileged position in the sequence of contests that feed into presidential nomination? For that matter, should *any* state – or any pair of states – have a guaranteed position in the calendar?

The 2008 Democratic contest has been commonly cited to justify Iowa's calendar position and to dispel concerns about the unrepresentative quality of the population. In fact, the resounding win by Barack Obama in the Iowa caucuses that year, a first step in the path to his ultimate nomination and election, carries the mythical allure of Jimmy Carter in 1976. Like the unknown governor from Georgia, Obama – just a first term US senator – poured his resources into grassroots organizing, including the development of neighborhood-level supporter networks, and the use of new technologies and data. Obama also leveraged his personal charisma, building relationships with influential Democrats across the state. His main opponent, then-Senator Hillary Clinton, placed less emphasis on the state and dispatched her campaign resources elsewhere. Obama's win was interpreted as validation of the Iowa caucuses as the promised land, offering a path to the nomination for those who don't have the benefit of traditional political resources and power. It was also taken as evidence that the state's relatively non-diverse activist pool can fall in line behind a candidate with appeal to a more diverse national electorate.

Those results from 2008 helped shore up the reputation of the caucuses, but it didn't last for long. The competitive 2012 Republican contest was volatile throughout fall 2011, with front-runner status shifting from candidate to candidate on an almost weekly basis. But the caucus result itself called into question the integrity of the process. As reported on caucus night, the results showed Pennsylvania Senator Rick Santorum with a small lead over former Massachusetts Governor Mitt Romney, the eventual nominee, who at that point was on top nationally. However, within days the Republican Party of Iowa reported that the results from a handful of precincts had been missing in the early count. Once those "lost" results were included, Romney took the lead. The optics of a system unable to track the results were bad enough, but the revised results made things even worse for the reputation of the caucuses. Romney had hardly campaigned in the state, making observers question whether Iowa really mattered.

By 2016, the Republican contest confirmed the traditional role of the state, rewarding Texas Senator Ted Cruz with a first-place finish. Cruz had flooded the state with volunteers from across the country, even housing some in a decommissioned college dorm, "Camp Cruz." This military-like organizing prowess (Zezima, 2016) was the state-of-the-art equivalent of Carter's 1976 and Obama's 2008 operations, and it would seem to warrant a caucus win. But Donald Trump came in a strong second, despite scant organization and a primitive data and analytics operation. In effect, Trump in 2016 – like Romney in 2012 – wrote his own Iowa user's guide, and his credible performance was interpreted as an affront to the caucuses.

The assaults directed at the caucuses over the years, whether because of their outsized importance, mechanical fails, or results that implicitly questioned the special nature of the contests, all paled in comparison to the onslaught after the Democratic caucuses in 2016. The contest that year, with Hillary Clinton and Vermont Senator Bernie Sanders as the leads, resurrected the same tensions that had marked 1968 at the national level, pitting the party establishment against outsiders who felt their voices were silenced in Democratic nomination politics. The 1968/2016 analogy doesn't end there. In both years, the internal division within the party fueled a strong push to reform the rules going forward. A general election loss by the eventual nominee – the establishment candidate – added determination to that push.

Clinton ran a different Iowa campaign in 2016 than she had in 2008. Obama's success had underscored the importance of a strong ground organization and cultivating relationships. So in 2016 Clinton organized heavily and showed up often. Entering the race officially in April 2015, she seemed the inevitable pick of the party – at least as inevitable as a female candidate could be. She already had a sizable campaign team as early as January 2015 and amassed strong support from establishment Democrats (Gearan & Balz, 2015). But in a world of internal party tension, this cut both ways, with the seeming strength tempered by Sanders' supporters charging the system was rigged in a way that disenfranchised those who are outside of the party mainstream, especially those newly mobilized into nomination politics.

The Democratic caucuses themselves gave some credibility to those charges. Turnout was pretty high, and some precincts were unable to accommodate the influx of new participants on caucus night, whether through procedures that didn't work well or meeting sites that were too small. The competition was close, so processes and results were examined with greater attention than usual – and they didn't always hold up well under scrutiny. The statewide results themselves, with Clinton holding only the slightest advantage over Sanders in the totals released by the state party, added to concerns by those who felt disadvantaged by the process. The logic was that inequities and irregularities in the Iowa caucus process, and even exploitation of obscure rules by insiders, might have thwarted the Sanders effort.

Not everyone agreed. State party leaders stood by the results, with then-state party chair Andy McGuire calling the contest some five hours after the caucuses ended. Sanders staff cried foul (Jacobs, 2016). Those with years of experience in the caucuses insisted that Clinton's success in part came from knowing the rules and tailoring strategies to optimize success under them, which is just good politics. What's more, they highlighted a straightforward way to change things: commit to the party for the long-term, not just to advance the cause of a particular candidate, and then improve the process. The Democratic National Committee (DNC) and the IDP for their part, following the playbook written after 1968, each commissioned groups to review caucus rules.

The Clinton/Sanders rift extended beyond the caucuses, simmering through the remainder of the nomination season. The lingering question after Clinton's nomination was how would Sanders supporters vote in November, or would they even vote. Brian Schaffner's analysis (Stein, 2017) of national data suggests that about 12% of Sanders supporters defected to Trump in the general election. Defection cut the other way as well, with a comparable percentage of supporters of losing Republican hopefuls ultimately voting for Clinton (Kurtzleben, 2017).[8] Nate Silver (2019), analyzing those same data, added that about 8% of Sanders primary voters cast a third-party vote in November, but very few stayed home. Final results in Iowa showed a resounding victory for Trump, 51% to 42%.

The Trump win shook Democrats, generating an immediate wave of activism and engagement nationally and locally.[9] This took multiple forms in Iowa, including resistance to the Republican policy agenda and recruitment of new candidates to run for lower-level elective offices, especially with the 2018 midterm elections in mind. Efforts were sometimes unifying, when Democrats coalesced around common goals, but they still highlighted residual internal tensions that had marked 2016. Sanders supporters maintained that the caucus system had been stacked against them, but even more that Democrats might have won in November had Sanders – and not Clinton – been the nominee. At the same time, the Clinton faction harbored the belief that Sanders and his supporters had not done enough to support the nominee.

In US politics, battles within parties are sometimes as contentious as those between them. These battles first played out in Iowa Democratic organizational politics in early 2017, with hotly contested party leadership elections marked by the same Clinton/Sanders divide. In the end, the pick for state party chair, a position filled by a vote of the state central committee, went to Derek Eadon, who had been involved in Iowa politics since the Obama 2008 campaign. He amassed enough support from both Clinton and Sanders factions, though not necessarily the first choice of either (Rynard, 2017a).[10] Under the new chair's leadership, the party continued exploring changes to the presidential nomination system that would be borne out in the next contest.

The Caucus Bubble

A "bubble" is a good metaphor for Iowa caucus politics, with broad utility. The caucuses represented an ecosystem of sorts, marked by unique – even quirky – rules and norms of behavior. They were shaped over time by a mix of developments, ranging from deliberate decisions by the formal parties, the candidates, and the media about presidential nomination to a host of factors that on the surface would seem to have nothing to do with the caucuses. Safe to say, the caucus bubble eluded simple explanation.

Over four decades, the bubble had been resilient, nothing pricking it enough to burst it. Not the calls that its privileged position made no sense or that the outcome in Iowa was imperfectly correlated with the nomination outcome (Hagen & Mayer, 2000; Hull, 2008; Adkins & Dowdle, 2001). Not even assaults by other states and presidential candidates on the caucuses. The reality had been that candidates treated Iowa as important, and the media did its part – intentional or not – to support that position. What's more, the national parties, wielding the ability to set the terms by which their presidential nominees are selected (Wekken, 1984), largely reinforced the bubble.

A bubble, however, is not impervious. The notion that the caucus bubble might burst, seemingly just an abstraction given the pattern of the previous four decades, took on urgency for Iowa Democrats in the 2020 cycle. The IDP, in a process begun after the 2016 caucuses with considerable pressure from the DNC, revised the rules to govern the actual caucus proceedings set for February 3, 2020, laboring under the threat that the future of the caucuses might be in doubt. At the same time, a record number of candidates would campaign in Iowa, even doubling down there, seeming to contradict any sense that the bubble had deflated or was at risk of doing so. Some would walk a particularly fine line, throwing shade on the bubble, even tossing some arrows at it, while still campaigning as if Iowa mattered.

The Political Climate circa 2019

Back when Jacob Hamblin first arrived in Iowa in March 2019, there was still some uncertainty about how the 2020 presidential nomination contest would play out and how the bubble would fare. But three things were certain for Democrats: the stakes were high, there was some reason for optimism, and the insider/outsider divide lingered.

At stake for Democrats was the risk of a second Trump Administration, and they were unified in their opposition to the president. In early March

2019, only 4% nationally of Democrats approved of the president's performance in office (Jones, 2019).[11] Data from a little later in the spring indicate that the electability of the nomination hopefuls – that is, the likelihood of winning against Trump – was key. A solid majority – 58% – opted for selecting "a candidate who has the best chance of beating the opposing candidate" in contrast to "a candidate who agrees with you on almost all of the issues you care about" (Brennan, 2019). December 2018 results in Iowa, like the May/June 2019 national readings, showed similar interest among Democrats in nominating an electable candidate. The Iowa Poll, the *Des Moines Register's* signature survey of Iowans which is prominent in nomination politics, recorded similar local support for electability, with 54% of likely Democratic caucus-goers giving the nod to picking a candidate who could beat Trump.[12]

The seeds of this laser focus on the president among Democrats had been planted in the immediate aftermath of the 2016 election. The backlash against the outcome and the new administration set the stage for a vocal, engaged resistance from progressives, women, minorities, members of the LGBTQ community, and others. Driven by what they saw as almost daily controversies coming out of the White House, a Supreme Court nomination battle that resulted in the Senate confirmation of Justice Brent Kavanaugh, anti-immigration rhetoric, and a surge in white supremacist activities, activists on the left prepared for electoral battles to come.

The 2018 midterms fueled Democratic hopes for 2020. In the 2018 midterm elections, a crush of new, non-traditional candidates carried Democrats to broad gains – including the recapture of the US House of Representatives. After the contested outcomes were settled, House Democrats held a 36 seat margin over the Republicans,[13] ultimately picking up 41 seats. Considered a solid Democratic win, perhaps even a "wave," this outcome reassured Democrats who had wondered whether they would benefit from the expected midterm vote loss phenomenon (Tufte, 1975; Kernell, 1977; Campbell, 1985) that typically plagues the president's party.[14] Given the party's emphasis on diversity, a few of the November 2018 results seemed especially significant: the first openly gay male governor, the first two Native American women and the first two Muslim women elected to Congress, as well as the first openly bisexual US senator, who also happened to be the first woman elected to the Senate from Arizona.

Most of the Democratic congressional candidates, successful or not, ran specifically in opposition to policies advocated by the Trump Administration. Those presidential priorities included efforts to limit immigration, cut taxes on wealthy individuals and corporations, and roll-back environmental regulation. These issues all took on a new light in the national agenda when, in the November 2018 election, Democrats won the US House and positioned themselves to drive policy alternatives to the administration and the Republican-controlled Senate.

In fact, a diverse group of four first-term Democratic congresswomen directly took on President Trump. As adept as the president at social media, the "Gang of Four" – a Latina, a Black woman, and two Muslim American women – highlighted their backgrounds and progressive ideals to both incite the president and push their new-majority House colleagues. Most prominently among these was "AOC," Alexandria Ocasio-Cortez (D-NY), who at 29 years old when taking office was the youngest congresswoman in US history. The success and prominence of these four women and their willingness to debate both the Republican president and the Democratic Speaker of the US House – Nancy Pelosi – were a clear and encouraging message to outsiders that their time may have arrived. But for many, it also foreshadowed what might become a 2020 version of the chasm between the establishment and insurgent Democrats.

Some of that division had been in play in Iowa during the midterms, too. At the same time that Democrats in Iowa had started work to revise their rules for presidential delegate selection, in part with that 2016 Sanders/Clinton divide in mind, they had hunkered down to nominate candidates to run for Congress, governor, and other state- and county-level offices. Like most states, Iowa uses primary elections to nominate down-ballot candidates, and a Sanders imprint marked a couple of contests in particular. Sanders endorsed Pete D'Alessandro, his 2016 Iowa campaign coordinator, among a wide field of candidates aiming to unseat the one-term Republican incumbent who held the congressional district including state capital Des Moines, also the state's largest population center. D'Alessandro failed to win the nomination, but the eventual Democratic nominee was victorious in November.

Even though Sanders never endorsed in the 2018 gubernatorial race, the insider/outsider dynamic was especially prominent. That six-way primary for governor featured a millionaire businessman/philanthropist as the establishment favorite against a union leader who earned the affection of Sanders supporters by running a campaign focused on universal health care and increasing the minimum wage. While the establishment Democrat would win the primary easily, the race was marked by fervent, unabashed activism by progressives, putting a spotlight on the internal divides within the party. In November, the sitting Republican governor was re-elected in a very close race, reinforcing the near-lock the GOP had on the Iowa governor's mansion over the previous half-century. Democrats won control of the state's congressional delegation, winning three of the four House seats, notably electing the state's first two female members.[15] For Democrats in Iowa, maybe it wasn't simply politics as usual.

Reading the tea leaves is a valued political skill. In fact, an entire industry of consultants labors to make sense of politics, project what will happen, advise, and strategize. Academics and pundits do a version of that too, with different emphases. That said, presidential nomination politics is a hard nut to crack, with lots of moving – though related – parts, as well as epic uncertainty.

Consider it from the perspective of a potential candidate, whose decision to run for the nomination might well be made without the critical knowledge of who else might run. More than a thought exercise, there are important ramifications, since supporters may well weigh each candidate against the others in the field (Bartels, 1987; Stone et al., 1992). Donors make those same calculations, too. And then add yet another dimension of uncertainty regarding rules, like wondering each cycle whether rules-focused Democrats will fine tune again. For good measure, layer on a host of other factors possibly at play in making an informed decision about running: the economy, global politics, not to mention how the media will respond.

All of this adds up to decision-making under uncertainty, with the real possibility of cascading effects – that is, developments that may well trigger or preclude what follows. But if you cut through the jargon, what it meant was that the men and women thinking about running for president, working for a campaign, or even heading to Iowa had no clue what was going to happen. And for 2020, perhaps more so than for any contest since 1976, the role to be played by Iowa was up in the air. All that uncertainty might have resulted in candidates holding off, resisting their instinct to run or to campaign in Iowa. For some it probably did. But others clearly made the decision to go all out in 2020. *Many others*. Maybe Iowa didn't conclusively offer a clear path to the nomination or even credibility. But just in case it did, it would be a risky state to ignore.

Notes

1 July 1, 2018 population estimate, US Census Bureau: https://factfinder.census.gov/faces/nav/jsf/pages/community_facts.xhtml?src=bkmk
2 Ware (2002) emphasizes that direct elections for nomination had been used on a limited basis since the mid-1800s. He is careful to point out that the direct primary, like the Australian ballot, was not forced on parties, but they found it in their interest to go along with adoption.
3 The Republican Party of Iowa had held its caucuses after the Democrats in 1972, not subject to the rules of the national Democratic Party and having some discretion about timing.
4 President Ford had never even been on a presidential ticket, becoming vice-president in 1973 when sitting Vice-President Spiro Agnew resigned.
5 Note that Democrats in Iowa can caucus either for a candidate or as "uncommitted."
6 See Kamarck (2019, chapter 2) for a comprehensive review of the jockeying of Iowa and New Hampshire.
7 Ia. Stat. § 43.4, "Political Party Precinct Caucuses," passed 1983 (Winebrenner & Goldford, 2010). New Hampshire followed suit, passing a law (Section 653:9 Presidential Primary Election) specifying that its primary must be at least seven days before a similar election in another state.
8 Schaffner data from the Cooperative Congressional Election Study, a large-N survey administered in November 2016.
9 Some 400,000 women and other activists marched on Washington, DC the day after Trump's inauguration. Five hundred concurrent marches around the country drew an estimated 3.3 million people (Frostenson, 2017).
10 Eadon's start with Obama in 2008 had come so early his first paycheck from the campaign bounced (Henderson, 2017). In 2017 he emerged from a field of seven

state party chair contenders to win the election. He resigned for health reasons in late June 2017 (Rynard, 2017b).
11 In contrast to Trump, Barack Obama's approval among Republicans at the same point in his first term was eight-points higher (Jones 2015).
12 Toplines for Study #2182 (http://cdn.cnn.com/cnn/2018/images/12/15/rel1iade mocrats.pdf). Note margin of error 4.6%, higher than typical surveys because of smaller sample size, produced by screening for likely caucus-goers. Pollster Ann Selzer conducts the Iowa Poll, which – though credited to *The Register* – is part of a three-way partnership also including CNN and Mediacom.
13 http://library.cqpress.com/elections/document.php?id=avg2018-3us1&type=toc&num=2313C83D-DC82-4EFB-BED7-FCB9D0D6D422
14 For a consideration of 2018 vote-loss forecasts, see Campbell (2018).
15 Iowa has a weak track record in electing women to high office. Republican Senator Joni Ernst, elected first in 2014, was the first woman in Iowa to hold any congressional seat, and while Democratic women have served as Lt. Governor, none have occupied the top state seat.

References

Adkins, Randall E. and Andrew J. Dowdle. 2001. "How important are Iowa and New Hampshire to winning post-reform presidential nominations?" *Political Research Quarterly* 54(2): 431–444.
Aldrich, John. 1995. *Why Parties?: The Origin and Transformation of Political Parties in America*. Chicago: University of Chicago Press.
Bartels, Larry M. 1987. "Candidate choice and the dynamics of the presidential nomination process." *American Journal of Political Science* 31(1): 1–30.
Brenan, Megan. 2019. "Electability of Democratic nominee outranks issue stances." *Gallup* June 25 (https://news.gallup.com/poll/259454/electability-democratic-nominee-outranks-issue-stances.aspx).
Brewer, Mark D. and Sandy L. Maisel. 2018. *The Parties Respond: Changes in American Parties and Campaigns* (5th edition). New York: Routledge.
Campbell, James E. 1985. "Explaining presidential losses in midterm congressional elections." *The Journal of Politics* 47(4): 1140–1157.
Campbell, James E. 2018. "The seats-in-trouble forecasts of the 2018 midterm congressional elections." *PS: Political Science & Politics* 51(S1): 12–16.
Converse, Philip E., Warren E. Miller, Jerrold G. Rusk and Arthur C. Wolfe. 1969. "Continuity and change in American politics: parties and issues in the 1968 election." *The American Political Science Review* 63(4): 1083–1105.
Farber, David. 1988. *Chicago '68*. Chicago: The University of Chicago Press.
Frostenson, Sarah. 2017. "New analysis: the Women's March in Washington, DC, drew half a million people." *Vox* January 27 (www.vox.com/policy-and-politics/2017/1/27/14364270/analysis-womens-march-washington-dc-half-million-people).
Gearan, Anne and Dan Balz. 2015. "Official or not, Hillary Clinton builds a massive team-in-waiting." *The Washington Post* February 6 (www.washingtonpost.com/politics/official-or-not-hillary-clintons-2016-campaign-is-already-well-underway/2015/02/06/a78fc358-ac8d-11e4-ad71-7b9eba0f87d6_story.html).
Hagen, Michael G. and William G. Mayer. 2000. "The Modern Politics of Presidential Selection: How Changing the Rules Really Did Change the Game." In *Pursuit of the White House 2000,* ed., William G. Mayer. New York, NY: Chatham House.

Henderson, O. Kay. 2017. "Derek Eadon is new Iowa Democratic Party chairman (AUDIO). Radio Iowa January 22 (www.radioiowa.com/2017/01/22/derek-eadon-is-newiowa-democratic-party-chairman/).

Hershey, Marjorie Randon. 2017. *Party Politics in America* (17th edition). New York: Routledge.

Hull, Christopher C. 2008. *Grassroots Rules: How the Iowa Caucus Helps Elect American Presidents*. Stanford, CA: Stanford University Press.

Jacobs, Jennifer. 2016. "Iowa's nightmare revisited: was correct winner called?" *The Des Moines Register* February 3 (www.desmoinesregister.com/story/news/elections/presidential/caucus/2016/02/02/iowas-nightmare-revisited-correct-winner-called-caucus-night/79702010/).

Jones, Jacob M. 2015. "Obama approval ratings still historically polarized." *Gallup* February 6 (https://news.gallup.com/poll/181490/obama-approval-ratings-historically-polarized.aspx).

Jones, Jacob M. 2019. "Trump job approval 43%; ties party polarization record." *Gallup* September 19 (https://news.gallup.com/poll/266906/trump-job-approval-ties-party-polarization-record.aspx).

Kamarck, Elaine. 2019. *Primary Politics: Everything You Need to Know about How America Nominates Its Presidential Candidates*. Washington, DC: Brookings Institution Press.

Kernell, Samuel. 1977. "Presidential popularity and negative voting: an alternative explanation of the midterm congressional decline of the president's party." *American Political Science Review* 71(1): 44–66.

Kessel John H. 1984. *Presidential Parties*. Homewood, IL: Dorsey Press.

Klein, Ezra. 2012. "Why Iowa gets to go first, and other facts about tonight's caucus." *The Washington Post* January 3 (www.washingtonpost.com/blogs/ezra-klein/post/why-iowa-gets-to-go-first-and-other-facts-about-tonights-caucus/2011/08/25/gIQAJtygYP_blog.html).

Kurtzleben, Danielle. 2017. "Here's how many Bernie Sanders supporters ultimately voted for Trump." *National Public Radio*. August 24.

Masket, Seth. 2016. *The Inevitable Party: Why Attempts to Kill the Party System Fail and How they Weaken Democracy*. New York: Oxford University Press.

Merton, Robert K. 1957. *Social Theory and Social Structure*. New York: Free Press.

Moore, David W. and Andrew E. Smith. 2015. *The First Primary: New Hampshire's Outsize Role in Presidential Nominations*. Durham, NH: University of New Hampshire Press.

Nardulli, Peter. 2013. *Popular Efficacy in the Democratic Era: A Reexamination of Electoral Accountability in the United States, 1828–2000*. Princeton, NJ: Princeton University Press.

Norrander, Barbara. 2015. *The Imperfect Primary: Oddities, Biases, and Strengths of US Presidential Nomination Politics*. New York: Routledge.

Parshall, Lisa K. 2018. *Reforming the Presidential Nominating Process: Front-loading's Consequences and the National Primary Solution*. New York: Routledge.

Ranney, Austin. 1975. *Curing the Mischiefs of Faction: Party Reform in America*. Berkeley: University of California Press.

Reichley, A. James. 1992. *The Life of the Parties: A History of American Political Parties*. Lanham, MD: Rowman & Littlefield Publishers.

Riordon, William L. 1948. *Plunkitt of Tammany Hall: A Series of Very Plain Talks on Very Practical Politics*. New York: A.A. Knopf.

Rynard, Pat. 2017a. "Derek Eadon elected Iowa Democrats Chair as party begins to unify." *Iowa Starting Line* January 21 (https://iowastartingline.com/2017/01/21/derek-eadon-elected-as-idp-chair-as-party-begins-to-unify/).

Rynard, Pat. 2017b. "Derek Eadon resigns as Iowa Democrats Chair." *Iowa Starting Line* June 29 (https://iowastartingline.com/2017/06/29/derek-eadon-resigns-iowa-democrats-chair/).

Silver, Nate. 2019. "How Bernie's 2020 map might change without the #NeverHillary vote." *FiveThirtyEight* February 21 (https://fivethirtyeight.com/features/bernie-sanders-was-helped-by-the-neverhillary-vote-what-does-that-mean-for-his-chances-now/).

Squire, Peverill. 1989. "Iowa and the nomination process." In Peverill Squire, ed. The Iowa Caucuses and the Presidential Nominating Process. Boulder, CO: Westview Press. pp. 1–17.

Stein, Jeff. 2017. "The Bernie voters who defected to Trump, explained by a political scientist." *Vox* August 24 (www.vox.com/policy-and-politics/2017/8/24/16194086/bernie-trump-voters-study).

Stone, Walter J., Ronald B. Rapoport, and Alan I. Abramowitz. 1992. "Candidate support in presidential nomination campaigns: the case of Iowa in 1984." *Journal of Politics* 54(4): 1074–1097.

Tufte, Edward R. 1975. "*Determinants of the outcomes of midterm congressional elections.*" *American Political Science Review* 69(3): 812–826.

Ware, Alan. 2002. *The American Direct Primary: Party Institutionalization and Transformation in the North*. New York: Cambridge University Press.

Wekkin, Gary D. 1984. "National-state party relations: the Democrats' new federal structure" *Political Science Quarterly* 99(1): 45–72.

Winebrenner, Hugh and Dennis J. Goldford. 2010. *The Iowa Precinct Caucuses: The Making of a Media Event, 3rd Edition*. Iowa City: University of Iowa Press.

Zezima, Katie. 2016. "Welcome to Camp Cruz — a little bit of 'Real World' on the trail in Iowa." *The Washington Post* January 24 (www.washingtonpost.com/politics/welcome-to-camp-cruz–a-little-bit-of-real-world-on-the-trail-in-iowa/2016/01/24/7c17c812-c076-11e5-bcda-62a36b394160_story.html).

2 The Promised Land

John Delaney had been all-in even before the dust had settled on the 2016 general election (Noble, 2017). A member of Congress when he started showing up in Iowa in 2017, the Maryland Democrat had a personal American Dream story, a kid whose Ivy League education was supported by a scholarship from his father's union, The International Brotherhood of Electrical Workers (IBEW). Largely unknown outside the Beltway, Delaney announced his intent to run for the presidency on July 28, 2017. He penned an opinion piece in the *Washington Post*, explaining that he aimed to fix the broken politics of the Trump Era, marked by excessive partisanship and an absence of leadership (Delaney, 2017). A few days later, just seven months into President Trump's term, the congressman filed his paperwork to officially declare his 2020 candidacy, just in time to stump at the Iowa State Fair, a mecca for presidential hopefuls.[1]

Enter the Candidates and Staff

Delaney's early candidacy went unnoticed by many Democrats. But they began to take note when he started logging significant numbers of days in Iowa, conjuring up the image of an unknown Jimmy Carter in 1976 showing up regularly, caucus politics potentially jump-starting his campaign. Candidate presence in the state is a predictor of success (Hull, 2008). And according to the *Des Moines Register's* "Candidate Tracker," by the end of 2017, Delaney had already held 24 events over ten days in Iowa.[2] But he wasn't alone. Other notable Democrats and Republicans made forays into the state, whether they were mulling a 2020 candidacy or not. Nebraska GOP senator and occasional Trump critic Ben Sasse, seen by some as a maverick, spoke at two high-profile Iowa events in 2017. The president himself had a big rally in June of that year. And then there were multiple Iowa appearances by eight Democrats who would enter the race and one who would not.[3] Those appearances hinted that Iowa would remain a crucial stop in the 2020 presidential nomination process, soothing concerns for Democrats who wondered whether the caucuses could withstand reputational damage leveled at them during the Sanders/Clinton 2016 nomination battle.

Things looked increasingly good for Delaney riding the conventional Iowa caucus model when he got a gift in February 2018 from a key Iowa Democrat. Jeff Link, a strategist, veteran of presidential campaigns back to Bill Clinton's in 1992, and consummate Democratic insider hosted a "meet and greet" for Delaney in his Des Moines home, inviting a wide array of Democratic activists. These included candidates and elected officials, local leaders, and rank-and-file partisans. Not necessarily a sign that Link supported Delaney, the event sent a signal to Democrats, especially the hundred or so in attendance, that they should take a look at the candidate. Delaney talked that day about his pragmatic, bipartisan approach to governing – an approach that resonated with Link. "I think that the main thing I took away from his message was that we need to take down all these attacks, bring people together."[4]

Over 2018, as Democratic congressional and state candidates fought in primaries and then geared up for the general election, presidential hopefuls beat a path to Iowa, spending a collective 66 days in the state and holding more than 220 events. Still, in that calendar year, only Delaney and Andrew Yang, the Silicon Valley entrepreneur, were declared candidates. Yang resurrected a concept from the early 1970s, which became his signature policy emphasis. Universal Basic Income (UBI), aka the "freedom dividend," was intended to be a monthly grant of $1,000 to each adult, regardless of need. The progressive/establishment division was already apparent between these two declared candidates, Delaney and Yang.

The late-September 2018 Iowa Poll had some good and bad news for Delaney. Despite his 96 cumulative stops over a month in the state, 36% of likely Democratic caucus-goers had not heard of him, though the remainder, on balance, judged him favorably.[5] There was no news for Andrew Yang. The Iowa Poll didn't even include him in the list of the 15 Democratic candidates about whom it posed questions. Hillary Clinton was constantly quizzed about a potential 2020 campaign, and she repeatedly insisted she had no intention of running again. The Iowa Poll took Clinton at her word, not listing her as a potential contender. Joe Biden, Barack Obama's vice-president, however, was a different matter.

Biden had contemplated a presidential bid in 2016, which would have been a natural move for a sitting and reasonably popular vice-president. But devastated by the 2015 death of his son Beau to cancer, the vice-president waited in the wings, telling late night host Steven Colbert that a candidate needs to be able to promise his heart, soul, and passion. "… I'd be lying if I said I knew I was there" (Kamp, 2017). Biden's decision paved the way for Clinton to be the 2016 standard bearer of the Obama legacy. After Clinton's loss, Biden exited the Obama White House with strong public support. His 61% Gallup approval rating in January 2017 was the highest of his eight years in office.[6] In the fall of that year, a new book by Biden brought him back into the public eye and foreshadowed the possibility of a 2020 candidacy. When the Iowa Poll tapped into Democratic sentiment in December 2018, his ratings were off-the-charts, a net 82% favorable. But Biden was 75-years old at that point, meaning he would be 78 at inauguration if he won. Still, he was just about a year younger than Bernie Sanders, who was signaling his intent to run as well. Both were only a few years older than the Republican incumbent in the White House.

By mid-April 2019, another 16 candidates had formally declared, joining Delaney and Yang and offering conclusive evidence that this would be a large field. It's not unusual for the out-party to see a large number of candidates competing. The GOP contest from 2016 was a recent reminder – with 17 Republicans vying for the nomination that Donald Trump eventually grabbed. The collection of Democrats with their sights set on 2020 included the usual suspects: former and sitting senators and governors, including Bernie Sanders giving it another try. But there was something different about the field beyond its size, even beyond the presence of Sanders, the Democratic Socialist, who continued to resist embracing the Democratic Party while seeking its nomination.

It was a diverse field in terms of gender and racial/ethnic composition. Six women were competing, including four sitting US senators. By mid-April, the field included six candidates of color as well as an openly gay man, a first for a major party nomination contest. Noticeably absent: Joe Biden, who hadn't formally declared despite signaling his intent to run. He was still lingering in the wings. The other candidates were active in the state – courting notable and elected Democrats, meeting with activists, and making themselves available to average Iowans. *Register* tracking data showed that as a group from February through the end of April 2019, the candidates logged 114 days in the state, hitting 214 cities and making appearances at 250 events. Candidates were doing the same in New Hampshire, but at about three-quarters speed (Rakich, 2019). By contrast, over *the entire pre-caucus period* in 1976 – Jimmy Carter's break-out year – the six Democratic candidates spent a total of 86 days in the state, with Carter himself logging only 17 (Winebrenner & Goldford, 2010).

The venues ran the gamut, but for the most part they were small-scale, sometimes specialized. On a swing through the state, Yang met one day with the "Drinking Liberally" group in Denison, a town of 8,400 in western Iowa, and the next took his high-tech message to a truck stop in suburban Des Moines where he warned truck drivers about the threat from artificial intelligence and robots. Minnesota Senator Amy Klobuchar, like many of her fellow candidates serving in Congress, divided her 2019 February President's Day recess between Iowa and New Hampshire. The neighboring-state senator hit several Iowa party events, including a soup luncheon, an annual dinner, and a winter banquet/fundraiser, all in different counties. Pete Buttigieg, mayor of South Bend, IN, and at age 37 among the youngest major party candidates ever to run, cut his way through university towns, meeting with Campus Democrats at Iowa State University and then stopping at a public library down the street from Grinnell College. In April, former Texas

Congressman Beto O'Rourke hit seven house parties in Central Iowa in a two-day period.

Massachusetts Senator Elizabeth Warren's early presence was a bit different. She was a known commodity in the state, a progressive favorite whom supporters had lobbied to run in 2016. That last Iowa Poll of 2018 had pegged her net favorable rating among likely caucus-goers at 64%, lagging behind only Biden and Sanders. Warren's events were more like rallies than the intimate get-togethers of many of the others. A three-day swing through Iowa in early January, when she was still running an exploratory campaign, drew an estimated 3,000 in total (Rynard, 2019), with an event in Sioux City, a blue collar, ag-processing city of 82,000 on the Missouri River across from Nebraska, drawing a crowd of 500 (Hayworth, 2019).

Even small events don't just happen; they require groundwork to find a space and put out the word. In many cases, local party organizations are the conduit because they know the area, the venues, and the people. Historically, local parties have been the key building blocks of US party organizations and, even now with generally stronger national and state party presences (Cotter et al., 1984), local structures are the basis on which the parties are organized (Epstein, 1986). In Iowa, as in most states, it's the county party which campaign staffers typically contact for advice.

It takes some political savvy to pull off events. Finding a space that's not too big – preferably a little snug for the expected crowd – will convey the image that there are more people interested than expected. The perfect situation: a partition that can be moved allowing an overflow crowd some breathing room. But bigger events – rallies like Warren's – needed more than just a few locals and clever aides to pull them off successfully. The more complex tasks would require real organization – teams of staff and volunteers performing specialized jobs.

Jacob Hamblin arrived in Iowa three weeks after Cory Booker declared and about the same time that a handful of other Iowa campaigns were beginning to staff up. In his late twenties, Jacob had worked campaigns for a few cycles, including general elections and primaries, in both Ohio and Texas. But now he was deployed to Iowa as part of the Booker organization, which would number 63 paid staff nationally by the end of March 2019.[7] Jacob was hired as a regional organizer, a mid-level position in the Iowa campaign structure, ultimately overseeing a team of organizers. Organizers were key to an Iowa presidential nomination campaign. They were the boots-on-the-ground, staff diffused through the state at the local level whose work had a clear endgame – getting Iowans to the caucuses. By March, Booker had filled many state-level positions and had a shell of an Iowa field operation in place: a state organizing director and at least three "regionals."[8]

Jacob would eventually set up shop in Iowa City, the fifth largest city in the state with 76,000 people, the home of the University of Iowa (UI) and a plum assignment for a Democrat. Located in Johnson County – historically a hotbed of progressive sentiment – which was dubbed by a former Republican governor as "The People's Republic of Johnson County." It's an affluent area, with a large population of university professionals, including well-compensated medical professionals from the UI hospital and medical school. Democrats almost always win in Johnson County general elections, but like other one-party areas, nomination races are hotly contested.

Life for campaign staff like Jacob was every bit as uncertain as it was for the candidates, and it carried its own challenges and risks. A campaign can fold on a dime when the money runs dry, the candidate fails to catch fire, or some scandalous behavior is unearthed. While pay and benefits are better than they used to be, campaign staffers won't get rich. Paid bi-weekly, the net pay for the Booker regionals would amount to just over $50,000/year, should the campaign last that long. And even in the best case, the job would end in November, 2020. But for state leadership and mid-level staff like Jacob, signing on wasn't just a shot in the dark.

Jacob had a strong commitment to Democratic candidates, and Cory Booker had impressed him back in Ohio when the senator showed up to campaign for local candidates. Booker stood out because he did more than the closed-door donor events for which other national candidates would swoop in. Jacob understood that campaigns are essentially "start-ups" hungry for money, but he liked that the senator would take time to talk to activists. Booker would shout out to people working events, like hotel staff. Jacob had been a bartender in college, so he "appreciated things like that."

For some campaign workers, experience on an Iowa presidential campaign was a box to check off. And with stakes high for Democrats in 2020, that box took on added importance. The need to beat Trump factored heavily into Jacob's decision calculus, and he reasoned that Iowa for campaign politics was "like Silicon Valley for tech." Still, he wondered, "[Do I] really want to move to another state and do a year-long primary?" In the end, he took a cue from an Ohio campaign colleague who had signed on with Booker. This gave him the confidence to know what to expect and some assurance that the campaign probably "wouldn't set up a terrible system," something that wasn't guaranteed for any campaign.

When Jacob was hired in February 2019, he joined dozens of others hired to staff Democratic nomination campaigns in Iowa, mostly in state leadership and regional management roles. By caucus time, 11 months later, staff numbers in the state would grow to more than 750. It was a seller's market with lots of job openings drawing young, educated workers, mostly in their twenties, to work in Iowa's caucus bubble.

Inside the Bubble

Presidential campaign work in Iowa wasn't like most other jobs. It often required that workers relocate from some distance, quickly learn the state geography, make friends, and meet people – and do it as if they were native

Iowans. This was no small feat for outsiders who needed to get inside the caucus bubble. Once in it, they played a direct role in helping to shape the campaign contours, much like the Iowans who are in it cycle after cycle. Contrary to common belief, the bubble is more than the wild ride of privilege and outsized importance that marked caucus politics since 1976, poised to collapse at any minute. It's also a rarified ecosystem with two parts. First, there's a miniscule pool of activists, including some with years – even decades – of involvement in caucus politics. And second, there's a professional staff, led by those with experience from past campaigns, often schooled in the science of politics, and armed with expertise and technology. This included the newly arrived campaign staff.

The Iowa side of the caucus bubble was always small. In the most exclusive sense, counting both Democrats and Republicans who were intimately involved – attending small events, volunteering for candidates – the bubble numbered seven or eight thousand Iowans at most. Toss in those who would eventually attend rallies or the caucuses themselves and the number can approach 350,000–400,000. In 2008, with competitive contests on both sides of the aisle, total caucus attendance was close to 355,000. But that's really just a fraction of the state's 2.3 million voting age population.[9]

Turnout is considerably lower in nomination contests than in general elections, almost without exception. And as a rule, caucus turnout is lower than primary turnout due to the heavy costs associated with attending a meeting compared to voting (Norrander, 2015; McDonald & Merivaki, 2015). Consider the 2016 contests nationwide, roughly similar in that both parties had no incumbent vying for re-nomination and meaningful contests that extended into the spring. Geoffrey Skelley's data show that at 11%, turnout in caucus states lagged way behind the 36% in primary states.[10] The situation in Iowa hadn't been quite as dismal as the average caucus state. In 2016, 15.7% of Iowa Democrats and Republicans caucused. Caucuses that same year in Nevada and Minnesota saw turnout in the 8% range, while Alaska's caucuses drew 6.2% of eligible voters and Hawaii's drew just 4.6%.[11] In comparison, Iowa looked pretty good. Still, a vast majority of Iowans do not caucus.

The common narrative in the press is that Iowans were all consumed with caucus politics.[12] This is partially right, but partially wrong. Those who were engaged in the process had extraordinary access to the presidential candidates, who were showing up in even the smallest towns. Some die-hard partisans *expected* to meet each candidate, withholding support until that happened. A joke among Iowans was that they wouldn't even consider a candidate who hadn't been in their living room, though realistically living-room visits were rare. But within the party activist crowd, it was not unusual for individuals to have attended candidate events for *each* of the candidates, even in large, multi-candidate fields. In the 2020 cycle, some Iowans built expansive collections of selfies, plastering social media feeds for friends to see. At the same time, a high percentage of Iowans were uninvolved, suspicious of politics, and only exposed to the candidates via TV and digital ads that were impossible to avoid as the caucuses approached.

Leslie Carpenter was part of that rarified world of engaged Iowans who understood how the caucuses could magnify their voices in politics, and with whom the staff needed to interact. Her focus was on the issue of mental health, having watched and supported her son, ill-served by the state's mental health system over many years. Leslie recalled when she was approached in 2015 at an Iowa City farmers market by Carlo Makarechi, then a field organizer for Hillary Clinton. It was Carlo's first day on the job and he walked up to Leslie, asking for her support and seeking a volunteer without knowing that she was already on board with his candidate. "So I turned to him and said 'Carlo, it's so nice to meet you. If I volunteer a lot with your organization, can you get me a meeting with Hillary Clinton?'" Leslie Carpenter might not be a typical caucus activist, but people like her were part of the bubble, recognizing that the caucuses gave them voice and access that they might not otherwise have.

Issues and ideas about a range of policies were part of the bubble as well, with many Iowans on the ground well versed in policies of particular interest to them. Conventional wisdom, inspired by some seminal thought (Key, 1956), holds that nomination voters are more extreme than general election voters, but for the most part empirical studies tell a different story. Nomination participants may be demographically unique and they are likely to be stronger partisans, but they aren't necessarily distinct in terms of issue positions or ideology (Geer, 1988; Norrander, 1989; Abramowitz, 2008; Sides et al., 2020). A few studies over the years have looked specifically at the Iowa caucus setting. One examining caucus attendees in 1984 found that activists were only somewhat more extreme ideologically than the typical partisan identifier, and they were just a little different in terms of issue positions from partisans nationwide. For example, and of some relevance to contemporary issue debates, Democratic caucus-goers in 1984 were more supportive of national health insurance than Democrats nationwide (Stone et al., 1989). A more recent study from 2008 showed that some issue differences between caucus attendees and registered voters were small, though in the expected direction (Redlawsk et al., 2011).

But the key conversations in the bubble – at least early on – were among an even more exclusive group than the already-small group of caucus attendees. They were not tracked systematically by pollsters or scholars, and these conversations were about more than just responses to survey prompts. The issues were borne out in the passions and concerns expressed by the people involved, and sometimes the unexpected.

Jacob Hamblin, the 2020 Booker regional, had grown up in a college town in Ohio. When he walked into that March 2019 gathering in Malcom, he mused, whether accurate or not, that "everyone in this room has knowledge that exceeds mine about Iowa politics." Jacob carried himself with a degree of ease, and maybe a little apprehension. He was an experienced outsider.

Although he was raised "very Midwestern, very white culturally," he is half Tunisian and as a kid looked a bit different from everyone else in Ohio. It wasn't until he went to Brazil – for a year as an exchange student – that he didn't feel so different. "… Brazil was the first time in my life that I wasn't asked, 'Oh, so what are you?'"

When Jacob talked about that Saturday in Malcom, he didn't mention that the small group of Democrats lacked diversity – or that he was decades younger than the average person there. What made an impression on him was the policy discussion, formally part of that Saturday's process, which held some surprises. Not all, but many Iowa party activists are informed and conversant about a range of issues, from the international to the local. So it would be unsurprising for conversation to turn to recycling, especially since communities in Iowa at that point, like those in other states, had been scaling back efforts due to increased costs globally of passing along the recyclable material. What surprised Jacob was some degree of expressed *opposition* to recycling. Afterall, these were Democrats, liberals, environmentalists. The logic for the counterintuitive position was that recycling gives corporate America what amounts to a pass, allowing it to continue to produce plastic products and packaging that degrade the environment.

Jacob had stepped into a bubble with committed people, sometimes staking out surprising positions. These people were willing to make issues, candidates, and party activism a central part of their lives. But it's a mistake to think of the bubble in monolithic terms, because there was considerable variation in it depending on who you are, where you live, and what you want. For example, the state might be mostly white and few among it might be primarily motivated by an issue like racial injustice. But there are Iowa activists for whom it is the most important issue, and they had an opportunity to jump into the bubble, engage with candidates, and expect some level of attention.

Among Democrats in 2020, a few lived in places that were knee-deep in hog confinement facilities and wanted something done. Though more of a state than a federal issue, jurisdictional boundaries never stopped activists from raising a concern. Others had seen record flooding and wanted either more funding for the Army Corps of Engineers or an expansive climate-change proposal. Some had concerns about guns and gun violence, while still others worried that focusing on guns might cost votes among moderates who liked to hunt. Every activist had an opportunity to bring their specific platform of issues to any candidate – or staffer – who happened to be in town on a given day.

Campaigns traditionally have used two primary ways to learn the lay of the land. Both of them tap into what might be considered legacy elements. The first was to make state-level staffing decisions that brought Iowa-specific knowledge and experience. There was a cohort of usual suspects who had worked on past statewide and congressional campaigns, some moving back and forth between campaign and government service, thanks to a candidate they helped elect, and others jumping from campaign to campaign. They tended to range in age from late twenties to mid-forties, sometimes married, occasionally with children. It is, after all, the kind of work that's taxing on family life.

Presidential campaigns don't vary too much organizationally, though there are always exceptions. The state director is at the apex of the organizational chart – the public face of the campaign. It's common to have strategists and consultants, whether on the payroll or on contract, weighing in on campaign specifics. In this regard, a "caucus director" might focus on turnout strategies, perhaps using analytics and modeling too. The political team is charged with courting support among political leaders and influencers, while pushing for endorsements and handling surrogates. Communications responsibilities, often media and outreach, are usually relegated to a "comms" person or team. And operations – or "ops" – can oversee a wide portfolio that might include HR, payroll, and handling leasing for headquarters. Some campaigns have state-level policy units, while others rely on the national campaign for policy development and guidance. Data and digital organizational units are relatively new additions to presidential campaigns, having developed at the same time that new data and digital technologies became available. Rudimentary versions of these organizational units, especially in the pre-Obama campaign world, were labeled with different names, like "voter file" or "website."[13] The number of staff in these divisions varied, depending on resources, strategic emphases, and the importance the campaign placed on the state. But for the typical campaign competing in Iowa, the "field" – which is the structure subsuming the organizers – numerically constituted the bulk of the personnel and provided the campaign with a *statewide* presence.

The standard early move for a campaign was to name a state director, an important development in both structural and symbolic terms. The director didn't have free rein, given that an operation in any state, even an important early one like Iowa, is tethered to the national. Still, the director likely had more discretion than anyone else locally about structure and staff choices. The symbolic element cuts a couple of different ways. Democratic insiders, just like everyone else operating in uncertainty, will read between the lines what the state director pick portends for the campaign – someone with experience, a winning track record, maybe a person known for innovation. These things are interpreted as potentially meaningful signals of what to expect. For the pool of campaign staff hopefuls weighing whether to shoot for or accept a position with a campaign, these early staffing decisions give important cues, especially for anyone who had worked with those already on board.

2020 was a banner year for women as state campaign directors in Iowa. Add the Trump reelection effort to the mix, and there were seven campaigns run by women. Their stories, like those of other staff, paint a picture of personnel making their way through an array of career opportunities, working for parties and candidates, with paths intersecting at times. Former US Secretary of Housing and Urban Development Julián Castro and Senator Elizabeth Warren had both declared early in 2019, and they each tapped women to run their Iowa campaigns. Cynthia Sebian-Lander with Castro had headed up Deidre DeJear's 2018 campaign for Iowa Secretary of State. While DeJear, a new Democratic leader, fell short in November, Sebian-Lander was still considered a rising star in Iowa politics. Warren's campaign was led by Janice Rottenberg. She had started in campaign politics as a summer unpaid fellow for Barack Obama in 2008 and had worked in a variety of positions since then, most recently heading up the state party's "coordinated campaign" in 2018. Legally speaking, the "coordinated" is an arm of the party, but in reality it tends to do the bidding of the candidate at the top of the ticket. Running the coordinated is a good way to get to know the entire state.[14] Another woman, Misty Rebik, headed up the Sanders campaign. Rebik had run the 2018 gubernatorial campaign for the "outsider" candidate and also had strong ties to the progressive, grassroots organization Iowa Citizens for Community Improvement (CCI), as did many of the other state-level Sanders staff. Klobuchar's state director, Lauren Dillon, was an Iowa native who had spent significant time in the Iowa governor's office and with the DNC. Her sister-in-law, Jen O'Malley Dillon, had been John Edwards' Iowa state director in 2008, was Beto O'Rourke's national campaign manager in 2020, and eventually moved to Joe Biden's campaign.

State campaign leadership brought knowledge of Iowa, and the party apparatus offered another route to the same. Campaigns came and went, but the party was around cycle after cycle. While state party chairs had relatively short tenures, some of the professional personnel who staffed the party had been around for many years. Similarly, the state central committee is a mix of veterans and newcomers. Organized along county lines, state parties have an inherent geographic diversity, offering meaningful contacts and relationships with local party leaders and activists. Put simply, the party apparatus provides connections and institutional memory. Talk to party officials and they'll tell you that the party offers both of these to all campaigns, a claim disputed by some campaigns, especially Sanders'. At the same time, having Iowans in charge and involved didn't mean there wouldn't be surprises or opportunities for learning, even when the candidate had run an Iowa campaign before.

Back in Malcom

In April 2019, Sanders' appearances in Iowa were limited to one weekend. But he was building out a broad, well-staffed organization and energizing – or reenergizing – activists. Scheduling a "town meeting" at the Malcom Auditorium on April 7th seemed a bit unusual because it was an obscure location for an event that would likely draw a big crowd. Malcom is much like hundreds of other small towns across the state: its population today is almost half what it was back in 1940. At one point the town – a station on the old Chicago, Rock Island and Pacific Railroad – had a school, a newspaper, banks, hotels, churches, three lodges, a grain elevator, and the auditorium. It also had a stockyard prompting the nickname "Little Chicago."[15] But over the years, more and more residents moved to cities, and local institutions closed their doors. The school merged with a nearby district, creating a much larger district that covers much of the eastern part of the county. Today, Malcom perseveres. It is home to a tavern, a well-known meat locker, and a chemical-processing complex owned by the German conglomerate BASF.

As the town meeting start time approached that Sunday, it was clear that Sanders' supporters had shown up in force: the main streets of the small town lined with parked cars. From the county names displayed on Iowa license plates, the event drew people from across the state, with good representation from out of state as well. Inside the auditorium, about 200 folding chairs were lined in rows facing the platform, with media standing in the back, cordoned off. The typical candidate event at this point in the cycle brought in a reporter or two, maybe a single camera crew. Sanders' media section hosted four crews, though one was the campaign's own. It resembled, to a degree, the press mob that would be present at events later in the cycle for competitive candidates. The campaign had its own sound system cycling through its usual playlist, including "Disco Inferno," with its "Burn, Baby Burn" refrain resonating with the "Feel the Bern" campaign meme. The ratio of Sanders volunteers at the event to plain old attendees was about 1:10. White, professionally printed "Bernie" signs were scattered on the folding chairs as people arrived, in place for the crowd to wave in approval for what they would hear, making a nice visual for the cameras.

Carl Birkestrand sat in the fourth row. Retired and his late sixties, Carl could pass for someone much younger. He was from Davenport, a river town of about 100,000, one hundred miles due east. Friendly and gregarious, Carl is quick to make friends and readily struck up conversation with those sitting close by. He had been in Sanders' camp for the caucuses in 2016, but had no trouble voting for Clinton in the general election. Pushed to elaborate on the 2016 move from Sanders to Clinton-as-nominee, Carl said that it was simple. He was just supporting the party. But with Sanders giving it another shot, Carl was back in his camp, spending this April weekend following the candidate on his swing through the state.

Outside the auditorium and 50 feet away, a merchandise vendor had set up a retail area to hawk Sanders t-shirts and buttons – something, like the array of press, rarely seen this early in a nomination campaign. The t-shirt and button vendors at campaign events in Iowa are seemingly without fail from the South, this one from Arizona. Despite the crowd inside, he said his business was "not good today." A lone female Sanders staffer stood in the street in front of the auditorium, splitting time on her phone between talking and texting. She wasn't up for idle chit chat while waiting, occasionally peering down the short street for the candidate's motorcade – or more accurately, the small line of cars and SUVs.

As the crowd inside was swelling beyond what the folding chairs would accommodate, national staff materialized outside. Out in front, one male staffer surveyed the scene, his eyes on a massive structure dominating the skyline two blocks away. "What are we looking at?" he asked a volunteer, a neighboring-county party chair who supported Sanders. "It's a grain elevator," he was told.

The staffer pushed for a little more. "And what's the population of this town?" The chair said he thought it was about 230, which puzzled the staffer. "Two-hundred thirty...?"

"Two-hundred thirty *people*," clarified the chair. It took a moment for the staffer to process that: "Wow. OK." Armed with new facts, he turned to brief his colleague.

"So what we're looking at is a grain elevator and we're in a town of 230." As if on cue, the colleague responded, "230 *people*?"

Inside, the candidate took the stage after a handful of local speakers and national surrogates – including Nina Turner, one of his most visible champions from 2016. Turner, moving between the platformed stage and the assembled chairs, fired up the crowd, dropping repeated references to "hashtag woke" in her message to Malcom and her introduction of the candidate. For his part, Sanders leaned on the podium, which bore a printed "Malcom" sign supplied by the campaign. The candidate, flanked by US and Iowa state flags, delivered a substantive speech, first – of course – acknowledging the setting: "I have been told that I am the first presidential candidate to ever come to Malcom, Iowa. The mayor tells me there are 287 people in this town, and we must have the whole town here," a line that the candidate delivered to wild enthusiasm from the crowd assembled from across the state and the Midwest, just a handful from Malcom.[16]

In the prepared speech and answers to questions, the senator presented his vision for progressive change and revolution, even engaging with the audience in a light-hearted manner that was not always his style. He acknowledged the obvious, signaling his attentiveness to place. "Rural America is hurting. We are losing family-based agriculture, we are seeing our kids leave the towns they grew up in because there are no decent jobs ... seeing downtowns boarded up and ... schools closing ..." Still, Sanders assured the audience that "a small town is a great place to live in." And possibly projecting, rather than reading the crowd, "[W]e should not be embarrassed about that."

Every political context has its peculiarities, and Iowa is hardly unique in that regard. But even with wide variation across communities and the lived experience of people across the state, Iowa presidential nomination politics is a world that can be unfamiliar to the deluge of political outsiders who arrive to work on campaigns, and even to some who are already in Iowa but are newcomers to the caucus bubble.

Notes

1 Legal status as a candidate comes with filing FEC FORM 2, a "statement of candidacy." It's a simple form, requiring very little information.
2 Hugh Winebrenner has studied the caucuses since the 1970s and tracked candidate days. Now the count is readily available, owing in part to new media, like *Iowa Starting Line*, and traditional media, like *The Des Moines Register*, which report candidate visits to the state.

30   *The Promised Land*

3 The *Register's* Tracker showed visits by future Democratic candidates Bill de Blasio, Pete Buttigieg, Tulsi Gabbard, Amy Klobuchar, Seth Moulton, Tim Ryan, Bernie Sanders, and Eric Swalwell, as well as Oregon senator Jeff Merkley, who would be highly visible throughout 2018 but never enter the race.
4 https://whotv.com/news/first-2020-democratic-presidential-candidate-visits-iowa/
5 Final late September 2018 Iowa Poll results in-full linked by *Iowa Starting Line* (https://iowastartingline.com/wp-content/uploads/2018/10/180919-Iowa-Voter-Survey-fin4.pdf.) Delaney favorable 24%, unfavorable 9%.
6 https://news.gallup.com/poll/202349/president-obama-leaves-white-house-favorable-rating.aspx
7 Disbursements shown in FEC reports filed quarterly by candidate committees offer a window on staff size. The itemized expenditures for "salary," "payroll," or some related entry reveal not only the number of staff on payroll but also the actual pay check of the staff member. The FEC data don't, however, tie staff to a particular state, since address listed may be a permanent one, not where a staff member resides during the campaign.
8 Digital resources make it much easier now than in the past to track campaign staff. Eric Appleman has documented staff – as well as other dimensions of presidential nomination and general election campaigns – since 2000. His websites (e.g. www.P2020.org for campaign 2020) offer the best available data on staff and their backgrounds. *Iowa Starting Line* and Ballotpedia also present data about staff.
9 www.census.gov/library/visualizations/2016/comm/citizen_voting_age_population/cb16-tps18_iowa.html. The record for Democratic caucus attendance was 236,000 in 2008. Republican attendance that same year, with a competitive contest as well, was 119,000. (www.electproject.org/2008p)
10 These reflect contests through April 21, 2016, which constituted about two-thirds of the contests – ones held while there was still some degree of competition in the party (Sabato, 2016).
11 www.electproject.org/2016P
12 See for example Pearce (2020).
13 Some state campaigns have additional structures, focused on specialized functions. For example, it's common to have outreach units focused on particular constituencies—like the Latinx or African American populations, or organized labor. Finance/fundraising is typically under the purview of the national campaign.
14 The coordinated model dates back to the mid-1980s in Democratic electoral politics across the nation (Corrado, 1996.) It reflects the conceit that "a rising tide lifts all boats." In other words, if campaigns for disparate offices under the party label coordinate their efforts, they should *all* benefit. In the 1990s, state coordinated campaigns were funded by then-abundant party soft money, something that changed under the McCain-Feingold (2002) soft money ban. Now, state parties extract contributions from campaigns to fund their coordinated efforts.
15 As reported in the "*Malcom Centennial*" book, http://grinnell.lib.ia.us/wp-content/uploads/2018/08/Malcom-Centennial-Book-1872-1972_optimized.pdf.
16 The senator was probably right about his status as first presidential candidate stopping in Malcom, though a September 1948 whistle-stop would have carried Harry Truman, then president and campaigning for the 1948 general election, through Malcom (Balducci, 2007).

References

Abramowitz, Alan. 2008. "Don't blame primary voters for polarization." *The Forum* 5(4):1–11.

Balducci, David. 2007. "Tall stalks and plain talk: Truman's 1948 whistle-stop campaign in Iowa." *Iowa Heritage Illustrated* Winter: 146–159.

Corrado, Anthony. 1996. "The politics of cohesion: the role of the national party committees in the 1992 election." In *The State of the Parties: The Changing Role of American Parties* 2nd ed. John C. Green and Daniel M. Shea, eds. Lanham, MD: Rowman & Littlefield.

Cotter, Cornelius P., James L. Gibson, John F. Bibby, Robert J. Huckshorn. 1984. *Party Organizations in American Politics*. New York: Praeger.

Delaney, John. 2017. "John Delaney: why I'm running for president." *The Washington Post* July 28 (www.washingtonpost.com/opinions/john-delaney-why-im-running-for-president/2017/07/28/02460ae4-73b7-11e7-8f39-eeb7d3a2d304_story.html).

Epstein, Leon. 1986. *Political Parties in the American Mold*. Madison: University of Wisconsin Press.

Geer, John. G. 1988. "Assessing the representativeness of electorates in presidential primaries." *American Journal of Political Science* 32(4):929–945.

Hayworth, Bret. 2019. "Elizabeth Warren in Sioux City vows to fight hard for working families." *Sioux City Journal* January 5 (https://siouxcityjournal.com/news/local/govt-and-politics/elizabeth-warren-in-sioux-city-vows-to-fight-hard-for/article_71d757da-b5a5-53f0-9b68-059a35a6ff1f.html).

Hull, Christopher C. 2008. *Grassroots Rules: How the Iowa Caucus Helps Elect American Presidents*. Stanford, CA: Stanford University Press.

Kamp, David. 2017. "Why Joe Biden didn't run … and why he's not ruling out 2020." *Vanity Fair* October 25 (www.vanityfair.com/news/2017/10/why-joe-biden-didnt-run-for-president-and-why-hes-not-ruling-out-2020).

Key, V. 0. 1956. *American State Politics: An Introduction*. New York: Knopf.

McDonald, Michael P. and Thessalia Merivaki "Voter turnout in presidential nominating contests." *The Forum* 13(4): 597–622.

Noble, Jason. 2017. "John Delaney's early, aggressive 2020 presidential bid is 'all in' on Iowa." *The Des Moines Register* October 20 (www.desmoinesregister.com/story/news/politics/2017/10/20/john-delaney-2020-presidential-iowa-caucuses/780497001/).

Norrander, Barbara. 1989. "Ideological representativeness of presidential primary voters" *American Journal of Political Science* 33 (3):570–87.

Norrander, Barbara. 2015. *The Imperfect Primary: Oddities, Biases, and Strengths of US Presidential Nomination Politics*. New York: Routledge.

Pearce, Matt. 2020. "'It's overwhelming': for Iowa Democrats, there's nowhere to hide from this presidential campaign." *Los Angeles Times* January 31 (www.latimes.com/politics/story/2020-01-31/iowa-democrats-nowhere-to-hide-from-presidential-campaign).

Rakich, Nathaniel. 2019. "The candidates who are going all in on Iowa or New Hampshire." *FiveThirtyEight* May 23 (https://fivethirtyeight.com/features/the-candidates-who-are-going-all-in-on-iowa-or-new-hampshire/).

Redlawsk, David P., Caroline J. Tolbert, and Todd Donovan. 2011. *Why Iowa?* Chicago: University of Chicago Press.

Rynard, Pat. 2019. "What Elizabeth Warren's Iowa swing told us about 2020." *Iowa Starting Line* January 7 (https://iowastartingline.com/2019/01/07/what-elizabeth-warrens-iowa-swing-told-us-about-2020/).

Sabato, Larry. 2016. "Primaries versus caucuses: the score so far in 2016." *Rasmussen Reports* April 21 (www.rasmussenreports.com/public_content/political_commentary/commentary_by_larry_j_sabato/primaries_versus_caucuses_the_score_so_far_in_2016).

Sides, John, Chris Tausanovitch, Lynn Vavreck and Christopher Warshaw. 2020. "On the representativeness of primary electorates." *British Journal of Political Science* 50(2), 677–685.

Stone, Walter J., Alan I. Abramowitz, and Ronald B. Rapoport. 1989. "How representative are the Iowa caucuses." In *The Iowa Caucuses and the Presidential Nomination Process*, ed. Peverill Squire, chap. 2. Boulder: Westview, pp. 19–49.

Winebrenner, Hugh and Dennis J. Goldford. 2010. *The Iowa Precinct Caucuses: The Making of a Media Event, 3rd Edition*. Iowa City: University of Iowa Press.

3 Setting Up Shop

The Iowa caucuses were different for each person, depending on perspective. For an unknown candidate without name recognition or personal wealth, they might have been the one shot at credibility. For a wealthy, self-financed candidate an afterthought – even a nuisance. For vendors selling digital campaign products or property owners with apartments for rent, a revenue stream. For an activist, a chance for access to prominent decision makers. And for a staffer, the caucuses were a career move.

Like many other organizers, Lauren Parker's first time in Iowa was when she arrived to work. Lauren was 29, a little older than the typical organizer, and her position with Senator Kirsten Gillibrand was her first paid position on any campaign. She had spent the previous ten years in New York City, attending college and staying there for work at a prominent film industry talent agency, followed by graduate school. Lauren had volunteered in 2016 for Hillary Clinton and then became interested in Gillibrand through contacts at work. A native of a southern state, Lauren's knowledge of the Midwest, let alone Iowa, was limited. But she was a true believer in Gillibrand and saw the candidate as the best out there for the job of president. She also was keenly interested in seeing a woman elected to the White House.

Her first night in Iowa, Lauren stayed in Des Moines with local Democratic royalty. Former IDP Chairman Scott Brennan and his family hosted her, something they'd done for many staffers and candidates over the years. Cory Booker, for example, had recently spent the night at the Brennan home. The next day, Lauren bought a used car – the first she had ever owned. It was a necessity if she were to organize her three, rural counties. In fact, a car is something almost every Iowa campaign staffer needs, a tool of the trade. Lauren had shopped online that first night in Des Moines, finding a car at a private auto lot, which struck Brennan as "a little bit dicey." The next day, Brennan drove her to the lot so she could take a look. He was happy to wait, but she insisted she'd be fine. Lauren returned to the house with what Brennan thought might have been "the ugliest car [I'd] ever seen"– an aging hatchback, with rust mixed in with the gold paint. Lauren wound up driving that car all over her vast rural territory, immersing herself in the place and its people and in the work of organizing.

For the parties in Iowa, the caucuses are the first and the most visible step in the multi-stage process that culminates in the selection of Iowa's national convention delegates. Fair to say, there's a mix of influences coming from both inside and outside of Iowa that structures the process. In fact, a dizzying array of national and state party organizations and state and federal governments, including the courts, are all involved at some level. The rules set down are hardly ever arbitrary, instead the product of political battles, some long ago and others more recent. And like rules in every other context, they're never neutral, working to the advantage of some and the disadvantage of others (Redlawsk et al., 2011).

For Iowa Democrats in 2020, there would be some important rule changes adopted by the state party, though under pressure from the Democratic National Committee (DNC). The internal party divisions of 2016 and after – sort of a 1968-lite dynamic – poured into the party planning. Part of this was to avoid a division that might doom a 2020 nominee, but it also represented the success of the voices of dissent from 2016 that had become part of the formal party apparatus. Generally speaking, US parties are permeable organizations (Pastor et al., 1999; Rapoport & Stone, 2005; Clark & Prysby, 2004). At least minimally there are some paths open to power and influence; after 2016, Sanders forces had successfully secured a voice in the decision-making structure, both at the DNC and the IDP. The rules in place for 2020 would be a combination of change and continuity, some provisions newly adopted and others used every cycle.

Basic Rules of the Game

Well in advance of every contest, the national parties set the basic terms of their presidential nomination season, technically spelled out in a "Call for Convention" document. Exacting and precise, mind-numbing in detail, the Call addresses a number of relevant details, for instance the national convention dates, originally set for July 13–16, 2020. The pick of Milwaukee, WI, as the Democrats' site would come later. The Call also sets the size of the national convention – 3,979 total pledged delegates in 2020, meaning that a candidate would need the support of 1,991 delegates at the convention – a majority – to pick up the nomination.[1] And it apportions to state parties a certain number of delegate positions to be filled in the caucus and primary processes.

That apportionment of delegate positions takes into consideration both the size of the state – small, in Iowa's case – and the strength of the Democratic vote in the past three presidential elections. That's a reward for past support of the party, giving a proportionately stronger voice to states with good Democratic track records, something that Iowa had in the Obama presidential general elections, but not in 2016. For a sense of the role the past support plays, consider a state like Utah with weak Democratic support, but a population only slightly larger than Iowa's. For the 2020 contest, it was apportioned just 29 delegates to be selected through its primary process, compared to Iowa's 41.[2]

This delegate apportionment provision is just a drop in the bucket holding the hundreds of rules that govern nomination politics. And it's a great example of how bias infuses every rule, in this case giving more delegates to the states which have been good party supporters. But the rules battles leading into 2020 in Iowa focused elsewhere, in large part placed on the agenda by concerns articulated by Sanders and his supporters. Some were prominent, visible to a moderately broad audience; others were obscure, the bailiwick of the sort of person who reads rulebooks for fun.

Concerns about just who can participate in a primary or caucus are long-standing, but they resonated with the Sanders charge that the Democratic nomination system is "rigged" in favor of the establishment. In Iowa, only registered partisans can participate in caucuses; the same provision is in place for primaries held for other offices.[3] Registering with a party or changing party registration is pretty easy, accomplished by filling out a registration or change of registration form at the primary or caucus and making sure to check the box of the right party. However, psychologically for some it's difficult, an effective barrier to participation.

Some voters and activists object on principle to the idea that only partisans should be eligible to participate in a party's primary or caucus,[4] a complaint dismissed by party advocates who feel that registration is a very low bar to pass in order to have a role in *the* fundamental activity of a party – selecting its nominee. For his part, Sanders had advanced a pragmatic argument about party registration, asserting that having independents in the mix for nomination would help produce a candidate more likely to win in the general election. This struck some as self-serving since Sanders tended to do better in contests with ready participation of independents (Stein, 2016). Still, changing caucus eligibility rules in 2020 was a non-starter. Not so for some other rules.

Provisions for what happens at the caucuses and after were fair game. Among the slated changes were how attendees would express candidate preference at the caucuses and how results would be reported and extended into later stages of the state's caucus-convention process. Democratic caucuses in Iowa have never used a ballot for attendees to disclose their candidate preference. Not a formal, printed ballot like in a primary or general election, not even a piece of paper to write a candidate's name.[5] Instead, under caucus procedures, attendees move – physically – into groups, with the number of people in each group being the indicator of support for a candidate. Add that up across the state and you would get a measure of candidate support akin to a raw vote if preferences were indicated on a ballot. But the IDP traditionally had reported a different value, a mathematical projection of how many delegates to the state convention a candidate could expect to receive given the precinct caucus results, that is after subsequent steps in the state's multi-stage process of delegate selection. These are state delegate equivalents (SDEs).

To critics, reporting SDEs and judging the caucus results on this basis were opaque and un-democratic because it potentially obscured the actual level of support for individual candidates among caucus attendees. The results from 2016 seemed to bear this out when Sanders thought he performed better than Clinton in caucus preference but lost in the SDEs. He asked the state party on caucus night to release a "raw vote count," which was a request impossible to fulfill because no such count existed (Roberts, 2016). For the state party, however, the delegate count has some value as an estimate of how things might theoretically look come summer when the party would be poised to select national convention delegates. In this sense, it's a nod to the caucuses as but one step in the selection of national convention delegates, the people who will ultimately make the call in nomination.

Additional concerns about those later stages in the caucus-convention process took on some steam in 2016 once attention – both of national observers and most people in Iowa – had shifted to other states. If SDEs hinted at inside baseball, this was worse. The events that followed the caucuses – the county, congressional district, and state conventions – were largely obscure from public view. Still, what transpired at those gatherings could matter, potentially shifting the results in favor of one candidate or another as the process played out. In what seemed like a familiar refrain, Sanders' supporters felt that these too were settings biased in favor of insiders, subject to gamesmanship by those in the know.[6] And the equally familiar rejoinder to that was that there's no shame in knowing the rules and effectively maneuvering within them to the advantage of your candidate.

Each Democratic state party drafts a "delegate selection plan" each cycle, submitting it to the DNC, which has final approval over it. A typical plan would largely repeat the past cycle's. But 2020 was no typical year for Democrats. Iowa Democrats drafted a plan that responded to some of the concerns of the Sanders faction, which was by then part of the state party apparatus. There was a little arm-twisting from the DNC as well, which had established the "Unity Reform Commission" – a small group of leaders representing the Clinton and the Sanders campaigns, including Sanders' champion Nina Turner. The commission issued a set of recommendations for the nomination season, many of which were ultimately adopted by the DNC.

Among the recommendations was the requirement that attendees cast their candidate preference in writing to ensure the possibility of an accurate recount, if necessary.[7] Preferences in writing would also make it easier to have a firm count of candidate support among attendees, which would facilitate another thing the commission had in mind for Iowa Democrats: reporting initial expressions of candidate preference, in addition to the SDEs. And to eliminate the possibility of those in-the-know gaming later steps in the caucus/convention system, the results of the caucuses were to be "locked in" for subsequent steps.

The typical Iowa Democrat, along with most Iowans, paid no attention to the rules rewriting process, at best skimming through a news article about some meeting of the national committee that was taking up plans for 2020. The only thing really resonating by early 2019 was the IDP proposal to hold a "virtual caucus." This addressed a persistent knock on the system over the years that the caucuses were exclusionary. By virtue of being a meeting held at a particular date and time, the caucuses left out some Democrats who might have wanted to participate – second-shift workers, parents with children at home, the disabled, the elderly. Essentially anyone without the luxury of dropping everything on a Monday evening in the middle of winter to spend a few hours at a party meeting was out of luck.

The Unity Commission had weighed in on this issue, recommending that caucus states offer absentee voting, making the process more inclusive. The problem for Iowa Democrats, though, was that any provision for absentee voting ventured into the dangerous territory of making the caucuses look like a primary, potentially sealing their doom. If the caucuses functioned like a primary, Iowa might no longer have claim on first-in-the-nation status, since New Hampshire had a lock on the "first primary" designation. The virtual caucus option, though mysterious in detail, seemed to offer the best of both worlds: headway on the issue of inclusiveness but no danger of crossing into primary territory. The early sketch had been included in the IDP's draft delegate-selection plan, ultimately approved by the state party in April 2019. It offered just enough detail to signal to rules-focused Democrats that the party had given careful thought to how this new system could comport with the basic provisions in place for traditional caucuses and delegate selection. For example, virtual caucus-goers were to express a ranked-choice preference among candidates. This would allow the virtual gathering to approximate a key component of long-standing in-person caucus rules.

Former IDP Chair Scott Brennan was mired in the plan from all sorts of angles. In addition to his state central committee membership, Brennan was a DNC member – and more to the point, sat on the Rules and Bylaws Committee, which is tasked each cycle with approving delegate-selection plans for each state. Party involvement can involve extraordinary commitments of time depending on the role. Brennan estimated that his party work took on average 10–15 hours/week, not including an enormous amount of travel over prior years as he worked to sell the virtual caucus plan to the national party and to other early states also involved in the Democratic nomination process.

Meanwhile on the ground in Iowa in spring 2019, State Democratic Chair Troy Price did his best to evangelize at local party gatherings, working to assuage lingering concerns about glitches from 2016 and new uncertainty about how the virtual caucus would work. Price had moved into the top spot at the IDP when Derek Eadon, that post 2016 pick, resigned shortly into his tenure because of health concerns. Price reported that the state party was making progress on operationalizing the virtual caucus concept, working with a group from Harvard – including a retired director of the National Security Agency – on technology "impregnable from hacking." He said that planning for the caucuses, then nine-months off, looked good, well ahead of where it had been in 2016 with respect to hiring personnel. And despite the plan to allocate 10% of the total caucus delegates to the virtual caucuses, the party's focus would still be on the traditional, in-person caucuses. "[T]hat's where the party building will take place."[8] A message like this was important to many party activists, because for them the caucuses were always about more than having a voice in the presidential nomination.

The interests of the party and candidates don't always align, but in the case of the virtual caucus plan they seemed to, at least for one candidate. For the IDP, virtual caucuses would solve a vexing problem of accessibility. For a candidate like Marianne Williamson, that 10% delegate take from the virtual caucus could land her support she might otherwise not get. Of the two dozen Democratic candidates in the mix that spring, Williamson was a non-traditional candidate, even more so than Donald Trump had been in 2016. She had entered the race in late January 2019, giving Iowans a few months to get to know her. But if they knew anything, it was that she was professed to be Oprah Winfrey's spiritual guru. An author and motivational speaker, Williamson asked Democrats to support her by joining the "evolution," a New Age twist on Sanders' "revolution." Based on those who attended events, Williamson appealed to a small slice of middle-aged suburban women – drawn to the candidate's message that "love will prevail."

Williamson didn't have enough support to register in the polls, but she did have an impressive 2.6 million followers on Twitter, with the Oprah connection undoubtedly helping. The campaign made a push for "virtual captains," capitalizing on Williamson's nationwide network by recruiting organizers in each of Iowa's 99 counties, though acknowledging that about 40% were from Iowa and the rest from across the nation (Rynard, 2019). A billboard in the state called out CNN, drawing its attention to her virtual chair success and hoping to parlay it into some attention by the network. It may have been a desperate move, but it revealed some strategic insight recognizing that the virtual caucuses might be a window of opportunity for certain candidates.

Beginning to Organize

Early in the cycle, it was mostly party and campaign leadership occupying themselves with the ins and outs of rules and strategy, plus a smattering of local party people, campaign junkies, and the occasional reporter. But most staffers and activists skipped right to the operative takeaways, void of much nuance. First, caucuses would be held on Monday, February 3, 2020 at 7pm. Second, those who showed up would indicate their preference for candidates with those results fueling judgments of who wins and who loses. And third, staff on the ground understood a critical imperative: *organize* in the interest of getting supporters to the caucuses.

The Organizers

Organizers are foot soldiers of modern mobilization efforts, both in electoral and nomination campaigns.[9] In Iowa caucus politics, the organizers established relationships with voters and activists, holding the long-term goal of mobilizing supporters to the caucuses and equipping them with information and skills necessary for a productive caucus experience. A common short-term goal was to construct an organization of volunteers to assist in that effort. A good organizer did this all effortlessly, combining the skills of both a salesperson and a preacher, bringing in supporters but also pushing them out to do the same.

By the start of June 2019, there were well over 100 organizers on the ground in Iowa. By that time, the field of candidates had grown to 23, with Buttigieg, Biden, Moulton, Ryan, and Swalwell having declared in April. Bullock, Bennet, and de Blasio joined the race in May, and Joe Sestak announced in June. Impressionistic evidence suggested that Warren and Harris were on their way to building particularly robust field organizations. Buttigieg seemed to lag behind, even beyond what would be expected for a candidate who declared moderately late in early April. Biden, having started his campaign at the end of April, had only a shell organization. The parameters of the Sanders campaign were a mystery to those outside of the tight Sanders circle. The campaign embodied stealth, eschewing traditional early paths to engaging with Democrats like attending local party meetings.

Each candidate and campaign is admittedly different, and the experience of a field organizer is also unique. That said, organizing is fundamentally the same across campaigns. In Iowa, the long-term focus was typically on caucus night and the potential caucus attendees who would express their preference for a candidate. In the short term, the organizer was tasked with meeting, engaging, and convincing Iowans to commit to the organizer's candidate – all tasks that might take some time. Along the way, the organizer tried to build their network of volunteers to assist with those same tasks – and more – as the caucuses approached.

Organizers working in Iowa were typically in their early to mid-twenties and college educated. Most were not native Iowans but came from across the country, though some states and regions seemed to be more prominent feeders. States proximate to Iowa, as well as New England and the DC beltway, were well-represented. Some organizers had previous campaign experience, though in many cases as a volunteer, not a paid staffer. Many were recent graduates, others had taken a break from their undergraduate studies, and still others were veterans of many previous campaigns – local, state, and national. Undaunted by the stories of long hours and low pay, they focused instead on the opportunity to affect an election outcome and the future of the country. They landed in the organizer positions through a number of different paths: online posts, personal connections, word-of-mouth, and even via party organizations.

Jennifer Koppess grew up in Colorado but came to Iowa to attend Drake University in Des Moines. At Drake, like other colleges and universities across the country located in state capitals, there's a well-traveled path into politics for students and alumni. Jennifer's path to the Booker campaign, where she started as an organizer the day after her college graduation, began with a friend and sorority sister who was a year ahead in school. The friend had taken a semester off to work for a state party entity that coordinates campaigns for the Iowa House of Representatives. And she pressed Jennifer to intern for the state legislative campaign of a Drake University professor. Though it was an unpaid internship, it was still a chance for Jennifer to cut her teeth on the sort of activities that would eventually be useful as a paid organizer: knocking doors/canvassing and making phone calls. Compensation came in the form of the occasional pizza.

Like this first foray into campaign work, Jennifer's path to Booker was in part paved by college connections. The classmate who had drawn Jennifer into the unpaid internship had signed on as a regional organizer with Booker, like Jacob Hamblin. For her part, Jennifer had been to a few nomination campaign events and saw Booker at one of his first appearances in the state. She applied to work for the campaign, but it took time to firm up the position, all while graduation was quickly approaching. "You send in your [application], then you talk with them, and then you wait. It's like 'Hurry up and wait.'"

There are as many paths to organizing for a presidential hopeful as there are organizers, and not all involve networks and political experience. Working for a presidential candidate in Iowa was an opportunity open to a wide swath of the population, at least theoretically. Specialized education, skills, and experiences were less important than enthusiasm and willingness to commit to a campaign and learn the ropes quickly. That said, there were effective barriers in place making the option of moving into campaign work less realistic for some, especially people whose personal situation – family commitments, financial responsibilities, even willingness or ability to tolerate risk and uncertainty – imposed demands too high to overlook.

By the 2020 cycle the terms of employment had improved due to a combination of factors, including the recognition that the work environment enhances quality of work. The extreme demands of campaign work had been in place for years, but some developments over the recent two decades had ratcheted up the reliance on organizers and expectations for their productivity. In the mix were an enhanced emphasis on grassroots mobilization and even new tools used in organizing, both arguably advances, but imposing hefty demands on organizers. This time around, improved conditions of employment reflected a greater attention to worker's rights, some advances in technology, and the experiences of campaign leadership who had worked their way up the ladder under more difficult workplace conditions and were now willing to commit to improvements. The seller's market didn't hurt, with the record size of the Democratic field meaning more jobs and a little more leverage for potential staff.

The salaries of Iowa organizers in place in the late spring/early summer 2019 hovered around $3,000/month, with health insurance and mileage on top of that. Campaigns had also made some advances in basic practices and tools that the business world had used for at least a decade. In the past, they were unsystematic about covering mileage. This expense could add up, with some organizers' territories covering multiple counties, plus meetings, training events, and campaign events scheduled in sometimes distant places. A common practice in the past was for the campaign to distribute gas station gift cards to compensate for gas – at worst and in rare cases cards aligned with stations outside the region. This cycle, some campaigns used centralized fleet cards to pay for gas, and even – another welcome development – prepaid cards for small expenses.

Organizers, like other campaign staff, sign a contract which, along with an employee handbook, details the terms of employment. This includes the weekly work hours and specified time off and holidays, acknowledging the importance of an improved work environment over the traditional 60–90 hour workweeks that were standard in previous campaign cycles. Those campaign handbooks commonly included confidentiality agreements prohibiting staff from discussing the campaign, sometimes extending beyond the life of the campaign. Handbooks addressed expectations for staff behavior, also reflecting lessons of the past, including charges of workplace harassment. After 2016, the Sanders campaign had been the subject of allegations about sexual harassment and a biased workplace culture. The 17-page document created by the 2020 Sanders campaign – "A Blueprint for Safety, Inclusion & Equity in Political Campaign Work" – was intended to address concerns about harassment and discrimination (Gambino, 2019).

Rachel Salas came from a rural area of a southern state, bringing her easy drawl to Iowa, a state known for a broadcast standard, neutral Midwestern accent. Rachel had graduated in May 2019 from a regional university, a journalism/political science double major who had picked up the politics bug during freshman year when the local elections board tried to block an on-campus voting site. She supported Sanders in her home state's 2016 primary and worked for him as a campaign fellow. She did the same for Clinton in the 2016 general election effort. It was during an internship at Emily's List, the long-standing organization committed to electing women, that Rachel met people who had staffed presidential campaigns in Iowa and promoted the idea of working there. "If [you want] to be in politics and make change … at a small level and then at a national level … you need to be an organizer, and you need to go to Iowa." Jeff Link, the Iowa operative who hosted the early Delaney gathering, calls the state an "incubator." He offered the compelling data point that David Plouffe, Obama's campaign manager, got his start in Iowa in the early 1990s. Rachel had been advised by the staff at Emily's List that she would need some more campaign experience to work in Iowa – something she found was not necessarily the case once she landed in the state. But not knowing this at the time, she followed that advice in her last year as a student, reducing her class load in fall 2018 and interning with a congressional campaign.

Kamala Harris was the real reason Rachel came to Iowa. Rachel had heard the California senator speak in early 2019, talking about the need to *stop thanking* Black women for electing progressive candidates and, instead, *start electing* Black women as progressive leaders.[10] When Harris announced her candidacy, Rachel made her move. "I just … went on her website, applied, and sent my resume off." That was in February 2019. At that point, Rachel was ready to graduate, and even though she didn't apply to any other campaigns, she sent out more than 100 resumes for other jobs. Like Jennifer Koppess, she then logged some time waiting. Finally in May, after graduation, she got a call from a Harris staffer in Cedar Rapids, Iowa. By July 1, 2019, Rachel was in Iowa.

One-on-Ones

When Rachel first set up shop in rural Iowa, she spent a few hours each day reaching out to known Democrats for "one-on-ones." These are face-to-face meetings, the first step in building a relationship with potential supporters. Definitely not unique to nomination politics or to Iowa, the one-on-one model is employed widely by field organizers in nomination and electoral campaigns. In fact, the Obama campaigns had formalized and tracked this technique, like many practices still followed today. Campaigns offer staff guidance to organizers like Rachel about these one-on-one conversations so they're not flying solo. This is critical for someone new to Iowa, especially with no prior campaign experience. Often using a public venue like a coffee shop or cafe, the organizer would follow a suggested script beginning with a hook to engage an activist, which varied from campaign to campaign. It might start with "What issues are important to you?" or "Tell me your story," and maybe even leaving the lead to the discretion of the organizer. Rachel enjoyed these conversations. "My journalism background came in handy because I never had a problem asking people questions. A lot of it was me asking people what their stories were, what their problems were, and then telling them how Kamala Harris would help."

Simple in concept, the one-on-one meeting has multiple purposes, a reminder that campaigns themselves are complex organizations with highly planned, refined, and frequently-tracked activities. For the organizer, the one-on-one was a chance to initially meet people, some small subset of those who will eventually show up at the caucuses. If the one-on-one yielded promising signals, maybe expressed interest in the candidate or better yet a willingness to volunteer, a follow-up meeting would be the logical next step. And if things went well, that initial contact would introduce the organizer to others. No doubt modern communication technology offers plenty of alternatives to these face-to-face meetings, and campaigns capitalize on those as well. But the in-person push at the outset allowed the organizer to hammer home the central role of traditional face-to-face communication and the power of cultivating new relationships while building a network of like-minded individuals working toward a common goal.

The emphasis on these face-to-face encounters was also a low-pressure way to introduce organizers to the work that would consume them, ramping up in complexity over the course of the campaign. The hope was that anyone hired to organize was at least immediately capable of having a comfortable and productive conversation, especially with a set of targets who shared an interest in the party. It's not as if they were reaching out to Republicans or those fundamentally antagonistic toward the Democratic cause. Rather, they were making a play for low-hanging fruit: Democratic activists in search of a candidate to support.

The Bubble Inside

It might be urban legend, but there's a story told by Democratic activists older than 40 about an alleged caucus-night brawl in 2000. The site was Carl's – or more formally Carl's Place – then, like in 2020, a dive bar in Des Moines' Sherman Hill neighborhood, just north of downtown. Back then, Sherman Hill was just starting down the path of gentrification. The Democratic battle that year was between Al Gore, the sitting vice-president, and Bill Bradley, a former US senator from New Jersey.[11] As the story goes, staffers from both camps were at a New Year's Eve party at Carl's – ready to celebrate the new millennium – when words were exchanged, threats levied, and, ultimately, punches thrown. It was, according to legend, a full-blown donnybrook. But the 2000 contest, both primary and general, was that sort of election.

As the fall 1999 campaign moved toward the early 2000 caucuses – that year scheduled for January 24th – Gore, the nomination heir-apparent, was looking a little vulnerable. In his brief 1988 presidential bid, Gore had famously avoided Iowa and skipped the caucuses. At the state party's fall 1987 fundraiser, then known as the Jefferson-Jackson Dinner, the "JJ," he had stunned the crowd. "There's something wrong when a dinky state like Iowa has so much influence." Gore's tune had changed by 1999 when it was time for that year's JJ, and Bradley was on his heels. "I believe in the Iowa caucuses!" (Barabak, 1999) In the end, Gore would win the Iowa caucuses easily and Bradley would leave the race in March 2000. But for a few months in the fall of 1999 and briefly into the new millennium, the race for the nomination looked to be a close one.

The caucus bubble, with devoted activists and staff focusing their energies on a high-stakes presidential nomination contest, had few options for releasing pressure when it would build. Given the state's prominence in the modern era, the traditional media – national and state – picked up on the slightest signs of minor tension, their coverage legitimizing these as real. And more recently, news media and social media outlets took the conflict online. To be sure, rarely was it an organizer or even a mid-level staffer weighing in publicly; campaigns tried to keep those staff in check. More often, it was the devoted supporters and political influencers on social media, only occasionally someone from the press-operation of the campaign, tossing verbal grenades.

There was tension in the air between the Clinton and Sanders camps in 2016, more than the norm for a contested nomination race. By fall 2015, the "Bernie Bros" label was attached to young, male Sanders supporters whose enthusiasm for the candidate and antipathy toward his opponent sometimes translated into aggressive, misogynistic online behavior. While many in Sanders' campaign questioned the accuracy of this portrayal – one observer calling it a "concoction… by pro-Clinton journalists" – the image persisted. People looking for drama could again find some at the JJ. By 2015, that event was more like a daylong series of activities, culminating in an evening dinner with speeches and plenty of attendant hoopla. Among the thousands of moments, big and small, that defined the 2015 JJ, one with staying power was Sanders' supporters walking out after their candidate spoke, before the other two – Clinton and O'Malley individually – took the stage. It was no Carl's brawl, but it was taken as a sign of bad blood within the Democratic camp.

From the perspective of Sanders and his campaign, Clinton and the Democratic Party were conspiring to shut down his insurgent 2016 campaign by stacking the rules in favor of Clinton. And from the Clinton corner, Sanders' supporters were spouting conspiracy theories and trying to change the rules in the middle of the game. In 2020, Sean Bagniewski was the Democratic chair in Polk County, home to Des Moines. But in 2016, he had simply been an activist seeing the tension up close and hearing the stories. Bagniewski recounted what sounded a little more like a 2016 version of Carl's: "A fistfight broke out in one county."

"Friendship 2020" was one path to a new 2020 era of good feelings, intended to be a bubble of kindness and affection among staff from rival campaigns. Before its use as a Democratic rallying cry, the phrase was used to promote a cruise ship voyage out of Miami. But in February 2019, senators Cory Booker and Sherrod Brown of Ohio – who would visit Iowa and briefly mull a run – were involved in a good-natured Twitter exchange, retweeted by a Booker Iowa staffer and directed to a former Clinton 2016 colleague who was in the Warren camp. That retweet had *#Friendship2020* attached, and it was retweeted the next day by Warren's digital media director, effectively birthing the cross-campaign lovefest.

State organizing leaders and local organizers invoked #Friendship2020 routinely as the campaigns staffed up in the spring, a conceptual promise that the staffer would end up supporting the nominee, whoever that might be. And along the way, they'd be good company for their compatriots in the other campaigns. If anything, this bubble within the bubble made for a handy hashtag woven through the organizers' Instagram and Twitter feeds.

Friendship 2020 existed in both a social and a social media context. Hundreds of posts using the hashtag went out, but for a variety of purposes. One tweet outlined its intent: "No matter which team you're on, we have the same goal to beat the current occupant of the White House! #Friendship2020." Another was celebratory: "Had such a blast at the @LatinoFestIA! Good #Friendship2020 vibes as always and so great to have some." Local Democrats would use it as almost a clarion call to all organizers: "Shoutout to all the organizers who have been incredibly helpful to the Calhoun Dems tonight and throughout this whole #IACaucus process. #organizing #friendship2020 #IA04"

It's impossible to isolate the impact of Friendship 2020. Jacob Hamblin with Booker thought, early in the cycle, that the organic dynamic of the big field in Iowa might itself pave the way for positive relationships among campaign staff. The 2018 battleground states including Iowa, as well as Virginia in the 2017 off year gubernatorial election, were feeders for early campaign hires.[12] Many of the rival 2020 top and mid-level staff had known and even worked with each other in recent contests, were mostly friendly, some even close friends. And as Jacob noted, the "culture at the top" relays a strong signal that can permeate through the ranks of the campaign. Even so, friendships come naturally among organizers, who are usually social people finding themselves sharing spaces – coffee shops, public libraries – and experiences with those from other campaigns. As for Friendship 2020, while some considered it a contrivance, many organizers at least publicly spoke fondly of it. The avowed interest in keeping rivals on good terms extended well beyond the Friendship 2020 crew. This time around, according to Polk County Chair Bagniewski, "There [would be] no tolerance whatsoever for the bullshit." In fact, there might even be an "overreaction" (Korecki, 2019).

Notes

1 See "Call for the 2020 Democratic National Convention," Chair Tom Perez, Adopted April 25, 2018.
2 Richard Berg-Andersson, "The Green Papers: The Math Behind the Democratic Delegate Allocation – 2020." www.thegreenpapers.com/P20/D-Alloc.phtml
3 Ia. Stat. § 43.38 establishes the requirements for participation. The IA Secretary of State refers to the system as "closed," though "partially open" used to describe Iowa's system by the National Conference of State Legislatures (www.ncsl.org/research/elections-and-campaigns/primary-types.aspx) is more apt.
4 See www.openprimaries.org, dedicated to removing partisan barriers to participation in primaries.
5 Iowa Republicans cast such a written ballot at their caucuses.
6 Blog post illustrates especially heated procedural conflict at a 2016 county convention – Bleeding Heartland, "The Polk County Democratic convention fiasco" at www.bleedingheartland.com/2016/03/13/the-polk-county-democratic-convention-fiasco/
7 "Report of the Unity Reform Commission," as adopted by the commission at its December 8 and 9, 2017 meeting.
8 Troy Price. April 14, 2019. Update delivered to Poweshiek County Democratic Party gathering. Grinnell, Iowa.

9 In Democratic nomination politics, most organizers worked for candidate campaigns, though NextGen and other progressive organizations had a strong organizing presence. In Democratic general elections, organizers tend to be hired by the party's coordinated campaign.
10 A prominent national storyline after the 2018 midterms was that the support of African American women had contributed to many Democratic wins, especially that of Senator Doug Jones in Alabama.
11 Bradley boasted broad credentials: Rhodes scholar, Olympic gold medalist, NBA Hall of Famer.
12 Virginia holds off year elections for statewide and state legislative offices. Larry Sabato reasons that having state elections unaligned with the federal cycle worked to the benefit of conservative Democratic segregationists through the early and mid-twentieth century. Dick Howard, law professor, offers that the schedule provides some insulation to the state from national moods (Paviour, 2019). It also serves as a haven for out-of-work staffers after presidential elections.

References

Barabak, Mark Z. 1999. "Forgetting the past, Gore now finds Iowa vote to his liking." *Los Angeles Times* October 12 (www.latimes.com/archives/la-xpm-1999-oct-12-mn-21569-story.html).

Clark, John A. and Charles L. Prysby. 2004. *Southern Political Party Activists: Patterns of Conflict and Change, 1991–2001*. Lexington: University of Kentucky Press.

Gambino, Lauren. 2019. "Bernie Sanders campaign unveils plan to prevent sexism among staff." *The Guardian* May 7 (www.theguardian.com/us-news/2019/may/07/bernie-sanders-campaign-plan-prevent-sexism).

Greenwald, Glenn. 2016. "The 'Bernie Bros' narrative: a cheap campaign tactic masquerading as journalism and social activism." *The Intercept* January 31 (https://theintercept.com/2016/01/31/the-bernie-bros-narrative-a-cheap-false-campaign-tactic-masquerading-as-journalism-and-social-activism/?comments=1).

Korecki, Natasha. 2019. "'No tolerance whatsoever for the bulls—': Iowa Dems warn against new Bernie-Hillary wars." *Politico* May 10 (www.politico.com/story/2019/05/10/2016-ghosts-1315854).

Pastor, Gregory S., Walter J. Stone, and Ronald B. Rapoport. 1999. "Candidate-centered sources of party change: the case of Pat Robertson, 1988." *The Journal of Politics* 61(2): 423–444.

Paviour, Ben. 2019. "A brief history of Virginia's off-year elections." *Virginia Public Media* October 25 (https://vpm.org/news/articles/7927/a-brief-history-of-virginias-off-year-elections.)

Rapoport, Ronald B. and Walter J. Stone. 2005. *Three's a Crowd: The Dynamic of Third Parties, Ross Perot, & Republican Resurgence*. Ann Arbor: University of Michigan Press.

Redlawsk, David P., Caroline J. Tolbert, and Todd Donovan. 2011. *Why Iowa?* Chicago: University of Chicago Press.

Roberts, Dan. 2016. "Bernie Sanders wants raw vote count released after tight finish in Iowa caucuses." *The Guardian* February 2 (www.theguardian.com/us-news/2016/feb/02/bernie-sanders-requests-vote-count-tight-finish-iowa-caucus-clinton).

Rynard, Pat. 2019. "Marianne Williamson recruits 'Virtual Captains' for virtual caucus." *Iowa Starting Line.* February 28 (https://iowastartingline.com/2019/02/28/marianne-williamson-recruits-virtual-captains-for-virtual-caucus/).

Stein, Jeff. 2016. "Bernie Sanders says Democrats should get rid of closed primaries. Is he right?" *Vox* April 28 (www.vox.com/2016/4/28/11469468/open-primaries-closed-primaries-sanders).

4 Summertime

Summer in Iowa is hot, arriving after a spring that could as easily be sunny and warm as it is socked by flooding, hail and tornadoes. In a typical year, school children are on their summer break by early June, unless they had blown through their cache of winter snow days and need to make up time. And unlike in most states, high school softball and baseball seasons run through the summer, keeping some families at the ballpark night after night. Other than that, the routine is much like it is elsewhere in the nation: for many a slightly slower pace of life. When June 2019 rolled around, the state had experienced all of the above, plus a trade war that left farmers anxious.

The Terrain

By the end of June, the candidate field had stabilized considerably. There were 25 in the race, with only a few contenders yet to formally enter, including billionaires Michael Bloomberg and Tom Steyer. Michael Bennet, Steve Bullock, Bill de Blasio, and Joe Sestak all declared in the May/June period. Meanwhile, the campaign structures of the other candidates continued to fill out. Biden's long-expected entry into the fray had come in late April, and once in he began to staff up his team. In reality, a candidate can do almost everything campaign-like without being a declared candidate, but staffing up has to wait until the papers are in (Ryan, 2015). So does raising money for the campaign, for that matter. One challenge in 2019 for candidates entering a little late was that many operatives had been snatched up by candidates who had already set up shop. Warren and Booker, for example, were bringing in second-wave staff hires in organizing positions (Debenedetti, 2019), while Buttigieg was just starting. In May, the mayor had only four total staff in the state, but added 30 new hires in June, including 12 organizers (Rodriguez, 2019).

With the caucuses still eight months off, it was too early to read much into what the polls said about candidates. Given so many in the race, the math worked against any single candidate walking away with commanding support. Biden – while remaining the top choice among likely Democratic caucus-goers – had others closing in. The early June Iowa Poll showed him leading at 24%, with a statistical tie among Sanders, Warren, and Buttigieg for second place. Sanders at 16% had slipped 9 points since March, granted there were more candidates in the mix by June, fractionalizing the support even more. But Warren and Buttigieg seemed to be gaining, Buttigieg in a dramatic way. His support jumped from 1% in March to 14% in June.[1]

Democrats grappled with the perennial electability question, wondering which candidate could beat President Trump in the 2020 general election. Scholarship has shown that no one factor explains candidate choice. But for activists, the prospects of winning in November factor into the selection of which candidate to support in the nomination contest (Stone & Abramowitz, 1986; Stone & Rapoport, 1994). In June 2019, likely caucus-goers pointed to electability as an important factor for the 2020 contest. The Iowa Poll showed that, at that point, almost two-thirds of those who planned to caucus prioritized beating the president, while just under one-third wanted a candidate who shared their positions on issues.

That same poll tapped into issues, asking respondents to indicate whether a candidate's position was key for them – a "must have" in the respondent's choice of who to support. Abortion rights and climate change were deal breakers for large majorities of Democrats. Seventy-nine percent indicated they would only back a candidate who supported a woman's right to an abortion.[2] For 75% it would be a deal breaker if a candidate didn't recognize the threat of climate change. Democrats were split on Medicare for All, the government-run health plan that Sanders and Warren had been pushing on the campaign trail. About one-half of the Democrats would only back a candidate who supported Medicare for All, but one in ten said they would oppose a candidate with that position, signaling a degree of discord among Democrats. There was a similar divide on the issue of free college tuition, the policy advocated by candidates on the progressive left. Twenty-three percent said that support for free tuition was essential, while 15% said they'd oppose a candidate with that position.

In past cycles, foreign policy had figured prominently in caucus politics. Candidate positions on the war in Iraq and on continued US involvement had been contentious, especially in 2004 and 2008 contests. Conventional wisdom holds that Iowans, influenced by the global impact of agriculture, have been historically attuned to international affairs.[3] But by summer 2019, other issues were weighing on Democrats' minds. In both April and August iterations of Monmouth's poll of Iowa Democrats, more than half of the respondents cited "health care" as a top issue, while an array of issues under the foreign policy umbrella registered very little.[4]

Still, trade was an issue with potential ramifications for Iowa farmers. The tariff war that President Trump waged with China, each socking the other with fees on imported goods, hit US agriculture hard, a potential "train wreck" (Parker, 2019) approximating the devastation leveled by the 1980s farm crisis (Guida & McCrimmon, 2019). Iowa farmers and organized agricultural interests lean Republican, but the implications of the trade war and its direct impact on the state's economy provided opportunities for Democratic candidates to weigh in.

That led to a flurry of rural white papers and manifesto-length policy statements from the campaigns, each seeking to extoll the rural and agriculture-focused sensibilities of their candidate. Money was no object in the content of the plans, so they were expansive and expensive. Most called for investments in rural broadband, electric grid improvements, and more, a blatant move to court Trump supporters in rural Iowa (Jaffe & Schor, 2019). These plans came with high price tags, in one case exceeding $1 trillion (Klobuchar, 2019).

Bottom Up

Cynics might call it pandering to their Iowa audience, but those rural plans addressed real concerns voiced by voters. After all, the caucus campaign gave Iowans the chance to hear what candidates have to say, but also to communicate with them and assess their promises. For Iowans, it was a breeze to see any number of candidates, provided access to a car and the time and resources to devote to politics. To be sure, not everyone had these; but generally speaking, direct access to powerful, national political leaders was more available to the average person in Iowa – and New Hampshire – than in the rest of the nation.

In modern electoral politics, communication between presidential candidates and voters tends to be top-down, even with new media technologies that presumably democratize politics (Stromer-Galley, 2019). Billions are spent each cycle on broadcast and digital advertising, neither one offering much opportunity for bottom-up communication. And despite the potential of new digital communications technologies – internet and cellular products – to make two-way communication between the campaign and the voter/activist feasible, they tended not to be exploited to their fullest (Stromer-Galley, 2019). The caucus campaign, on the other hand, put the candidate face-to-face with average people, giving them an unmediated shot at those running. The combination of the physical candidate presence and the state's small population meant that Iowans were able to inject issues into the public discussion. The multitude of town halls and meet-and-greets, where candidates fielded questions from those attending, were signature elements of Iowa's retail-focused politics. Questions came from all directions, from all sorts of people. The events provided a snapshot of the issues important to voters at that given moment, things that pollsters might not bother asking about. Yet at times, organized interests offered a little nudge.

The Des Moines Register tracked the questions candidates were asked in April 2019, finding a broad range posed in a variety of ways. "Many of the questions were pointed. Some were rambling" (Phannenstiel, 2019). Questions on education, climate change, and health care made up a quarter of the more than 300 queries the newspaper tracked that month. But even those broad categories can be deceptive. Health care questions, for example, could touch on anything from Medicare for All to the Affordable Care Act to prescription drug pricing. Routinely the issue of mental and behavioral health arose, often in the context of a question from a voter with a personal experience. The topic was a hot button for many Iowans, since the state suffered from dramatic shortages of providers and had seen state mental health institutions shuttered. Suicides were on the increase, and numbers among farmers could approach levels unseen since the 1980s. In addition, Iowa had been hit by the crisis of opioid addiction that had crushed many rural communities across the country.

Typically it was just an average person asking a question of personal interest. But sometimes the question was the result of an organized effort to force the field of candidates to address issues, using techniques developed over the years. In 2019, Bill Holland worked in government affairs for the League of Conservation Voters, a Washington DC-based environmental advocacy group. But 20 years earlier, he had been a college student in Iowa, fighting some of the same environmental battles. Involved in high school in clean water issues, Bill aligned in college with a national network of environmental groups. Among his tasks in the lead up to 2000 was "bird-dogging" – following candidates and asking pointed questions at each stop. He worked for Ozone Action, a group which would eventually merge with the international powerhouse Greenpeace. Their focus was on global warming, which in later years was broadened to "climate change." In the 2000 cycle, activists wore buttons with the question "What's Your Plan?" – short for "What's your plan to address global warming?" They asked that question wherever and whenever they had a chance to quiz a candidate of either party. By Caucus Day, the candidates had been asked about their plan so many times they had a pat answer and often recognized the questioner.

Sometimes props help. In the five weeks before the caucuses that year, Bill and a partner worked 18-hour days, showing up at candidate events with a 20-foot tall inflatable ear of corn meant to convey the message "global warming kills corn." With the help of a generator, inflating the giant corncob wasn't too hard, but deflating it was a different story. They'd have to jump on it – literally throw their bodies on it – to get the air out. Bill recalls that as an activist on the ground in Iowa, he was able to push the envelope. A colleague from the national organization had told him, "In DC, we have to play it safe."

The Routine

By summer 2019, field organizers like Rachel, Jennifer, and Lauren began to settle in – and settle *into* the routine that would remain largely in place through the fall, though with important distinctions across campaigns. First things first: find housing, which itself has some unique opportunities and challenges.

A Place to Live

Democrats have been using the "supporter housing" practice for decades, asking locals active in the party and connected to the campaigns to offer up space in their homes – a room, a sofa – for staff. It's almost a rite of passage for field organizers to live in supporter housing, and expansive networks of now-senior campaign operatives across the country have the common experience of having lived with Iowans. No surprise, it can work out well or poorly for either or both parties, the staffer and the host. But generally speaking, those volunteering their space and the staff are committed to making the relationship work.

Melanie Cloud and Mitch Gross were in their mid-twenties when they started dating around the time of the 2000 caucuses. Melanie was the data director for the state party and Mitch was on staff with the Secretary of Agriculture, an elected executive position in Iowa. Now, 20 years later, Mitch is a high school principal and the mayor pro tem of Coralville, a community adjacent to Iowa City. Melanie works for a non-profit that provides services to developmentally disabled young adults. Their family – they have three daughters – has routinely hosted staffers. Their first was Lindsay Scola, who arrived in February 2007. Lindsay tells the familiar story, still relevant today: "I quit my job, bought a car and moved to Iowa to campaign."[5] She stayed through January in 2008, that very early caucus year, going on eventually to work on the advance team in the Obama White House, with other political career stops before landing in the entertainment industry in Los Angeles.

Hosting Lindsay turned the Gross family into likely suspects for hosting others. "I know Lindsey stayed with you. Can we have somebody else coming into town [stay with you]?" Over the years, they've hosted approximately ten others, reflecting fondly on the experiences, feeling a strong familial tie to some. They remember well the traditional Rosh Hashanah dinner Lindsay arranged at their house – about 20 guests standing around the dining room table, with printed prayers for the largely non-Jewish crowd to recite. Though more than a decade has passed, there's still a tinge of embarrassment in Mitch as he describes what happened. The now-vintage multi-disk CD player, used to play a solemn, sung prayer, shuffled unexpectedly to the *Pulp Fiction* soundtrack – then advanced to the equally inappropriate Imperial March from *The Empire Strikes Back*.

The state is peppered with households like Melanie's and Mitch's, willing to host staffers. Former Davenport mayor Thom Hart is another perennial host, often opening his house to multiple staffers at a time. In the 2020 cycle, he had nine from three different campaigns live with him. Over five years, 53 different campaign workers had called his house home. Of course, there's as much variation in the situations – the people, the ambient fun of the household, the physical settings – as there is variation in the state. Relative to other parts of the country, there are few apartment dwellers in Iowa, so most supporter housing took place in single-family houses. But the arrangement might just as likely have been a suite-like setup with a separate entrance, a sofa in a home of a single parent and multiple children, or a spare bedroom of an older Iowan in a retirement community. The contention is that it didn't really matter since the staffers would be logging long work hours. But for sure, living circumstances affected the overall experience. That said, there was typically not enough supporter housing to go around, especially in a cycle like 2020 with so many candidates. Danny Shelton, a digital specialist who works with Jeff Link, got his start in organizing. He advises staffers weighing their options to read between the lines: "If there isn't supporter housing offered in a campaign, you should question your choice of campaign."

Whether by necessity or choice, many staffers rented. The market varies across the state, but generally speaking rents are moderately low at about 75% of the national median.[6] High-rent pockets, like Iowa City and Coralville, with strong demand from University of Iowa students, have the added challenge of a rigid academic calendar rental cycle. Leases typically stop at the end of July and start on August 1. In 2019, the apartment stock in Des Moines, especially downtown, was in high demand. Property manager McKenzie Waldroup noted that people were "flooding into the city," an observation consistent with the stated draw of the city – low costs, available jobs, livability – noted by a variety of entities that rank urban areas. Smaller towns and rural areas have their own challenges, often lacking broad rental options. Still, the uncertainty of campaign politics cast perhaps the biggest challenge, with the possibility that a campaign could fold at any point, leaving a renter in a long-term lease out of luck.

Part of what drew Jim Flores to sign on as a NextGen organizer in Iowa was the assured security of a campaign in it for the long run. Unlike candidate campaigns, NextGen was a Super PAC with a broad commitment to progressive candidates who shared its concern about the threat of climate change. NextGen had been organizing in Iowa since 2014, back when it was still shepherded by Tom Steyer, who initially bankrolled the PAC. It was particularly active in the 2018 midterms, focusing its organizing work on mobilizing college campuses. Jim was new to Iowa, but he wasn't new to organizing, having worked a state legislative race in the southwest. He reasoned that working for NextGen was not only consistent with his values but offered security through the general election, since it would mobilize for the left no matter who received the nomination. Jim didn't think twice about signing a long-term lease extending through November 2020.

For organizers and staff more generally, finding a place to live was the big personal task. As for work, most were expected to hit the ground running, backed up by a little in-person training. Campaigns typically spread out instruction on workplace expectations, technology, and caucus politics more specifically over a long expanse of time, asking staff to gather at somewhat regular intervals in regions or at a central state location. But the initial onboarding and training was especially important, a crash course aimed at turning individual hires into a team with shared values. It was also a chance to introduce the new team members to the technology and data that would be central to the campaign.

VAN Work

Data and data-driven practices are now hyped in politics, as in all other aspects of modern life, for that matter. But data have always been central to campaigns. Maybe they weren't digitized. Maybe the data were simply information, things that party people and campaign workers knew, stored in the recesses of their minds or on index cards. Today, the organizing arm of modern campaigns in particular runs on digitized data about individual voters. The core building block for these data is the voter file – that is, the state-collected information about registered voters. Organized at the individual level, the voter file includes the information the state collects through the voter registration process. Since there's party registration in Iowa, the voter file includes party affiliation. The individual's record also gives the history of voter participation in general elections, primaries, and even caucuses. To be specific, it tells *whether* the person participated and – for nomination politics – in which party's contest. Why do states keep this information? Beyond serving as the official record of who can participate, it allows a check on the integrity of the process.

NGP-VAN is the prominent vendor whose products are used by Democratic parties and campaigns to support direct voter contact and other campaign activities. From the organizer's angle, "VAN" – or "the VAN," depending on syntactical preference – is the multipurpose tool for accessing, adding, and updating information about potential supporters and volunteers. Ultimately it supports a number of critical tasks associated with organizing. In terms void of jargon and glossing over nuance, VAN is where organizers turn to access contact information for people with whom they want to engage, to add data gleaned from their interactions with individual voters, to extract groups of people – and contact information – for phone banks, canvassing, and more. Equipping the organizer with basic VAN skills and access is typically one of the prominent components of training. Much of the organizer's routine, starting early and extending over the expanse of the campaign season, will use VAN technology to help build the relationships with those who will attend the caucuses and to construct and manage the volunteer organization which will assist in the enterprise. The VAN is significant on many levels beyond its straightforward utility for the staff. Its history is a story of technology with implications for the distribution of power within the party. It also says a little something about career possibilities for staff.

The software products of for-profit NGP-VAN are a mainstay for essentially any campaign using digitized voter lists to support efforts to reach voters. FEC records show that it dominates in the federal campaign space, but even those are a little misleading, only reflecting contracts with federal committees. It's a powerhouse at the state level as well. In addition to software, NGP-VAN maintains the Democratic Party's voter list, "Vote Builder." These two products, the software and the voter file combined, mean that the Democratic Party and the campaigns that run under its label are very much dependent on this private organization. Of course, firms like this typically serve parties and groups on just one side of the political spectrum. And it's common for people who've cut their teeth in the campaign world to transition to private industry, sometimes developing the new products that populate the array of tools campaigns will buy. That's essentially the VAN story, one that carries through that same "Iowa as incubator" thread that has marked campaign staff.

Twenty years ago in Iowa, the state party itself was a data broker, purchasing the voter file from the state of Iowa then selling it to presidential nomination campaigns. A solid revenue stream for the party, especially when caucus contests were contested, it was also a service to candidate campaigns, arguably a useful function that the party served. This is consistent with an abstract understanding of modern US political parties as service providers (Aldrich, 1995; Cotter et al., 1984), unable to exercise heavy-handed control over candidates and their campaigns, but able to forge a relationship, and maybe a little leverage, based on the critical services they could provide.

The transition from party control of data and software to having a for-profit enterprise with national reach was subtle. Mark Sullivan was a tech consultant in 2001, working for then-Senator Tom Harkin from Iowa. Harkin, along with sitting Democratic governor Tom Vilsack, largely called the shots in state Democratic Party politics.[7] Sullivan and business partner Scott Adler built the first iteration of the VAN in 2001 for the Iowa Democratic Party (IDP), which was focused that year on Vilsack's 2002 reelection campaign. Sullivan later noted that "[h]andling the voter file was this extraordinary complexity and nobody did it well."[8] Then, in characteristic diffusion of successful campaign technology, the VAN spread to other state Democratic parties, first Missouri, then others, and eventually was picked up by the Democratic National Committee (DNC) for use with its national database. Along the way, internet-based VAN technology extended to a variety of other platforms, new at the time, from Palm Pilots circa 2004 to iPhones beginning in 2010. Now it's used in contests up and down the ballot. FEC data show that all but one of the declared 2020 candidates directed expenditures to NGP-VAN. The only holdout: Wayne Messem, mayor of Miramar, FL, whose presidential nomination campaign lasted for eight months, operating on a shoe-string budget.[9]

The general storyline – a product hatched on the campaign trail making its way into a commercial enterprise – is common, certainly predating this VAN case, and repeated over and over in campaign politics. Admittedly, the for-profit space on both the left and right has always shown a strong imprint of campaign staff. At present, the commercial world of data and fundraising in particular bear the signature of veterans of Barack Obama's campaigns. Check out the principals of the top firms and you'll find employment records that include presidential politics – and in many cases, Iowa experience. It's a useful reminder that the skills imparted and refined on the campaign trail transfer into other domains, some with more money-making potential and maybe even more job security.

A Tale of Three Events

In the Iowa caucus calendar, summer was the beginning of the high-season for events showcasing multiple candidates. The "cattle call" label pinned on some of these events conjures up the notion of an open audition – a cattle call – for actors, rather than something related to agriculture. These multi-candidate events would continue through the fall, in most cases open to all declared candidates along with any person who could pay the price of admission, which varied considerably. On the surface, they were all about allowing Iowans a vantage point for comparing candidates. But of course, there was more to it, usually something good coming to the sponsoring organization. Often the interests of the candidates aligned with those of other partisan-leaning groups in the state: exposure and media coverage for both, a cash haul for the sponsor. Back-to-back cattle calls on July 13 and 14, 2019, and a well-attended birthday party in between, illustrate this well.

Old School

The United Auto Workers (UAW) Local 838 Hall in Waterloo had seen its share of Democratic Party events over the years. Organized labor remains one of the party's core constituent groups, even though it's politically weaker than in the past. In Iowa, like much of the country, labor lost influence when traditional manufacturing floundered. A community like Newton, 30 miles east of Des Moines, was historically a hotbed of union strength back when Maytag, the appliance manufacturer with UAW employees, was headquartered there. Since Maytag left Newton in 2007, the wind energy industry has become the core employer of blue-collar workers, though the vast majority are not unionized. In Waterloo, a city of 67,000, labor still has clout, with workers at its major employer – John Deere – organized under the UAW umbrella. Deere, a manufacturer of farm equipment, sells to domestic and international markets.

The Saturday event in Waterloo wasn't a labor event, but it was at a labor venue. Technically the cattle call was sponsored by the 1st District Democratic Central Committee, the party organization at the congressional district level, a rung between the county parties and the IDP, with a special interest in protecting the congressional seat then held by first-term incumbent Abby Finkenauer. For the party, hosting this event was a way to pull in some cash, with tickets for individuals at $25, proceeds going to the party.

The labor venue was significant, a reminder to all that the relationship between the party and unions goes way back – visible in messages both subtle and overt about the priorities of labor. The union hall in Waterloo is decidedly old school, complete with a parking lot reminding visitors that this UAW local is committed to protecting US manufacturing. "ATTENTION IF YOU ARE DRIVING A FOREIGN CAR THAT IS NOT MANUFACTURED IN NORTH AMERICA BY UNION LABOR, YOU NEED TO PARK IN THE BACK OF THE LOT BETWEEN

THE SIGNS!"[10] Walking inside that day, attendees confronted a gauntlet of tables, young campaign staff close by, ready to chat up their candidate or cause. Plenty of printed material was available, too. Inspect the material of Democratic candidates and causes – mail pieces, cards, placards, yard signs, and the like – and you should see the "bug," the tiny union emblem shown on the material, signaling it was printed by a union shop.

The main space in the union hall held five long tables running perpendicular to a raised stage. If sitting, even the most distant attendee would be within 100 feet of each of the seven different presidential candidates who attended and spoke. Many in the audience, made up of mostly 60-somethings, wore union garb and drove in from across the vast 1st District, which extended from the northeast corner of the state southwest to near Des Moines. The admission ticket covered a picnic fare of locally smoked barbecue, but not alcohol, which was available at a cash bar. Despite valiant efforts of the event organizers to move people to the tables, many campaign staff, attendees, and the occasional candidate found the bar/food area a convenient place for networking, even if it was a distraction for those there to listen to the candidates, each delivering a 15-minute speech. The audio had some glitches, jarring feedback at times. Many events like these include a signer perched on stage for the hearing-impaired. This one relied on an off-site transcriptionist, with a feed projected behind the speakers.

Each candidate took a slightly different approach to the event, though the speeches were heavy on bio. Retired admiral Joe Sestak, who had declared just three weeks before, regaled the crowd with stories of life at sea. John Delaney, the well-known commodity, there with his wife and daughter, included what many Iowans had heard before, that he owed his Columbia University education to a union scholarship. Ohio Representative Tim Ryan, towering over most, seemed to be thinking of President Trump's 2016 inroads with the working class, emphasizing that in fact Democrats are the party of ordinary people – with an obligation to help them "do something extraordinary." And Amy Klobuchar, not far from the border of her home state, got a big laugh and a few groans with the story of her first campaign slogan, used back in an elementary school election: *All the way with Amy K.* The candidate admitted it was best to abandon that one. She also displayed some political savvy, giving a shout out to Waterloo's mayor Quentin Hart, signaling either presence of mind or good advice from staff. The mayor also received a wave and praise from Pete Buttigieg, playing up their mayoral ties.

Candidates cycled in and out of the event. While Senator Michael Bennet spoke, New York City Mayor Bill de Blasio lingered outside, close to the parking lot, waiting to make his entrance. Flanked by one staff member, the mayor was in from New York for the weekend, one of his few visits to the state, with no obvious sign of an Iowa-based staff. This was a frantic weekend for many of the candidates. The mayor hadn't yet decided what his entire Iowa weekend agenda would look like, though this was the second barbecue event of the day for him. Others – like Bennet – planned six events for that day alone, intending to rotate campaign staff among them.[11]

New School

Most of the candidates who had spoken in Waterloo on that Saturday, and a few who hadn't, made their way about 60 miles south for a pair of events on Sunday, a steamy day with temperatures in the 90s. The Sunday events skewed a little younger, their feel more twenty-first century, maybe also more "progressive" than Waterloo, though the firm lines that would eventually form over the course of the campaign separating progressives and moderates were not yet fully congealed.

The Sunday morning event carried new school elements but hosted a title definitely old school: a birthday party. In party politics, a birthday party is a euphemism for fundraiser, historically exploited by machine bosses and other powerful political figures, grateful recipients of the attendees' gifts of money – campaign contributions or just plain cash. In the early 1980s, a powerful Ohio state legislative leader, House Speaker Verne Riffe, routinely pulled in more than $1 million[12] in his annual birthday party, with funds used by Riffe for his own reelection bids and to assist other Democratic office-seekers in exchange for allegiance to the speaker in the future (Suddes, 1994, p. 166). That Sunday in Iowa, the birthday celebration wasn't for a machine boss or an old pol calling the shots. It was for a charismatic young Democratic state senator, Zach Wahls.

Wahls had the national spotlight turned on him in 2011 when, as a 19-year-old college student, he testified before the Iowa Legislature in support of same-sex marriage, telling his story of growing up with two moms and defending their right to marry. A landmark 2009 Iowa Supreme Court decision had legalized same-sex marriage, just the third state in the nation to do so. In the aftermath of the decision, the state legislature took up a constitutional amendment to reverse the decision, and Wahls' testimony before the House Judiciary Committee went viral. Wahls was elected to the state Senate in 2018, and he was seen as the state's fastest-rising Democratic star. That made him a target for presidential contenders, reaching out to him as early as 2018. He had turned down a request to be the state chair for one of the major contenders, reasoning that his plate was full as a first-term state senator. His party/fundraiser for Senate Democrats was a destination for 2020 hopefuls, his birthday date fortuitously tucked between two cattle calls, optimizing potential to draw in the presidential crowd.

Wahls invited about 12 campaigns, and others not on the official list found out about it through the grapevine. He recalled getting a call from Sen. Michael Bennet's campaign, asking if the senator could attend and speak. "I'm not going to say 'no' to a sitting US senator," Wahls said. He added that Biden's team didn't follow up, and it struck him that Bernie just "didn't care." Other candidates like Booker were out of the state. De Blasio, who had planned to attend, was a no-show, derailed by a New York blackout.[13] Wahls celebrated his birthday with Bennet, Buttigieg, Delaney, Hickenlooper, and Klobuchar, giving each candidate a chance to speak. With contributions directed to the Senate Democrats, Wahls estimated the crowd at approximately 200, mostly from the Iowa City/Coralville area, with a final fundraising total of about $30,000.[14]

Later that day and 20 miles away in Cedar Rapids at the New Bo City Market, host organization Progress Iowa held its annual "Corn Feed." Cedar Rapids and Iowa City are proximate cities, but they have a different feel, one the ultra-liberal university town, the other more of mix, with industry giants from ag processing, insurance, and aeronautics. The market is located in the historic New Bohemia neighborhood, highlighting the city's Czech heritage. Cedar Rapids, especially the New Bo neighborhood, had been ravaged by flood waters multiple times in the previous 20 years, and the market, a non-profit retail space and business incubator, was a cornerstone of economic revitalization. A park-like space outside the indoor market hosts community events like weekly farmers markets and a three-day summer "Fields of Yogi" yoga event – definitely not the union hall in Waterloo.

The outdoor setting was the right size for the crowd of almost 3,000 that gathered; attendees sat on the ground and in lawn chairs, eventually hearing ten of the presidential hopefuls. Though people were asked to register for the event, admission was free. But as a fundraiser for Progress Iowa, there were plenty of opportunities to contribute or even sponsor the event. Four of the most prominent candidates in the field – Biden, Harris, Sanders, and Warren – did not attend, but their organizers and other staff did. Near the space where people plopped down to hear the candidate speeches, campaigns and interest groups set up tents and booths, a few grabbing prime shaded areas, most others with at least a canopy offering some protection from the sweltering sun. The Buttigieg campaign had the most elaborate setup: a large tent providing shade and activities around the perimeter. Whether any of this truly mattered politically, beyond a measure of fun and comfort that it offered, was never clear. But these setups did require advance planning, and it's tempting to read something meaningful into the quality of the campaign's preparation. Staff for Washington governor Jay Inslee sat uncovered with no protection from the sun until someone took pity and tracked down a canopy to cover their table.

The Corn Feed was a well-oiled machine, running on schedule with virtually no delay between one candidate's ten-minute speech and the next. The speeches varied in content, some with a nod to agriculture, most taking on the President, Seth Moulton from Massachusetts even making a case for impeachment. For those who had stumped in Waterloo the day before, there was considerable consistency. Many candidates lingered in the air-conditioned indoor market space before and after taking the stage, along with lots of attendees seeking respite from the heat and a chance to mingle with the featured guests, maybe take selfies. In fact, at times the crowd inside seemed more densely packed than outside. But inside and out, the mood was hopeful and positive.

Most people there probably missed what may have been the most overtly confrontational development of the day: a digital, mobile ad on a truck, parked prominently across the street from New Bo, slamming de Blasio, who by that time had decamped to New York. Touting that the mayor "puts working people last," the ad was sponsored by the Police Benevolent Association (PBA) of the City of New York – the police union – introducing a little out-of-state labor sentiment to Iowa caucus politics. It would have been hard, on the other hand, to miss the buzz building around Buttigieg at the event, including the entourage of press following him as the budding celebrity worked his way through the crowds, a signal of things to come.

Outside the Bubble

For most of the caucus campaign in the summer months, candidates traveled the state staffed by a small number of campaign aides, maybe just one or two, often including the state director. Others, especially regionals and organizers, helped staff and mobilize supporters to the events, but it was usually only a select set of the top-level personnel with direct and regular access to the candidates. Even so, they're more likely to be in a car with the candidate occupied with "call time" than to be engaged in a substantive conversation. Not surprisingly, campaigns are like many other large organizations, with specialized roles and a vertical structure that, despite what might seem like an ever-present candidate presence, offers rather few opportunities for most campaign staff to engage directly with the candidate. This makes sense, because the candidate is often juggling both the campaign and the demands of an elected position. Ohio Congressman Tim Ryan, when asked in Waterloo if he had a sense of what his staff on the ground were doing, noted that news of staff problems will make its way up the ladder to him. Short of that, "My job is to raise money, give speeches and shake hands." Even though candidates were the central figures in the caucus bubble – the reason the bubble even existed – they largely lingered outside of the day-to-day work occupying most staff.

Others symbolically distanced themselves from the caucus bubble. Not everyone involved in caucus politics was in the bubble – or wanted to be there. The Sanders campaign appeared to deliberately separate itself from the other teams of organizers, as well as Democratic Party structures. Early on, while staffers from a broad cross-section of campaigns used party events, parades, and other gatherings to make connections or catch up with colleagues from previous cycles, the Sanders team was often conspicuously absent. This was not surprising, given the animosity that existed among Sanders, his supporters, and elements within the party since 2016. The Sanders crew appeared to be out-of-step with the common refrain among organizers that their ultimate focus was electing a Democrat in 2020. One regional lead commented that everyone was committed, except for "He Who Shall Not Be Named."

An obscure but telling incident came at the annual summer "Meskwaki Pow Wow" at the Sac and Fox tribe's settlement in Tama County, an event that drew five candidates and a slew of campaign staffers who had volunteered for shifts at the county party booth. Though in the mid-80s that day, it felt hotter, and the Tama County Democrats had a cooler of iced bottled water for the volunteers. The local Sanders staffer was at the event, but was not among the campaign workers who volunteered to help to staff the party's booth. One organizer recalled reaching out to the staffer at the event, offering water to counter the heat, an offer politely declined – and interpreted, right or wrong, as proof of Sanders' "go-it-alone" approach.

At the same time, some Sanders staff were part of the Friendship 2020 crew. In the summer, Casey Clemmons, a Clinton 2016 veteran who was state caucus director for Gillibrand, organized a weekly Friendship 2020 happy hour at a brew pub in Des Moines' trendy East Village, a designation that makes native New Yorkers snicker. "We were really intentional to be inclusive of everyone. We had a spreadsheet with a point person from every campaign… to invite them every week." Casey added, "There were Sanders staffers at almost every gathering I attended." Still, some opposing camps saw the Sanders crew as standoffish and less-than-committed to the party. Others reasoned that this was strategic, part of the campaign's stealth effort, not seeking to trumpet the strength of their organization, maybe even obscure it. In this way, the Sanders campaign was both under the radar and outside of the bubble.

Some campaign staffers found that the bubble wasn't for them. Monica Johanssen was eager to work on a campaign and attracted to the candidacy of former Texas congressman Beto O'Rourke. O'Rourke, who had narrowly lost a bid to unseat incumbent senator Ted Cruz in 2018, had become a national symbol for Democrats seeking to reverse policies launched during the Trump Administration and highlight progressive alternatives. His entry into the 2020 race drew much fanfare; he landed on the cover of Rolling Stone magazine and drew the largest crowds of the cast of candidates early in 2019. Monica, like many other organizers, was a recent college graduate with a work and volunteer history in campaign politics. She graduated, took the job with O'Rourke, and moved to Iowa in the early summer, landing in a small town. She seemed to be a natural at interacting with new people: a gregarious woman at ease in different situations. But Monica found that once in Iowa, work overwhelmed the other parts of her life. It was "difficult to make friends or have real connections outside of [her] identity as an organizer." The pressure to "seamlessly integrate [friendships] with the work of the campaign" was something that she "really, really did not like." Campaign work always has the potential to blur the lines between the professional and the personal, but perhaps more so in the caucus bubble, given the intensity of the work in a relatively small state. Monica resigned after about six weeks on the job, moving to DC and landing an entry-level position on the Hill. She reflected later that she might have found the work in Iowa more enjoyable had she been assigned to a more urban area, but predicted that even then she would probably have eventually left.

Notes

1 The Iowa Poll (#2190) cautioned that a shift in methodology from March to June made the overtime comparisons shaky. The June poll weighted responses to approximate the impact of virtual caucus-goers, who were to control 10% of the delegates in February 2020.
2 Figures reported here for likely in-person attendees.
3 Much of this is tied to trade, since international markets – for decades – have been destinations for Iowa grain. But connections to notable foreign leaders also have piqued the state's interest. At the height of the Cold War, Soviet leader Nikita Kruschev had visited the farm of Roswell Garst in tiny Coon Rapids. The current Chinese President Xi Jinping had visited Iowa in 1985 as a young party official, forging a relationship with the state's Republican governor and even staying in the home of a family in Muscatine, a city in southeast Iowa on the Mississippi River (Osnos 2012).
4 In both April and August 2019, immigration occupied the minds of 14% of Iowa Democrats, foreign policy/world standing 5% (April) and 3% (August), and terrorism/national security 4% and 1% over that same time frame. Monmouth survey of likely Democratic voters, April 2019 at www.monmouth.edu/polling-institute/documents/monmouthpoll_ia_041119-2.pdf/, August at www.monmouth.edu/polling-institute/documents/monmouthpoll_ia_080819.pdf/.
5 "4 UAA Alums in the Obama Administration." October 2009. www.washington.edu/alumni/partnerships/undergrad/200910/obama_alums.html
6 The 2018 American Community Survey (www.census.gov/programs-surveys/acs/) reports median gross rent, including estimated heating and cooling, at $777 in Iowa, compared to $1,058 nationally.
7 It's common for statewide elected officials to exert a strong influence on a state party. With recent GOP dominance in the US Senate and gubernatorial contests, there's no comparable elected leadership of the party like there was in the past.
8 Voter Activation Network described by Personal Democracy Media (https://personaldemocracy.com/company-reviews-2010/voter-activation-network).
9 Democratic nomination campaigns showing payments in NGP-VAN Vendor Recipient Records through October 23, 2020: www.opensecrets.org/campaign-expenditures/vendor?cycle=2020&vendor=NGP+VAN)
10 The details are significant, careful to signal that the union's concern is not with foreign cars as such, but foreign cars built abroad or in non-union US factories.
11 Any inconsistencies between stated candidate plans and published tracking reports – in this case and more generally in the campaign – are a reminder that either plans change or the data have errors, likely some combination of the two.
12 The equivalent of close to $2 million in 2020 dollars.
13 The day before in Waterloo, shortly after he had addressed the union-hall crowd, the mayor got word of the blackout affecting 72,000 residents on the west side of Manhattan, raising immediate questions about a possible terrorist plot. Back home, a local newspaper headline asked this question: *The power went out. Where was de Blasio?* (Mays 2019).
14 Despite the presence of national candidates, this was a state-level event, meaning contributions were disclosed to the Iowa Ethics and Campaign Disclosure Board, the state-level equivalent of the FEC. Technically, they were directed to the Iowa Democratic Party, which holds the Senate Majority Fund accounts in a segregated fund, making it difficult to identify with complete certainty those birthday party receipts.

References

Aldrich, John. 1995. *Why Parties?: The Origin and Transformation of Political Parties in America*. Chicago: University of Chicago Press.

Cotter, Cornelius P., James L. Gibson, John F. Bibby, Robert J. Huckshorn. 1984. *Party Organizations in American Politics*. New York: Praeger.

Debenedetti, Gabriel. 2019 "Cory Booker and Elizabeth Warren are making massive bets on Iowa." *New York Magazine* June 4 (https://nymag.com/intelligencer/2019/06/cory-booker-and-elizabeth-warren-are-betting-big-in-iowa.html).

Guida, Victoria and Ryan McCrimmon. 2019. "Trump's trade wars thrust farmers into desperation loans." *Politico* June 24 (www.politico.com/story/2019/06/24/trump-trade-farmers-loans-1547826).

Hart, Gary. 1987. "Transcript of Hart statement withdrawing his candidacy." *The New York Times* May 9 (www.nytimes.com/1987/05/09/us/transcript-of-hart-statement-withdrawing-his-candidacy.html).

Jaffe, Alexandra and Elana, Schor. 2019. "2020 Democrats target Trump gains in rural areas." *AP News* August 7 (https://apnews.com/67111b75b34043deaad1e89fd9eb0a5b).

Klobuchar, Amy. 2019. "Senator Klobuchar's plan from the Heartland: strengthening our agricultural and rural communities." *Medium* August 7 (https://medium.com/@Amy_Klobuchar/senator-klobuchars-plan-from-the-heartland-strengthening-our-agricultural-and-rural-communities-405cb6b3234d).

Mays, Jacob C. 2019. "The power went out. Where was de Blasio?" *The New York Times* July 14 (www.nytimes.com/2019/07/14/nyregion/bill-de-blasio-nyc-blackout.html).

Osnos, Evan. 2012. "Xi's American journey." *The New Yorker* February 15 (www.newyorker.com/news/daily-comment/xis-american-journey).

Parker, Mario. 2019. "Record floods and Trump's trade war are threatening to make this year a 'train wreck' for corn farmers." *Time* June 14 (https://time.com/5607318/floods-trade-wars-hurt-farmers/).

Pfannenstiel, Brianne. 2019. "What's on Iowans' minds going into 2020 caucuses? A look at 300 questions they asked candidates in April." *The Des Moines Register* May 10 (www.desmoinesregister.com/story/news/elections/presidential/caucus/2019/05/09/iowa-caucus-2020-questions-campaign-health-climate-change-education-president-trump/3587082002/).

Rodriguez, Barbara. 2019. "Democratic presidential candidate Pete Buttigieg hires 30 more Iowa staffers." *The Des Moines Register* June 20 (www.desmoinesregister.com/story/news/elections/presidential/caucus/2019/06/20/democrat-pete-buttigieg-indiana-mayor-hires-30-additional-staffers-iowa-organizing-poll-caucuses/1505073001/).

Ryan, Paul S. 2015. "'Testing the Waters' and the Big Lie: How Prospective Presidential Candidates Evade Candidate Contribution Limits While the FEC Looks the Other Way." *Campaign Legal Center Report*. February (www.campaignlegalcenter.org).

Steger, Wayne P. 2016 "Conditional arbiters: the limits of political party influence in presidential nominations." *PS: Political Science & Politics* 49(4): 709–715.

Stone, Walter J., and Alan I. Abramowitz. 1986. "Ideology, electability, and candidate choice." In *The Life of the Parties, Activists in Presidential Politics*, eds. Ronald B. Rapoport, Alan I. Abramowitz, and John McGlennon. University Press of Kentucky, pp. 75–96.

Stone, Walter J., and Ronald B. Rapoport. 1994. "Candidate perception among nomination activists: a new look at the moderation hypothesis." *The Journal of Politics* 56(4): 1034–1052.

Stromer-Galley, Jennifer. 2019. *Presidential Campaigning in the Internet Age, 2nd Edition.* New York: Oxford University Press.

Suddes, Thomas. 1994. "Panorama of Ohio Politics in the Voinovich Era, 1991-" *Ohio Politics.* Ed., Alexander P. Lamis. Kent, OH: Kent State University Press, pp. 157–180.

5 New Again

There's never a steady state in campaign politics; some innovation, evolution, or change is always brewing. Even if the rules are the same, the players, the political context, and any number of other factors are different. At the same time, much of what seems new might well be just a version of some existing – even old – practice or development. Look hard enough and there's often something to that familiar adage: Everything old is new again. Still, the 2020 Democratic contest was marked by a number of seemingly new developments, even beyond the early start, the record size of the field, and the scheduled rule changes.

The Debates

Candidate debates are now expected features of presidential nomination campaigns, routine ways in which a national audience checks in on the contenders. Democrats in the 2020 cycle faced the same problem Republicans did in 2016: too many candidates to fit easily into a typical debate format. The plan devised by the Democratic National Committee (DNC) to deal with this challenge filtered down to practices on the ground in Iowa.[1] Primary debates are at least potentially significant for several reasons, and so who's included can matter. Debate history is replete with debate performances that seemed to advance some candidacies, like Republican Newt Gingrich in 2012 (Streitfeld & Steinhauser, 2012) while derailing the chances of others, like Rick Perry in that same cycle (Gardner & Rucker, 2011). There's also some systematic empirical evidence that debates matter.[2]

In the 2020 cycle, Democrats struggled with a basic challenge. If the debate is too small or exclusive, an adequate range of voices may not be heard. If it's too big, then things become unwieldy.

The DNC announced an agreement in early 2019 with the TV networks, specifying as many as 12 debates and indicating its openness to holding single debates on consecutive nights to accommodate what might be an extremely large candidate field. Back in 2016, the networks had imposed on the large Republican field a tiered format for some of the debates, with top candidates in prime time and the others in an "undercard" session scheduled before the main debate (Hopkins, 2018). These "happy hour" or "kids' table" debates were widely derided. While they commanded a relatively small viewing audience, they were described as "brutal" and "ignominious" with those candidates relegated to them labeled "also-rans" (Allen, 2015). For the 2020 cycle, Democrats set up a "two-path" system for candidates to qualify for each debate. One featured a polling threshold and the other grassroots fundraising. Candidates would need to qualify for each debate, and over the course of the nomination season the thresholds became higher and higher, making it more difficult to make the stage. The rules in place for each of the first two debates, one in June and the other in July, specified that in order to be invited, a candidate needed at least 1% support in three different qualifying polls. As for fundraising, a candidate needed 65,000 *unique donors* – in other words, a count of individuals who contributed with no concern for the contribution size or how many contributions are made, either by the individual or in the aggregate.[3]

The DNC insisted that these criteria for debate inclusion were consistent with providing party grassroots a "bigger voice than ever before." The 1% support threshold *is* a reasonably low bar to pass. But in summer 2019, the presence of 20-some candidates made getting to 1% more difficult. The unique donor requirement gave candidates whose backers lacked deep pockets a fighting chance to get on the debate stage. Observers reasoned that the DNC viewed amassing a large number of small donors as a good indicator of enthusiasm (FiveThirtyEight, 2019). As it turned out, only a few candidates were excluded from those initial debates. But even though the criteria did little to limit the number of candidates, the fundraising threshold made a mark on the incentive structure for candidates. And it trickled down to campaign behavior in Iowa.

Raising money is a perennial challenge for campaigns, but the unique donor metric prompted a scramble to amass large numbers of contributors in order to qualify for each debate. Even a request for $1 does not come organically. It requires an investment in fundraising, a significant expenditure of resources. According to the *New York Times*, "campaign after campaign said the party's donor requirements skewed the way they allocated resources" potentially shifting them from organizing to fundraising. Reportedly, campaigns were pouring money into digital ads, and the vendors doing the work were charging up to $40 for a single $1 donation (Goldmacher & Lerer, 2019).

Regardless, a drumbeat for some nominal contribution became standard at campaign events. As early as March of 2019, Marianne Williamson had campaign staff and volunteers ask anyone attending her events to donate a dollar so she could meet the unique donor threshold. And by early summer, "unique donors" was a term that everyone seemed to understand. For field staff usually immune from fundraising, this meant collecting money and the accompanying paperwork, in some cases asking for money in addition to caucus night commitments.

It is commonplace in politics for some rule or reform to have unforeseen consequences, sometimes at odds with the rule's intent. Whether intentional or not, the DNC thresholds created a scramble for cash and encouraged campaigns to expend resources in ways they might otherwise not have. This pressure may have been most-pronounced for the lesser-known candidates, for whom clearing even one of those bars – polling numbers or unique donors – was a considerable challenge. Adding insult, those ostensibly inclusive criteria just as easily cut the other way; they were definitive metrics of failure in the nomination season, well before the caucusing or voting began. Even before the second debate at the end of July, the rules had snatched their first victim. California Congressman Eric Swalwell's withdrawal from the race was blamed in part on his difficulty making it to the second debate. But the rules also signaled something more abstract: they institutionalized a role for an extended party network (see for example, Bernstein, 2000; Herrnson, 2009; Koger et al., 2009) of organizations in the DNC-run debate process. The normal quarterly reporting periods established by the FEC for campaigns didn't cut it for the counts of unique donors needed for the schedule setup for the debates. In a lesser-known aspect of the DNC's rules, the party advised candidates that they could validate their donor count using data from Act Blue, the powerhouse Democratic fundraising non-profit, or from NGP VAN.

Relational Organizing

Like almost every other enterprise, campaign politics often feature some new practice or technique that piques the attention of insiders and carries a certain cachet. In 2019 campaign circles, "relational organizing" filled that role. It was a twist on the fundamental organizing principles showcased in the first Obama campaign and seen as contributing to the 2008 win. Whether driven by true advances in campaigning or plain old pragmatism, relational organizing affected the conduct of organizing in Iowa.

To the Obama campaigns, "organizing" meant deliberately emulating community organizing, following a playbook more routinely found in movement politics than in electoral campaigns. Obama wasn't the first candidate to do this, but he had the highest profile. The campaign drew inspiration and practical tactics from Harvard-based sociologist Marshall Ganz, whose early hands-on organizing experience in both the civil rights and the California farm workers movements influenced his understanding of organizing. Ganz had advised the Howard Dean campaign on organizing in the 2004 cycle and – drawn to the candidate Obama – sought out a relationship with the Obama campaign in 2007. By summer that year, Ganz was setting up for Obama "intensive community organizing–style training camps" (Abramsky, 2011).

Key to Ganz's community approach was that volunteers would take on leadership roles, recruiting and managing other volunteers. The job of the field staff – the organizers – was to recruit and manage the volunteer leaders. The Obama campaign called this a "team model," or more colloquially a "snowflake model," placing the paid organizer in the middle, and building out a volunteer structure centered on team leaders. The snowflake imagery, in contrast to what spokes of a wheel might suggest, conveyed that while there was centralized coordination, lines of accountability permeated the entire volunteer structure.

By the time the 2020 cycle started, organizing was old hat, and even the term "relational organization" had been on the radar. Under the Obama model, it had meant staff building relationships, starting with getting to know and understand the community (McKenna & Han, 2015, pp. 102–103). Ganz himself (2009) used the term, emphasizing the importance of "ongoing working relationships." But in the 2020 cycle, "relational organizing" carried a nuanced meaning with practical implications for the campaigns. It meant that in building a field organization, staff found volunteers who leveraged their personal networks. The Buttigieg campaign was perhaps the most overt practitioner of this model, putting a fine point on starting with "friends and family" in its field strategy. By summer, as the Buttigieg field structure took shape, organizing staff were quick to signal in one-on-ones that they were doing something special this time around, not following the same old organizing model in place for the past few cycles.

Greta Carnes, Buttigieg's national organizing director, acknowledged that the campaign "didn't invent relational organizing," though it was a central part of their approach. "[W]e asked people to talk to their friends and family about Pete, filling them in on him. That he speaks multiple languages. That's he a military veteran. That he came out as gay while South Bend mayor and then was re-elected with 80% of the vote." This was the campaign's strategy to build an organization, which had been slow to take shape, even though the candidate had become a media favorite and his support was surging in Iowa. Carnes admitted that they had started in a hole. "We were already behind on staff on the ground, ... so we built a different kind of program from the very outset." She emphasized it was more than a tactic tacked on to a traditional organizing program (McGowan, 2020).[4]

In the abstract, the logic behind organizing is that the personal relationship can be leveraged to extract from volunteers greater levels of commitment and contribution, whether or not couched in "relational organizing" terms. Over the course of the campaign, the "ask" made of volunteers expands. Inviting someone to attend a small meeting of supporters might be a first step toward drawing in a volunteer, followed later by a request to bring others to another meeting, and finally a push for significant time commitments in the form of phone calls, knocking doors, or recruiting and managing volunteers as the caucuses approached. Presumably, the volunteer's commitment to the campaign strengthens, both with time and added responsibilities. Still, the paid organizer/volunteer relationship remains an important lever for the campaign to use. A Klobuchar organizer reflected on its utility: having a volunteer who "wouldn't want to let a friend down" is a useful asset for the campaign. Being able to start with "friends and family," as touted by the Buttigieg campaign, had the added allure of running an organizing campaign even if the campaign's data were not great, something rumored of the Buttigieg campaign in the summer.

Lauren Parker with Gillibrand was well aware of the utility of relationships, but she approached organizing in what appeared to be a more holistic and less-overtly strategic fashion. Establishing relationships with both volunteers and would-be caucus-goers, she complemented the utilitarian model with what can only be described as deeply personal connections. Lauren, for example, established close working connections with several high school students she knew were committed supporters. With the campaign in mind, she relied on those students to help her organize other students who would be 18 by Election Day, 2020, and thus permitted to caucus under Iowa law. But her relationships with the students went beyond the nuts and bolts of organizing. She spent time with them, their families and friends, establishing a close rapport that extended beyond their ten-plus year age difference. Like an older sister or aunt, she attended high school events in which her young group of volunteers performed, and she would maintain that contact even after the caucuses.

Lauren engaged the other end of the age spectrum as well, accepting an invitation from another volunteer. Marge Drake recalled that Lauren had expressed interest in meeting some local knitters. "I introduced her to the Thursday afternoon [knitting group] of primarily retired women … with an average age around 75," not counting a few working women and the occasional visiting daughter or granddaughter. Lauren had no illusions about activating the knitters politically, sensing members' political leanings covered a wide spectrum, including the right. Still, she managed to cultivate a number of new friends and fans. The group, according to Marge Drake, "was beyond thrilled to welcome a young, outgoing visitor" who was in town for the "caucus madness."

New Tech

Occasionally, something truly new enters the world of caucus politics, often involving technology. In the 2020 cycle, communication technology permeated Iowa caucus politics in countless ways. Thirty years earlier, radio reporters would feed their caucus stories from a pay phone. In 2020, they could upload studio-quality sound from their iPhones. The erstwhile communications staffer posted to Instagram and Twitter from a candidate event, and was sure to check as a reporter left, "Did you tweet?" Candidates traveled, even to coffee-house events, with their own sound systems, featuring battery-operated hand-held mics and credible speakers. While organizing still turned on some old-school technologies, like cell phones and the occasional email, newer platforms like Slack facilitated messaging among staffers. And on the organizing front in 2020, one product – peer-to-peer (P2P) texting, introduced only four years earlier – became widely diffused. This untethered the campaign from the sort of VAN dominance that had marked the Obama era and in doing so shook up the power dynamics within the campaign.

The Obama prowess in organizing in 2008 and 2012 was built on record numbers of grassroots volunteers (McKenna & Han, 2015), but it relied on a high degree of centralized control. The campaign was tightly structured around distinct lines of authority, routine practices, and rigid control of data. By the time Obama had entered the caucus scene, parties and campaigns in Iowa had been VAN-reliant for a couple of cycles. But access to the VAN itself had been limited, usually only to staff in the upper rungs of an organization, which would pass down the chain VAN-generated information. Under Obama, VAN was front and center even more so than before. And while technology by then permitted VAN access to paid staff at the local level, those staff still took their marching orders directly from the top, following tight protocols for precisely who the campaign should contact and how to engage these contacts on the phone or at their doors. There was little discretion for paid organizers, even less for volunteers, and heavily circumscribed paths to potential supporters with scripted phone calls and appeals at the door.

The situation started to change in 2016 when the Sanders campaign introduced P2P texting tools, allowing a staffer or volunteer to send out a text to a large numbers of voters or activists. These personalized texts, coming from a real person, cater to how people now communicate: on the fly, texting on their phones. Increasingly, the public screens phone calls and ignores emails, successfully tuning out communications from campaigns (Stanley-Becker, 2020). But P2P texts look like the messages that arrive from friends or co-workers, one person to another.[5] After the Sanders launch in 2016 of P2P texting, the practice took off in the 2018 midterm. By 2020 it was a mainstay of organizing. Among the platforms used by the 2016 Sanders campaign was Hustle, which would be widely adopted by more than ten of the 2020 nomination campaigns.[6]

Texting approaches vary in intent, but a common strategy is to invite a low-effort response, in effect seeding a longer conversation in hopes of generating active involvement with the campaign. Event invitations are particularly useful hooks, and engaged Iowans found their cell phones buzzing with notifications of texts arriving, starting especially in the late summer. An August text from a Bullock organizer pitched a volunteer shift at a local animal shelter as part of a statewide day of service promoted by the campaign: "I thought I would reach out and give you the opportunity to help our furry friends. Text or call me back if you are interested." The chance to meet a retired senator from a neighboring state was what the Biden campaign offered, perhaps more attractive to an older crowd of Democrats. "We are excited to open up our new office [this] Saturday at 1pm. Senator Bob Kerrey will be there too! Are you free?" Sanders pitched to a younger demographic in this late-season text: "Did you hear? We're having a Caucus Concert with musical guest Bon Iver ... Are you able to join us?"

Read between the lines of this now widely-adopted P2P campaign technology, along with relational organizing, and there's a familiar story of innovation – namely, necessity as the mother of invention. At the same time, sometimes it's old wine in new bottles.

Michael Silberman has one of those stories about starting his political career in presidential nomination politics. In 2019 he was global director for Mobilisation Lab (MobLab), a non-profit that had early ties to Greenpeace. MobLab has a global presence and it focuses on "people-powered" movements.[7] But back in 2003, after he graduated from Middlebury College, he worked for Howard Dean's 2004 nomination campaign. As Silberman tells it, the campaign was short on money, which contributed to the mindset that "they had nothing to lose." Having nothing to lose, in turn, gave them the license to "try new stuff." They ceded control to volunteers, asking them to make their own signs and even organize events. The signature Dean innovation was Meetup, a social media platform for bringing together – on- and off-line – groups of people with shared interests, in this case a shared interest in the Dean candidacy (Kreiss, 2012). Silberman, reflecting in 2010 on the 2004 Iowa caucus campaign, referred to its approach as "distributed organizing," a core component of which was to give campaign volunteers license to innovate and organize on their own. That same term carried considerable cachet in the 2020 cycle, especially in Buttigieg and Sanders organizing circles.

Like Dean in 2004, those two campaigns – Sanders in 2016 and Buttigieg in 2020 – also conveyed a "backs against the wall" quality. In 2016, Zack Exley worked for Sanders. He was in charge of technology in the later states – that is, the states with contests later than the first four. Exley emphasized that going into the 2016 campaign "there wasn't a whole lot of preparation" which translated into the campaign organically adopting technologies that volunteers were using. His comments both acknowledge the technological sophistication of average Americans and celebrate the campaign's wisdom in building from that. "There's no way this sixty-year-old nurse … is telling me about her Slack team."[8]

Two-Way Street

Nomination campaigns work to enlist supporters and activists, but it's also a two-way street. Issue-focused individuals use their energy and skills to leverage access, including personal time with prominent national staff and even with the candidates themselves. Mental health advocate Leslie Carpenter hadn't missed a beat in 2016, trying to broker a deal with unsuspecting organizer Carlo Makarechi on his first day on the job. In the end, Leslie volunteered, but never did get that meeting with Hillary Clinton. By 2020, she was able to break through. Leslie had ramped up her game.

It's difficult to believe Leslie when she says that Scott, her husband and partner in advocacy, is more comfortable with public speaking than she is. She is articulate and compelling with a kind demeanor, a woman who retired early in order to devote her energy to advocacy. The Carpenters are nationally known mental health advocates, and they used the caucuses as a platform for raising issues and pushing solutions directly to decision makers. They were often present at candidate events in blue t-shirts, hers posing the question "WHY DOES IOWA HAVE ONLY 64 BEDS FOR THE MENTALLY ILL?" His shirt answered, noting that the federal government incentivizes the state to limit its beds (Carpenter, 2019). Their explanation for Iowa's worst-in-the-nation ranking on mental health facilities had relevance beyond Iowa, casting the issue in national terms.

Leslie claims to have been "not that sophisticated" in 2016. In the 2020 cycle, the Carpenters approached campaigns with a curated PowerPoint, downloaded to a pdf on an iPad, sharing their policy proposals with anyone they could – elected officials, presidential campaign staff, local or national. They cast a wide net in cultivating relationships with nomination campaigns, wanting their message out there and knowing the value of getting on a candidate's agenda even if that candidate never took off. Staffers were important in their own right. Whenever approached by a staffer, Leslie and her husband took the time to interact because the staff "are people in our future." Down the road, a few will make it to the White House or other important political venues. They will be "educated people on our issue, going into higher positions of power throughout the whole country." She had a long-term vision when it came to Iowa campaign staff.

The Carpenters had several points of contact within the 2020 campaigns. They met with multiple field staff and the state policy director from the Warren operation, and they were on phone calls to Warren's national policy team. Jacob Hamblin entered the Carpenters' sphere when they reached out to the Booker campaign, extending an invitation to the senator to join the annual community walk sponsored by the National Alliance on Mental Illness (NAMI). The walk had been in April, the same day as Booker's fiftieth birthday, which he had proposed to celebrate with community service. In the end, the candidate didn't attend the NAMI walk, but Jacob Hamblin did. The Carpenters also went to their share of cattle calls, tracking down candidates with forethought and planning. From Leslie's perspective, "Wing Ding" in early August 2019 was her "most productive and efficient night" of the campaign.

North Iowa Wing Ding is another one of those summer political mainstays, a showcase event on a Saturday evening, with Friday night and Saturday daytime activities too. Wing Ding started in 2004, a fundraiser sponsored by a handful of North Iowa counties which were "out of sorts" and one of them financially broke. As with other caucus-related phenomena, Obama, then the ascendant star, helped put Wing Ding on the map. It was like many other political events in the state, organized by a bevy of party volunteers logging long hours and pulling together an experience, this one involving chicken wings. In other locales, an event of this scale might well be contracted out to event-planning firms. Initial feelers to candidates about the 2019 event were sent out in October 2018. Candidates who showed up got five minutes to speak and, in the ever-present quest of Democrats for equity, candidate order was random (McNett, 2019).

With over 20 candidates on the program, Leslie saw Wing Ding as a prime opportunity and went prepared with material for each candidate. For most of them it was the second batch that they would have received from her that season. "I made friends with the security guys offstage, so that I [could]… be in that offstage area where the candidates are entering and exiting," in a prime position to get their attention. She "got to every single candidate that evening," giving them a five-point plan generated with material from an online poll of experienced mental health advocates.

Leslie's interaction with Bernie Sanders stands out in her mind. She noted that she'd met him before in 2015 and 2016. Certainly, candidates meet far too many people to remember them all, but in her signature blue t-shirt Leslie's focused concern on mental health would likely have been clear to the candidate. "[I handed him] the information, and he just stood there in front of a gaggle of reporters, put his hand in my face and screamed at me: 'My Medicare for All plan will solve all this. Read my plan. Read my plan. Read my plan.'" Leslie adds, "He must have said ['read my plan'] ten times to me."

She tried to interject that insurance wasn't the issue, since she and her husband each had employer-based insurance. She continued to push, "Would you take this packet." The candidate acquiesced, "I'll take it, but you need to read my plan." Jane Sanders, the candidate's wife, standing close by, reinforced the message for Leslie: "Dear, you need to read the plan." Leslie read the plan and tried to reach out to Sanders later in the campaign but got no response.

Leslie had more luck getting through to another candidate, this time via campaign staff, working up the chain of command. The Carpenters' greatest champion was Booker staffer Jacob Hamblin, who had gotten to know them well, talking frequently about mental health and their personal experiences as well as their advocacy work. He felt that the Booker campaign needed to work with the Carpenters, given their connections both to the community and a national network. Like other staff in Iowa at all levels, Jacob logged time on regular calls with the campaign staff and he'd routinely talk up the Carpenters in his weekly reports. He considered it his personal challenge to connect the Carpenters with the candidate. "Whenever I talked to our state director or any of our political people, I was constantly the squeaky wheel … with a smile." He'd say "Hey, I know I'm terribly annoying, but these people are amazing." Jacob said he knew if they "got [the Carpenters] in front of the right people, both sides would fall in love with each other."

The Carpenters would get 25 minutes face-to-face with Cory Booker in the fall, thanks to Jacob, even though his job ostensibly was managing a regional team of field organizers. Leslie Carpenter said that one of the candidate's top national aides, Matt Klapper, told her after the meeting with Booker, "You need to thank Jacob." She already knew that Jacob was "relentless" in landing the meeting for them. From Jacob's angle, this was just his "shoot your shot" approach, which he described as his region's mantra.

Exiting the Bubble

Nomination politics is essentially about winnowing the field of candidates,[9] and one of the roles refined by the Iowa caucuses over the past half century was to do just that. But winnowing starts well before the caucuses, for a variety of reasons. Sometimes candidates can't sustain the time away from other elected positions, others are felled by scandal, and some just never get traction. In the 2020 cycle, those national criteria for making it to the debate stage had a unique effect on who populated the caucus bubble. And when a campaign folds, it's not just the candidate who exits but the staff as well.

New York Senator Kirsten Gillibrand, who had entered the race in January 2019 with some reasonable expectation of success, never gained her footing. In national polls, her support rarely exceeded 1%, no better in Iowa. Some speculated that the contest had an undercurrent of gender bias plaguing the female candidates. "[Male] candidates are the subject of flashy profiles and media buzz, affording them an inherent advantage over their female counterparts" (Siddiqui, 2019). Some Democrats harbored ill feelings toward the New York senator, remembering that two years earlier she had urged Minnesota Senator Al Franken to resign, which he eventually did, presumably ending the political career of a popular, liberal star.

By mid-August, the buzz about Gillibrand pointed to impending doom, a quality spreading at the point. She spent $1 million on TV ads in Iowa and New Hampshire to try to boost her standing and qualify for the third debate, for which the DNC had raised the bar, upping required polling and unique donor numbers (Shepard, 2019). Over an eight-day period, Hickenlooper, Inslee, and Moulton would withdraw. On August 28th, the DNC announced Gillibrand would not be on the debate stage.

Around this time, Lauren Parker had been reflective, assessing the work she was doing for Gillibrand and the impact she had on the campaign. She understood the bind the campaign was in, though when the candidate withdrew it still came as a surprise. In fact, Lauren did not learn Gillibrand had dropped out until after a meeting with a likely caucus-goer. She missed the invite to the staff call announcing the withdrawal because she didn't want to glance at her phone during the one-on-one.

Casey Clemmons, Gillibrand's caucus director, praised the candidate for the timing of her departure. "I personally give Kirsten a lot of credit for dropping out when she did," for acknowledging that "maybe it wasn't the right time, maybe it wasn't the right year." Casey thought it was a smart decision for the candidate's political future, but also for her staff who had "a really tough job." Still, the withdrawal was a blow for staffers, many who had left behind other jobs, family and friends to move to Iowa to work for the senator.

"I felt a lot of emotions, including anger and heartbreak," noted Lauren. But one of her Iowa City-based colleagues faced something more concrete: the need to exit a six-month lease only two days after signing it. This organizer, a recent college graduate, had spent a good part of her first two months in Iowa City in supporter housing. When signing her lease on August 26, she had anticipated a fall and winter in Iowa City. Luckily, her landlord found someone else to take the lease and even returned her entire deposit.

The campaign may have folded but Gillibrand's state leadership team went to work, transitioning to a make-shift career development office to assist staff whose last paycheck would come September 17, less than three weeks away. Casey Clemmons said that state leadership put out a quick call for staff to update and submit resumes. They also explicitly asked the staff what they were interested in doing next. "Do you want to continue on a presidential [campaign]?" "Do you want to do a senate race?" "Who are some of the folks you're interested in?"

Within just a few days of Gillibrand's withdrawal, the campaign had sorted the resumes in Google folders for individual campaigns and then "blasted out the Google Drive with everyone's resume, saying 'hire these folks, hire these folks, hire these folks.'" Gillibrand staff from across the state came to the Des Moines state headquarters one last time, depositing the physical remnants of their campaign work – material, things to shred – but also for exit interviews and career advice from senior staff. Gillibrand's withdrawal was well-timed as other Iowa campaigns were expanding their staffs. Casey estimated that as much as 80% of Gillibrand's Iowa staff landed positions.

Lauren would spend the following week calling and visiting, saying goodbye to Gillibrand supporters and volunteers, the people she had cultivated in her organizing work, as well as new friends from rival campaigns. She weighed signing on with another presidential candidate, having multiple options. In fact, within three hours of Gillibrand's withdrawal announcement, Lauren had received offers from three different campaigns, one asking for an immediate start, another offering a higher-level position. Knowing that Gillibrand's withdrawal would not be the last before the caucuses, Lauren contemplated whether she really wanted to go through that again. In the end, she made plans to fly home for a few weeks, poised to return as an organizer – in the same turf – for another female candidate. When Lauren's Iowa City-based colleague left, she did not come back. A Gillibrand person through and through, she declined moving to another campaign and went home instead.

Notes

1 The party and media outlets – or some combination of the two – set the rules for primary debates. In contrast, general election debates are regulated by the Commission on Presidential Debates, a non-profit, bipartisan commission, set up for the distinct purpose of organizing and managing general election debates.
2 Given a "comparative lack of knowledge" among voters in primaries compared to general elections, there's room for substantial impact on attitudes (Benoit et al.,

2002, p. 318), especially early in the nomination campaign. Nomination debates can increase audience knowledge, factor into candidate evaluations, including judgments of electability, and even contribute to voter confidence in their evaluations (Yawn et al., 1998).
3 True to form for Democrats, the stated rules were more exacting, specifying which polls, over which specific time frame, would be considered. They also stated expectations for geographic diffusion for donors. And if the two paths turned out to be too inclusive, not weeding out enough candidates, the party would include those who had met both grassroots support and fundraising criteria (DNC Release February 14, 2019, "DNC Announces Details For The First Two Presidential Primary Debates." https://democrats.org/news/dnc-announces-details-for-the-first-two-presidential-primary-debates/)
4 Tara McGowan, who conducted the Carnes interview, was herself a principal in political tech firm ACRONYM, which sold digital products to the Buttigieg campaign.
5 Federal Communication Commission (FCC) rules on political texting (www.fcc.gov/rules-political-campaign-calls-and-texts) are in practice quite permissible, allowing even unsolicited text communications, provided an actual person hits "send" for each (Zarroli, 2020).
6 Payments to Hustle in Vendor Recipient Records through October 23, 2020: www.opensecrets.org/campaign-expenditures/vendor?cycle=2020&vendor=Hustle+Inc
7 https://mobilisationlab.org
8 Zach Exley in "Lessons from the Sanders Campaign," Personal Democracy Forum, New York City, June 2016 (www.youtube.com/watch?v=JLoaMVq1OLk)
9 Norrander (2006) conceptualizes presidential nomination as a game of "attrition," finding rules less important than assets – popular support and money – a candidate had at the outset in explaining how long candidates stay in the race.

References

Abramsky, Sasha. 2011. "A conversation with Marshall Ganz." *The Nation* February 3 (www.thenation.com/article/archive/conversation-marshall-ganz/).
Allen, Jonathan. 2015. "It was brutal to be in the "kids' table" debate." *Vox* August 6 (www.vox.com/2015/8/6/9114283/kids-table-Republican-debate-brutal).
Benoit, William L., Mitchell S. McKinney, and Michael T. Stephenson. 2002. "Effects of watching primary debates in the 2000 US presidential campaign." *Journal of Communication* 52(2): 316–331.
Bernstein, Jonathan. 2000. "The new presidential elite." In *Pursuit of the White House 2000*, ed., William G. Mayer. New York, NY: Chatham House, pp. 145–178.
Carpenter, Leslie. 2019. "It is about the beds." *Bleeding Heartland (blog)* September 15 (www.bleedingheartland.com/2019/09/15/it-is-about-the-beds/).
FiveThirtyEight. 2019. Podcast: "Who is winning the fundraising primary so far?" (https://fivethirtyeight.com/features/who-is-winning-the-fundraising-primary-so-far/).
Ganz, Marshall. 2009. "Organizing Obama: Campaign, Organization, Movement." In the Proceedings of the American Sociological Association Annual Meeting, San Francisco, CA, August 8–11.

Gardner, Amy and Philip Rucker. 2011. "Rick Perry stumbles badly in Republican presidential debate." *The Washington Post* November 10 (www.washingtonpost.com/politics/republican-presidential-candidates-focus-on-economy/2011/11/09/gIQA5Lsp6M_story.html).

Goldmacher, Shane and Lisa Lerer. 2019. "New Democratic debate rules will distort priorities, some campaign say." *The New York Times* May 30 (www.nytimes.com/2019/05/30/us/politics/democratic-debate-rules.html).

Herrnson, Paul S. 2009. "The roles of party organizations, party-connected committees, and party allies in elections." *Journal of Politics* 71(4): 1207–1224.

Hopkins, David A. 2018. Televised debates in presidential primaries in *Routledge Handbook of Primary Elections* ed., Robert G. Boatright. New York: Routledge, pp. 307–319.

Koger, Gregory, Seth Masket, and Hans Noel. 2009. "Partisan webs: information exchange and party networks." *British Journal of Political Science* 39(July): 633–653.

Kreiss, Daniel. 2012. *Taking Our Country Back: The Crafting of Networked Politics from Howard Dean to Barack Obama*. New York: Oxford University Press.

McGowan, Tara. 2020. Podcast: "FWIW Episode 11: campaigning amidst a pandemic." (www.fwiwpodcast.com/fwiw-episode-11-campaigning-amidst-a-pandemic).

McKenna, Elizabeth and Hahrie Han. 2015. *Groundbreakers: How Obama's 2.2 Million Volunteers Transformed Campaigning In America*. New York: Oxford

McNett, Jared. 2019. "What it takes to make the Iowa Wing Ding sing." *(Mason City) Globe Gazette* August 7 (https://globegazette.com/news/local/govt-and-politics/what-it-takes-to-make-the-iowa-wing-ding-sing/article_aec6513b-c2e0-5b15-a536-931074b1055c.html).

Minow, Newton N. and Craig L. LaMay. 2008. *Inside the Presidential Debates*. Chicago: University of Chicago Press.

Norrander, Barbara. 2006. "The attrition game: Initial resources, initial contests and the exit of candidates during the US presidential primary season." *British Journal of Political Science* 36(3): 487–507.

Shepard, Steven. 2019. "Gillibrand launches TV ads in bid to stay on debate stage." *Politico* August 9 (www.politico.com/story/2019/08/09/gillibrand-tv-ads-democratic-debate-1456107).

Siddiqui, Sabrina. 2019. "Kirsten Gillibrand can't break through – is sexism to blame?" *The Guardian* May 20 (www.theguardian.com/us-news/2019/may/20/kirsten-gillibrand-cant-break-through-is-gender-bias-to-blame).

Stanley-Becker, Isaac. 2020. "She sends texts to put Bernie Sanders in the White House — she and 12,000 others." *The Washington Post* February 1 (www.washingtonpost.com/politics/she-texts-to-put-bernie-sanders-in-the-white-house-she-and-12000-others/2020/02/01/88a9e252-3ebe-11ea-baca-eb7ace0a3455_story.html).

Stone, Walter J., and Alan I. Abramowitz. 1986. "Ideology, electability, and candidate choice." In *The Life of the Parties, Activists in Presidential Politics*, eds. Ronald B. Rapoport, Alan I. Abramowitz, and John McGlennon. University Press of Kentucky, pp. 175–198.

Stone, Walter J., and Ronald B. Rapoport. 1994. "Candidate perception among nomination activists: a new look at the moderation hypothesis." *The Journal of Politics* 56(4): 1034–1052.

Streitfeld, Rachel and Paul Steinhauser. 2012. "Gingrich delivers show-stopper at beginning of South Carolina debate." *CNN Politics* January 20 (www.cnn.com/2012/01/19/politics/gop-debate/index.html).

Yawn, Mike, Keven Ellsworth, Bob Beatty and Kim Fridkin Kahn. 1998. "How a presidential primary debate changed attitudes of audience members. *Political Behavior* 20: 155–181.

Zarroli, Jim. 2020. "Getting lots of political messages on your phone? Welcome to 'The Texting Election.'" *NPR* October 7 (www.npr.org/2020/10/07/920776670/getting-lots-of-political-messages-on-your-phone-welcome-to-the-texting-election).

6 The Party Umbrella

September 2019 began with a clear understanding among everyone – candidates, staffers, journalists, activists, and rank-and-file partisans – that with five months until Caucus Day, the Democratic race was wide open. Even with the spate of late-August withdrawals, 21 candidates remained. One billionaire had already joined the race and another was yet to come. One thing, however, was certain: the rhetoric directed by the contenders at each other in debates and on the stump had become aggressive, at times harsh. At a national level, former vice-president Joe Biden remained the perceived leader. National polls showed him ahead, but a surging Elizabeth Warren had caught – or even passed – Bernie Sanders for second. In Iowa, the same scenario was playing out, though Pete Buttigieg had emerged as a serious contender, passing California senator Kamala Harris in some polls to move into the top four.[1]

Warren's strong showing came as no surprise to those on the ground in Iowa. She had built a juggernaut of an organization, placing operatives in offices across the state and mobilizing a passionate volunteer base. In some ways, her model replicated that of Sanders – both in 2016 and 2020 – but her engagement with local Democratic party organizations differed vastly from Sanders'. Warren and her staff frequently espoused a desire to elect Democrats up and down the ballot and build a strong bench of future candidates. But from a policy perspective, she and Sanders had similar, progressive agendas that left them competing for an active base of largely young voters. They were eager for a "revolution" if they were for Sanders or seeking "big, structural change" if they preferred Warren.

Meanwhile, the front-runner was not acting the part. Biden was trailing both the two progressives and the surging Buttigieg in fundraising and the development of a finance infrastructure. On top of that, Biden was getting negative press as President Trump lobbed corruption accusations at his son, Hunter, who served on the board of a Ukrainian gas company while his father was vice-president. Yet polls still had Biden in the lead and doing well among Democrats drawn to electability.

Biden's standard stump speech played up his eight-year partnership with Barack Obama, emphasizing it as a defining experience that made him the best prepared and most electable Democrat in the race. But while Obama remained a wildly popular president among most Democrats, he kept his distance from the nomination race, willing to express encouragement but holding off on endorsing (Epstein, 2019). As for Biden's ties to the former president, some progressives felt the Obama Administration had been two terms of missed opportunities (West, 2017) while others were too young to have been enamored with the 44th president or his vice-president.

Another flash point between the establishment Biden and the two progressives was the issue of health care. While Sanders and Warren continued to extoll Medicare for All and the transformational potential of a national health care plan, Biden believed in the pragmatism of Obamacare – whether carrying that label or the more commonly heard Affordable Care Act. He felt that allowing Americans access to the health care plan of their choice, whether through a private insurer or a government marketplace, was the better option. The progressive senators disagreed, saying that unless there was a guarantee of health care coverage, someone would always be left out. The establishment vs. progressives battle within the Democratic Party, ongoing since 2016, would not abate. It rose up at multi-candidate events, within social media, and even at kitchen tables as parents and voting-aged children hashed out their differences. It would only become more heated as the caucuses neared.

Into the Weeds

Not all of that went into caucus politics captured the attention of the media and the public, or for that matter most campaign staff. Some things flew under the radar for even close observers on the ground, depending on their positions and roles. Laying the groundwork for the caucuses involved decisions made and resources expended by state and local party organizations in Iowa, starting about a year in advance of the caucuses. Mixing metaphors, these are the weeds of the bubble, obscure decisions and actions affecting the way campaigns and the caucuses played out. In some cases, those obscure decisions could affect the eventual outcome.

On that March 2019 day in Malcom when Jacob Hamblin had shown up at the county party's off-year caucus, the agenda had touched briefly on the topic of planning the *second* event in the Iowa Democratic caucus/convention process – the 2020 county convention. The event was a year off, to be held about six weeks after the February 2020 precinct caucuses, and even most of the hardcore party activists at the meeting gave it little thought. But the rather obscure decision about convention size – a task delegated to county parties by the Iowa Democratic Party (IDP) – could matter in terms of the caucus outcome, especially in very small, rural precincts. In short, it could mean the difference between a winner-take-all or a proportional distribution of delegates, the former giving an extra boost to the candidate who succeeded in mobilizing supporters to those small caucuses. It might translate into a marginally stronger voice for a candidate who did well in rural areas.[2]

There was another early decision – a task, really – that occupied local parties, less esoteric than convention size, but potentially impactful: securing venues for the caucuses. This was a little trickier than it might seem, a job typically undertaken by county party chairs, who in their volunteer positions shouldered increasingly burdensome responsibilities as the caucuses approached. In all, the Democratic Party would need to secure sites for 1,678 precincts, with a given chairperson responsible for anywhere from 4 to 177, depending on the county. In an earlier era, caucuses would routinely be held in homes of Democrats. David Nagle, the state party chair who served in the 1980s, estimated that in 1976, 30–40% of caucuses were in the living rooms of Democrats (Kilen, 2016). Over time, this became a less-attractive option, in part because of an emphasis placed on accessibility. Caucus turnout was another factor as it grew to the point that even a large home could not accommodate the attendees. In 2016, caucuses were held in homes in only five precincts (Kilen, 2016). In 2020 none would be. However, relying on other options – school gyms and cafeterias, libraries, community centers, and the like – didn't necessarily solve the space challenge, with larger caucuses in the state requiring space for several hundred or even close-to 1,000 in a competitive year. Space like that isn't particularly abundant anywhere, even in urban precincts. Iowa code stipulates that public spaces – like those in schools and libraries – be offered at no cost to the parties,[3] but some counties occasionally resorted to renting event space.

The challenge for county chairs was to line up sites, appropriate both in location and capacity, all available at the same time on that Monday night. It helped that they weren't chasing the same spaces as Republicans, which happens when there are competitive contests in both parties. Even though Iowa Republicans would also hold caucuses on February 3, they didn't expect high turnout given the minimal competition for President Trump.[4] There was added psychological pressure for the Democrats to secure large-enough spaces. In 2016, crowded caucuses in some of the larger precincts contributed to the Clinton/Sanders tension.

Much of the work associated with organizing the caucuses-as-events fell to the parties themselves, with the state party holding ultimate responsibility. It's a costly proposition. The IDP October 2019 budget[5] estimated caucus-related expenses for the 2020 cycle at more than $1 million, not an insignificant sum for a party with a total budget of around $3 million. Included were sizable outlays for technology and security, constituting over three-fourths of the projected caucus expenses. But even with a reliance on technology, explained IDP Executive Director (ED) Kevin Geiken, the state party still trafficked in paper. It allocated funds for printing documents to record all the information at the caucuses and postage to have it sent back to the state party. Those projected caucus expenses did not include the ramped-up staffing, which Geiken estimated to be another $500,000–700,000. In addition to its core IDP team of 13 staff, the party planned to staff up with an additional 14 hires; by October it was well into this staff expansion. Geiken was fully aware of the benefits accrued to Iowa Democrats by holding these high-profile events. But the costs – literal and figurative – didn't escape him either. He emphasized that the caucuses ran on the labor of the party in the state, funded in large part by monetary contributions from Democrats themselves – in contrast to "taxpayer supported" presidential primaries.

The staffing of the formal party is not dissimilar to that of the campaigns, though the work is permanent and not just seasonal. In fact, this is one of the key distinctions between a candidate-centered campaign and the formal party apparatus; the party organization is in it for the long haul. Many of the positions in campaign organizations have analogues in the party – a state chair, a director, and posts in finance, digital, and data, to name a few. The additional caucus staff interfaced with the statewide party structure, assisting the county parties in organizing and administering the caucuses. There were also dedicated staff for engagement with key constituency groups in the party (e.g. Latinx, African American, and organized labor) as well as individuals focused on accessibility. The employment profiles of those working for the party – both in core and caucus-focused positions – often show past involvement in campaign politics, perhaps no better illustrated than with the state chair Troy Price.

Price brought to the top position his past experience as IDP ED, having also filled political director positions for both Obama in 2012 and Clinton in 2016. He was known more broadly outside of campaign circles for his work defending marriage equality in the state as ED of One Iowa, an LGBTQ rights-focused organization. Kevin Geiken had been the deputy ED in a prior midterm cycle, having started in the field as an organizer with Obama in 2008 and 2012. The party chair/ED distinction is analogous to the top leadership roles in a campaign organization. The chair is more visible, with responsibilities focused on symbolic and outreach tasks, while the ED is focused on nuts and bolts, remaining behind the scenes.

Just Who Decides?

In the aftermath of 1968, the new presidential nomination system set by the Democrats wrested control from party insiders and placed it in the hands of rank-and-file Democrats, ostensibly democratizing the process. This was manifest in the broad brushstrokes of the post-reform system, like the mandate that national convention delegates are chosen not in some opaque process or by a heavy-handed governor or party leader, but via primaries and caucuses, broadly publicized events open to participation by average Democrats. Schier (1980) paints a picture of Iowa caucuses operating in that pre-reform era – as they had for some 60 years – with little openness. When one progressive activist, a McCarthy supporter, inquired of her local Polk County party leader in 1968 about where and when to caucus, she was told, in effect, not to bother: "[The] few established Democrats in the neighborhood took care of it, and what concern was it of [hers]" (Schier, 1980, p. 86).

The post-reform changes adopted by Democrats extended beyond adding transparency to the caucuses. The democratic impulse was borne out in a variety of details marking the new system. Though the McGovern-Fraser commission recommendations hadn't used the language of "proportional representation," instead invoking "fair representation" or "fair reflection," the party inched toward a full articulation of that rule over the first few cycles after 1968 (Kamarck, 2019). Proportional representation, required now by the Democratic Party but only permitted by the GOP, is considered to be more democratic in that minority voices – both in terms of number and embodied diversity – are more fully represented than under winner-take-all systems.

Acting on democratic impulses for a party is one thing. Creating a set of rules associated with losing elections is another. The reality is that the reformed Democratic system produced nominees who lost in the general election, at least two-thirds of the time initially. The 1972 landslide loss of McGovern to Richard Nixon and the 1980 loss of then-incumbent Jimmy Carter to Ronald Reagan overshadowed Carter's 1976 win. It was easy to discount that 1976 outcome as the good fortune of Carter being from the South and going up against a Watergate-stained Republican.

In the trusted Democratic spirit of revising rules to solve a problem, the party created a new delegate category – automatic, unpledged delegates who attend the national convention not because they are selected through primaries or caucus/convention processes but because they are party leaders or elected officials. These delegates would become known colloquially as "superdelegates," a term eschewed by many Democrats holding those positions, preferring the "automatic" label instead. Regardless, the introduction of this type of delegate meant an enhanced path for input in the nomination process by party insiders – and the reintroduction of "peer review" into the presidential nomination system.[6]

Ever since the introduction of superdelegates, there had been some attendant internal party debate about the appropriate role and the merits of these unpledged delegates, with candidates trumpeting outsider status recognizing that superdelegate support could even be a disadvantage. It wasn't until 2008 that the internal debate moved to a public stage. Obama's campaign, observing that the unpledged delegates were lining up behind Hillary Clinton, argued that they should be following the popular will of the Democratic rank-and-file, confirming the choice of the primary voters (Kamarck, 2019). The 2016 contest reignited both the internal and external debates, with concerns by the Sanders campaign that the automatic delegates were yet one more manifestation of a rigged system, working to the advantage of the establishment. This argument had weighed heavily on the recommendation of the Democratic National Committee's (DNC) Unity Commission, and for the 2020 cycle the party adopted its first major change to superdelegates since their inception in 1984. They would only cast votes at the convention if no candidate received a majority of the pledged delegates on the first round of voting.

Historically the actual vote of automatic delegates had never changed the outcome of a contest. Still, there was always the chance that this rules change could be more-than-symbolic with the big 2020 field potentially splitting delegates. And like other structural aspects of the post-reform system that opened up the process, the rules affected the conduct of campaigns, what candidates did, and the role that rank-and-file Democrats played. That's why Democratic nomination campaigns have looked much different in the post-1968 era than they did before. At the same time, despite the democratization of the process, the ultimate winner of many contests looked like someone the party insiders might have picked.

The Party Decides (Cohen et al., 2008) contends that after a few cycles under the new rules, the players – Democratic elected officials, as well as other party-related influencers – adjusted to the new system in a way that reinforced the power of party insiders. They might not be able to call the shots on delegate selection or actions at the conventions, but they could convey signals that could drive supporters into particular candidate camps. The authors, putting a fine point on it, conceptualize one way this happens: "a deliberative process spread out over the entire nation" in which the endorsements reflect "who can best represent [the endorser's] own concerns, unify the party, and win the general election" (Cohen et al., 2008, p. 172). Using evidence from party insiders – state and national election and party officials, activists, and even non-political celebrities – *The Party Decides* shows that endorsements more often than not coalesce behind one candidate. And when that happens, that candidate wins the nomination. The contention that the party converges around the establishment candidate was especially compelling over the time frame analyzed by *The Party Decides*, but it was challenged by the nomination of Obama – who didn't start out as the pick of the establishment. Trump's nomination offered yet another strong challenge.[7]

Campaigns tend to be unconcerned about academic debates, and so – as usual – the field simply made its pitch to the pool of likely endorsers. Every cycle candidates of both parties dedicate a significant amount of staff time to this task, often undertaken especially by state leadership and the campaign's political unit, usually with not much direct organizer involvement.

Some of the 2020 endorsements were unsurprising – like former US Agriculture Secretary and one-time Iowa governor Tom Vilsack's endorsement of Joe Biden. The two worked together for eight years in the Obama Administration, and Vilsack and his wife Christie, a one-time congressional candidate, hosted an event for Biden in the summer. Their formal endorsement, however, would not come until later in the year. By fall, there were still many would-be endorsers still uncommitted. Then Elizabeth Warren's well-oiled campaign machine began to make inroads with some influential Democratic legislators, including State Senator Zach Wahls, who jumped on board with Warren in October, despite strong overtures from Pete Buttigieg.

Endorsements by the party apparatus had been historically hard to secure, with party leaders feeling a certain obligation to demonstrate an unbiased structure. That mindset began to crumble in 2008, and it continued to do so in 2016, when party officers lined up early behind the candidates in the

Clinton/Sanders showdown. Local party leaders were initially reluctant to endorse in 2020, encouraged by the state party to remain neutral,[8] but this changed as 2019 progressed and chairs and vice-chairs signaled their preferences.

In theory at least, there are tangible by-products of an endorsement. For the presidential candidate, it could bring an existing network of supporters and volunteers, perhaps an elected official's campaign organization or members of a union. Despite the weakening of organized labor, a union endorsement is still valuable, assuming it translates into support among rank-and-file union members. Sometimes endorsements have some symbolic value as well, a sign that a key constituency group is aligned with the candidate or that prominent political leaders think that candidate is electable.

Good things can accrue to the endorser as well. Though rare and pushing the ethical envelope, presidential candidates can make contributions to lower-level federal candidates in exchange for an endorsement. To be legal, however, this *quid pro quo* transaction needs to be disclosed to the FEC, displayed in both the disbursements of the presidential campaign and the receipts of the other. For candidates for Iowa state-level offices, the situation is different and represents an overt disconnect between federal and state law. While federal law allows a presidential candidate's campaign committee to contribute to a state or local candidate, Iowa law bans those candidates from accepting the contribution, creating a headache for staff at Iowa's campaign finance and ethics board. Tom Steyer's state political director was forced to resign in late fall 2019 amidst charges that he was attempting to orchestrate money-for-endorsement exchanges with a number of down-ballot candidates (Rodriguez, 2019).

A substantial amount of the money flowing from the presidential candidates to other Iowa candidates, at both the federal and state levels, comes via federal leadership PACs. Corrado (1992) dubbed these "pre-candidate PACs" when they functioned as an arm of a presidential hopeful. Most of the 2020 field had PACs in place prior to their candidacies, and many – 14 – made contributions to federal candidates in Iowa in the 2017/2018 cycle.[9] The giving pattern of each PAC hints at a strategy, though admittedly reading motive into a financial contribution is always a tricky business (Wilcox, 1989; Currinder, 2003). Still, considering midterm cycle giving in the first four nomination states, it looked like those who would be front-runners, like Warren, Sanders, and Biden, wrote off the early states a little more than the lesser-knowns. This suggests that PAC giving might have been seen as more important for the underdogs.

PAC-facilitated contributions to Iowa candidates pale in comparison to spending by Super PACs, which can spend unlimited amounts provided they do so independently of campaign committees – no coordination is permitted. Much of the spending goes toward media.[10] However, some Super PACs fund organizing efforts, much like candidates and parties do. NextGen was the big caucus player in this regard, as it had been in Iowa in previous cycles, since 2014. The group planned to invest $3.5 million in the state, hiring 16 field organizers and focusing its effort on college campuses (Hytrek, 2019). Super PAC involvement in Iowa in 2020 ventured into the product space in a prominent fashion, with tech development vendor ACRONYM, tied to Super PAC PACRONYM, selling its texting product to the Buttigieg campaign and eventually an app to the IDP to relay and tabulate results on caucus night.

Centripetal Tech

The twenty-first-century nomination ecosystem is populated with disparate actors, from traditional organizations like parties, campaigns, and profit-driven vendors to entities taking new organizational forms. Think of it in the aggregate as a complex organization, while hardly united, with at least some level of affinity among the parts. This image applies equally to the national scene as it does to Iowa. Bringing the disparate parts together after a contentious nomination contest isn't the only challenge. Another is to muster some degree of coherence from year to year. In the distant past, the formal party organization might have provided that coherence, persisting from one cycle to the next, the prime repository of expertise, technical skill, and memory about campaign politics. But today, formal parties have plenty of competitors. And data-driven politics and technology have only increased the challenge.

For all of the focus on data and technological innovation marking the first few contests of the twenty-first century – from Dean to Obama, to the 2016 contest – the party had no central repository of data. The typical campaign in Iowa accesses the voter file via VAN, fueling contacts between organizers and the voters, on the phone and at their doors. Increasingly, other commercial products used by campaigns sync with VAN. But the party had lacked the ability to build a broad infrastructure of data under its own umbrella, refined and enhanced by the day-to-day work of campaigns, and available the next cycle to Democratic campaigns, parties, and progressive organizations. Somewhat ironical given the focus of the Obama campaign on data and analytics, the situation hadn't much improved under Obama's leadership of the Democratic Party.

Though advances in data were credited to Obama-the-candidate, many practitioners considered President Obama's performance as head of the Democratic Party to have been lackluster (Debenedetti, 2017). In particular, the move to transform the 2012 general election campaign into a non-profit structure, operating independently of the DNC and even arguably competing with it for donors, seemed to represent the president's overwhelming concern with Obama-as-brand, rather than with the Democratic Party (Milkis & York, 2017). And despite the advances in data and analytics by campaigns and the progressive left in this era, the party itself was not much of a player. Hillary Clinton, after her defeat in the 2016 election, bemoaned the party's data. "I get the nomination ... [and] I inherit nothing from the Democratic Party." She added that "its data was mediocre to poor, non-existent, wrong" (Lapowski, 2019).

Even worse for Democrats, the GOP seemed to have its data act together. In 2011, Republicans created a private company – Data Trust – to serve as a data clearinghouse, structured so that it did not run afoul of the FEC prohibition of coordination between campaign committees and Super PACs. Under this model, campaigns could license data to the Trust, and then other groups could purchase it without violating FEC regulations (Lapowski, 2019). The Democratic version of this, announced in 2019, was a "data exchange," an effort supported by DNC chair Tom Perez and chaired by 2004 presidential hopeful Howard Dean, who had served as DNC chair under Obama. Chairman Perez reportedly "cajoled" state party chairs in 2018 to release data to the clearinghouse. And touting the promise of the ready exchange of data, Dean boasted that "one door knock in Iowa can benefit the entire ecosystem" (Lapowski, 2019).

Alfred Johnson's concern with the party and data had a slightly different focus: volunteer recruitment and building organizations. He was another veteran of Obama's 2008 campaign in Iowa – having organized in Ames, home to Iowa State, another university town and the University of Iowa's intrastate rival. Johnson worked in the White House after the 2008 win, moving between finance and tech afterward. After the Trump election, he noticed the surge in Democratic activism, especially online, but worried – as many others have – about whether that "authentic organizing momentum" could be converted into political campaigns.

Mobilize[11] is an events platform, a startup co-founded by Johnson in 2017 and used by some 20 Democratic presidential nomination candidates in 2020 (Green, 2020). The product addressed the problem for the left that Johnson had observed: "[T]he tech used by campaigns and groups … didn't allow for collaboration." The Mobilize platform allows people to sign up for campaign events and volunteer shifts, sign petitions, and other types of actions. Because the platform syncs with the VAN, the Mobilize data can inform contact strategies of a campaign. One thing that's notable is that each volunteer gets a unified profile across every campaign that persists with them. Johnson sees this as a plus for the party, but in more abstract terms as a way to protect against inefficiency and loss. It helps counter the prevailing norm of "technology [dying] with the campaigns."

The DNC Hammer

The allure of the data exchange or a platform like Mobilize is that it opens the door for cooperation. But in some instances cooperation is mandatory. The saga of the 2020 virtual caucuses in Iowa came to an abrupt end in late August 2019, when Iowa's plan to offer an option to caucus remotely was vetoed by the DNC, a stark reminder of the national party's clout in the broader party organizational structure (Wekkin, 1984) – not to mention the snail's pace at which complex organizations move. The development also underscored the tension between values of accessibility and security.

The Unity Commission had adopted its recommendation for a more inclusive and accessible process in December 2017. The IDP had taken up the charge early on with its own reform committee, and eventually the delegate-selection proposal featuring a virtual option. How, precisely, these virtual events would work was a mystery to most Democratic activists and local party leaders, not certain whether it would be online or through an app, or some sort of call-in system. One thing was settled: the state party had been firm from the start that the delegates apportioned to the virtual caucuses would comprise 10% of the delegates to be awarded on February 3, which seemed a reasonable number – not too many, not too few. Following the formal state party process, the state central committee approved the delegate-selection plan, including the virtual concept, in April 2019.[12] At the end of June, DNC committeeman Scott Brennan presented details of the plan to the national Rules and Bylaws Committee meeting in Pittsburgh, the first hurdle in the path toward final DNC approval.

The plan Brennan described to the committee was a call-in system, structured to comply with the provisions for the traditional in-person caucuses. Brennan noted he fielded a lot of questions from the committee about the plan, but that it "seemed fine." In the end, the Rules and Bylaws Committee granted provisional approval to the Iowa plan. Brennan noted that another virtual plan, proposed by Nevada, also an early state with a caucus system, appeared to generate harsher committee questions, which Iowa party leaders read as a cautionary signal that they had better engage with the DNC tech team. When they did engage, however, the DNC tech team simply advised them to "build out the process." Brennan regrets not pushing the DNC tech people "to tell us that [the virtual plan] was a problem or that they had concerns."

The IDP went to work on building out the system, but when Rules and Bylaws met later in the summer, DNC chair Tom Perez told them in a closed-door meeting that security experts convened by the national party had been able to hack into a conference call between Iowa and Nevada Democrats and the Rules and Bylaws Committee. This reportedly "enraged party officials in caucus states who [said their virtual] systems were not fully built and the hack of a general teleconferencing system was not comparable" (Pager, 2019). Some speculated that the DNC's approach was especially cautious for several reasons. First, it had been hacked in 2016. And second, dismissing security concerns would be akin to what Democrats saw as a cavalier attitude toward cyber security by President Trump and the GOP. IDP chair Troy Price, while clearly angry about the DNC thwarting what he felt was a good-faith effort, used the microphone to slam the opposition party: "We have seen time and again the increased threat by foreign state actors and the continued reluctance by Donald Trump and Republicans in Congress to take this threat seriously."[13] The national committee finalized its decision to reject the virtual caucus plan for both Iowa and Nevada on August 30th.

The DNC's veto of the virtual caucus, which would have allowed remote participation, was a blow to those pushing for a more inclusive Democratic process. Presidential hopeful Julián Castro, struggling to gain traction, tweeted that day his dismay over the decision: "The DNC has disallowed plans to increase participation in the first-in-the-nation caucus state. I strongly urge the DNC to embrace our party's values and allow absentee voting, either through a virtual caucus, mail-in, or early voting process."[14] But absentee or mail-in voting, though used widely in Iowa general elections,[15] carried some risk for Democrats in the caucus context, a swipe at what was considered the fundamental essence of a caucus – a meeting, with deliberation, and ultimately the allocation of delegates. And while absentee voting wouldn't necessarily turn the caucus system into a primary system, it was a movement in that direction, potentially threatening Iowa's privileged first-in-the-nation position. As for 2020, the IDP was left with five months to make the caucuses more inclusive.

So by September 2019, Iowa Democrats were effectively starting to compile their "to do" list for 2024: tackle the problem of how to pull off remote caucuses but still heed the concerns of security experts who caution that no system could provide 100% protection from predators. The more immediate concern: how to make the 2020 caucuses more inclusive, short of using a remote system.

Driving

Sanders supporter Carl Birkestrand landed a volunteer gig, but not a typical one. After that early April weekend when Carl saw Sanders in Malcom, the campaign reached out, asking if he'd be interested in driving in the caravan of cars that accompanied the candidate on his trips through the state. Carl became a regular, switching roles in the usual three-car caravan between driving the "lead car," with a staffer riding shotgun, giving directions, and driving the "drag car," hauling supplies and on-the-ready should someone need to go in another direction. Carl didn't drive the candidate, who would ride in a third car, but did observe him up close, getting a feel for what he's like: "All business, all the time." Carl was impressed with the entire Sanders team and grateful for getting to spend a little time one-on-one with the candidate in the summer. But he felt like he "had arrived," when once Jane Sanders just walked up and said, "How are you doing, Carl?"

Notes

1 FiveThirtyEight, "Latest Polls: Who's ahead in Iowa?" (https://projects.fivethirtyeight.com/polls/president-primary-d/iowa/)
2 The logic is somewhat complicated. But at the heart of it is the reality that the decision about how many delegates will attend the county convention affects the number of delegates allocated to each precinct, keeping in mind delegates are allocated to precincts in much the same way that the national party allocates delegates, based on past party performance. That said, a very small precinct might be allocated one vs. two delegates, depending on the decision about county

convention size. If one, the results in the precinct on caucus night will necessarily be winner-take-all. With two to award, there would be some basic semblance of proportional distribution. The same principle applies more prominently in a different context – namely in the distribution of legislative seats in proportional representation systems. It holds that proportionality is inversely related to the number of legislative seats to distribute (Rae, 1967; Lijphart, 1990) – or delegates, in this case.

3 Ia. Stat. § 43.93 1986.
4 Republican parties in nine states chose to cancel their nomination contests, handing their delegates to the president in a show of support for him (Hutzler, 2020). The declared Republican candidates beyond the president – Bill Weld and Mark Sanford, both former governors, and conservative talk-radio host Joe Walsh, who had represented Illinois in the US House – had a minimal presence in Iowa. Sanford was even a no-show at an event he had scheduled. Joe Walsh displayed some ingenuity, late in the caucus campaign meeting Iowa Republicans by walking the line of people who were waiting to get into a big Trump rally in Des Moines.
5 Provided by IDP Executive Director Kevin Geiken.
6 In each election cycle, the national party tweaks the numbers of automatic delegates who will attend the convention, with their delegate share ranging from 14% of the total convention delegates in 1984 (www.belfercenter.org/publication/history-super-delegates-democratic-party) to a planned 16% in 2020 (https://ballotpedia.org/Democratic_delegate_rules,_2020). Scholar Elaine Kamarck, whose political credentials include long-term membership on the Democratic National Committee and service as an unpledged, automatic delegate, is a vocal proponent of peer review in the nomination. Kamarck touts the value of including in the process the voices of those whose experiences position them to judge a potential nominee in terms of potential for success as president (Kamarck, 2019, p. 195)
7 Steger (2016) suggests a concrete refinement to *The Party Decides* to account for Trump's nomination, and Bawn et al. (2012) – dealing more conceptually – propose a modified definition of party, with implications for the dynamics of nomination.
8 Endorsement of presidential candidates by DNC officers was precluded by the national party, as described in the DNC Officer Endorsement Policy, issued in December 2018.
9 Candidates can be freer in donating money through the PAC vehicle, since limits in place for contributions to leadership PACs are higher than limits to candidate committees, meaning that funds can be replenished more readily. FEC guidelines for contribution limits specifiy the details. (www.fec.gov/help-candidates-and-committees/candidate-taking-receipts/contribution-limits/).
10 Wesleyan Media Project reported that by caucus time, Biden's Super PAC had spent over $3 million on TV ads: "$44 Million on Presidential Ads in Iowa" January 9, 2020 (http://mediaproject.wesleyan.edu/releases-012920/)
11 Also known as "Mobilize America."
12 IDP Release April 6, 2019 "State Central Committee Approves Iowa Democratic Party 2020 Delegate Selection Plan" (https://iowademocrats.org/state-central-committee-approves-iowa-democratic-party-2020-delegate-selection-plan/)

13 IDP Release August 30, 2019. "Iowa Democratic Party Statement on DNC's Recommendation Not to Approve Iowa's Virtual Caucus Plan" https://iowademocrats.org/iowa-democratic-party-statement-dncs-recommendation-not-approve-iowas-virtual-caucus-plan/
14 https://twitter.com/JulianCastro/status/1167492375020736512
15 Iowa has permissive early voting procedures for general elections and primaries, allowing any voter a mail or in-person early vote option. Figures reported by the US Election Project (www.electproject.org/) for general elections in 2010 through 2018 show that consistently over 40% of votes by registered Democrats were cast through early or mail-in processes, exceeding in each year the early vote of Republicans, which hovered in 32–39% range. Since 2000, Democrats in Iowa have incorporated elaborate early voting initiatives into their campaigns.

References

Bawn, Kathleen, Martin Cohen, David Karol, Seth Masket, Hans Noel, and John Zaller. 2012. "A theory of political parties: groups, policy demands and nominations in American politics." *Perspectives on Politics* 10(3): 571–597.

Cohen, Martin, David Karol, Hans Noel and John Zaller. 2008. *The Party Decides: Presidential Nominations Before and After Reform*. Chicago: University of Chicago Press.

Corrado, Anthony. 1992. *Creative Campaigning: PACs and the Presidential Selection Process*. New York: Routledge.

Currinder, Marian L. 2003. Leadership PAC contribution strategies and house member ambitions *Legislative Studies Quarterly* 28(4):551–577.

Debenedetti, Gabriel. 2017. "Obama's party-building legacy splits Democrats.' *Politico* February 9 (www.politico.com/story/2017/02/obama-democrats-party-building-234820).

Epstein, Kayla. 2019. "Obama tells Democrats worried about the primary field to 'chill out'." *The Washington Post* November 22 (www.washingtonpost.com/politics/2019/11/22/obama-tells-democrats-worried-about-primary-field-chill-out/).

Green, Joshua. 2020. "Democrats just got the digital machine they need to keep winning." *Bloomberg Businessweek* November 30 (www.bloomberg.com/news/articles/2020-11-30/everyaction-and-mobilize-give-democrats-the-app-they-need-to-keep-winning).

Hutzler, Alexandra. 2020. "Trump's 2020 challengers accuse GOP of trying to protect the president as increasing number of states scrap primary contests." *Newsweek* January 8 (www.newsweek.com/trump-2020-challengers-slam-gop-scraping-primary-contests-1481121).

Hytrek, Nikoel. 2019. "NextGen Iowa making another big investment in youth turnout." *Iowa Starting Line* December 3 (https://iowastartingline.com/2019/12/03/nextgen-iowa-making-another-big-investment-in-youth-turnout/).

Jaffe, Alexandra. 2019. "Tom Steyer aide in Iowa offered money for endorsements." *The Des Moines Register* November 7 (www.desmoinesregister.com/story/news/elections/presidential/caucus/2019/11/07/election-2020-tom-steyer-iowa-aide-pat-murphy-offered-money-endorsements/2519204001/).

Kamarck, Elaine. 2019. *Primary Politics: Everything You Need to Know about How America Nominates Its Presidential Candidates*. Washington, DC: Brookings Institution Press.

Kilen, Mike. 2016. "The home caucus: cozy tradition nears extinction." *The Des Moines Register* February 4 www.desmoinesregister.com/story/news/elections/presidential/caucus/2016/02/04/home-caucus-cozy-tradition-nears-extinction/79696102/).

Lapowski, Issie. 2019. "Inside the Democrats' plan to fix their crumbling data operation." *Wired* April 9 (www.wired.com/story/democrats-fix-crumbling-data-operation/).

Lijphart, Arend. 1990. "The political consequences of electoral laws, 1945–85." *The American Political Science Review* 84(2): 481–96.

Milkis, Sidney M. and John Warren York. 2017. "Barack Obama, organizing for action, and executive-centered partisanship." *Studies in American Political Development*, 31(April): 1–23.

Pager, Tyler. 2019. "Virtual Caucus at Risk after DNC Experts Hacked Conference Call." *Bloomberg* April 25 (www.bloombergquint.com/politics/dnc-virtual-caucus-at-risk-after-experts-hacked-conference-call)

Rae, Duncan W. 1967. *The Political Consequences of Electoral Laws*. Yale University Press, New Haven.

Rodriquez, Barbara. 2019. "Tom Steyer's Iowa political director resigns after money-for-endorsements allegation." *The Des Moines Register* November 8 (www.desmoinesregister.com/story/news/elections/presidential/caucus/2019/11/08/tom-steyer-iowa-political-director-resigns-after-money-endorsements-allegation/2534771001/).

Schier, Steven E. 1980. *The Rules and the Game: Democratic National Convention Delegate Selection in Iowa and Wisconsin*. Washington, DC: University Press of America.

Squire, Peverill. 2008. "The Iowa caucuses, 1972–2008: a eulogy." *The Forum* 5(4):1–9.

Steger, Wayne P. 2016 "Conditional arbiters: the limits of political party influence in presidential nominations." *PS: Political Science & Politics* 49(4): 709–715.

Wekkin, Gary D. 1984. "National-state party relations: the Democrats' new federal structure" *Political Science Quarterly* 99(1): 45–72.

West, Cornel. 2017. "Pity the sad legacy of Barack Obama." *The Guardian* January 9 (www.theguardian.com/commentisfree/2017/jan/09/barack-obama-legacy-presidency).

Wilcox, Clyde. 1989. "Share the wealth: contributions by congressional incumbents to the campaigns of other candidates." *American Politics Quarterly* 17(4):386–408.

7 Doubling Down

Removing the virtual caucuses from the table meant that by fall campaigns had a little more certainty about the process they could expect on February 3. Even so, Democratic caucuses as events are quite complex and seem shrouded in mystery for the uninitiated, whether Iowans who had never attended one or staff new to the state. That mystery persisted despite monumental efforts made by campaigns to clarify what to expect. In the 2020 cycle, the new rules on the books complicated – but also simplified – things.

Caucus Basics and Twists

Eligible participants – that is, registered Democrats who will be 18 by the presidential general election – can caucus in their precincts. Precincts are considered the smallest political unit in the state, but population across precincts varies considerably statewide. Within a county or city, though, they have roughly comparable populations.[1] Caucus turnout also varies dramatically statewide, in a competitive year from a handful of people to around 1,000. Variation is due to a combination of factors: population and concentration of Democrats in a precinct, as well as basic turnout patterns. Turnout tends to be higher in urban than rural areas.

Not surprisingly, the feel of each caucus varies. But there is a set agenda for them all which falls into three basic categories: basic party business, platform work, and activities connected to presidential nomination and delegate selection. In a typical caucus, the vast majority of people attending aren't much interested in party business or the platform. Same for the campaigns which have mobilized people to attend. For them, like almost all attendees, it's all about expressing support and – whether or not the attendees realize it – having a voice in the process of allocating to candidates the precinct's predetermined number of delegates to the county convention. Those delegates will then attend the county convention, the next step in Iowa's longer, tiered process that will ultimately select the pledged national convention delegates.

This delegate-related work commands the most energy and time in a typical, competitive year. For that matter, as the caucuses approach, the process will capture the attention of the media, which will dutifully describe it, these days resorting to graphics and interactive displays when the platform permits.[2] At the caucuses themselves, once the presidential nomination work begins the attendees express their candidate support by physically moving – "aligning" – into preference groups. Groups that constitute at least 15% of the caucus attendees are "viable" and are eventually awarded county convention delegate slots proportionate to the size of the preference groups. Imagine a precinct that has ten county convention delegates to award to candidates. Imagine further a percentage breakdown for candidate support of 50/30/20, say in 2016, Clinton, Sanders, and O'Malley supporters. In that case, it would be a similar 50/30/20 split in delegates awarded to each as well. The process ends with the preference groups selecting people to serve in those delegate positions. Of course, in practice the process is more complicated, governed by precise mathematical formulas and number counts that rarely calculate to integer outcomes,[3] with norms of behavior and nuance that add some intrigue.

In past cycles, any number of "realignments" followed that first expression of preference when caucus-goers moved into initial candidate groups. In these realignments, groups that fell short of the 15% threshold could try to persuade individuals in larger, readily-viable groups to jump ship, knowing that they wouldn't jeopardize the viability of their preferred candidate by lending support to make another group viable. Likewise, two or more groups that failed to meet the 15% cut-off could merge, forming a newly-viable group. Any number of scenarios could play out, the product of different motives of multiple attendees, possibly with a nudge from campaigns. Some might reflect sincere behavior, choices made that seem to be a straightforward expression of the preferences of caucus attendees. Others might be strategic, perceived paths to a desirable goal not necessarily transparent to an observer (Shepsle & Bonchek, 1996; Redlawsk et al., 2011). Toss in the possibility that moves could be effectively random, a compelling explanation if attendees, in fact, have incomplete knowledge of the detailed rules. Whatever the dynamic, the largely open-ended realignment process in the past could take a lot of time, maybe an hour or more, contributing to the burden imposed on attendees. What's more, it was a process in which insiders – the party establishment – would seem to have a comparative advantage.

The single realignment round permitted under the new 2020 rules would – theoretically – expedite proceedings, freeing up participants from the constraints of a long, drawn-out event. Another change in store for 2020 was – for the first time – a documented indication of candidate preference. Caucus attendees would record on a "presidential preference card" their initial candidate pick, as well as the candidate whose preference group they landed in after realignment. This might sound like a ballot, but the IDP was careful to avoid that language, instead casting it in terms familiar to the traditional caucus process of preference groups and alignments. The preference card would offer two things to the process. It would first generate a formal measure of caucus attendees' initial preferences that would be made public. That measure would then be coupled with the party's traditional go-to metric of caucus outcome: the state party's state delegate equivalents (SDE) projection. Second, the new preference count would serve as a paper trail, essential for a recount should the precinct caucus results be questioned.

A Change of Seasons

In campaign politics – and the actual campaigns themselves – everything ramps up a notch in the fall. But that increase in activity looked different for each campaign. In 2020, the usual money chase took on a new level of import, thanks to the DNC's debate-access criteria – thresholds that grew more demanding as the season progressed.[4] Of course, the fundraising bar posed more of a challenge for some than others. For Sanders, consistently breaking records in small-donor fundraising, it was no challenge at all. By November, the DNC had thrown a lifeline to some candidates facing a wall with the unique donor requirement. They could also hit 5% support in two polls of early voting states. With the exception of Senator Warren, women and candidates of color struggled. Both Booker and Castro complained that DNC debate rules prevented them and other candidates of color from participating but allowed a billionaire, implying Bloomberg, "buy his way onto the stage" (McCaskill, 2019).

On the ground in Iowa, campaigns ramped up in visible ways. Some candidates started spending money with abandon, running traditional broadcast ads or signing contracts for them, complementing the digital ads that had been greeting Iowans for months. Most chose to start visiting the state even more frequently. Though they were fewer in number, the remaining candidates were even more present than they had been in the spring and summer. In total, candidates logged 166 Iowa events in September and 131 in October, compared to double-digit numbers in the months prior – including the big August draw of the Iowa State Fair, a traditional stop for candidates on the circuit.

A few campaigns were in a position to double-down on field operations, bringing in additional staff while maybe shifting initial organizers to regional positions. Organizer Lauren Parker, who had worked for Gillibrand, returned to the state after signing on with Kamala Harris and took over part of Rachel Salas' territory. New to Iowa and to organizing when she had started with Gillibrand, Lauren had a stockpile of additional factors to consider when weighing offers from other campaigns, including one dangling a regional director job. In the end, the Harris position would allow her to organize the same counties she had previously worked, reducing startup costs and offering the chance to enlist her Gillibrand-focused organizing relationships into the Harris effort. Lauren could remain in her same supporter housing and, importantly, work alongside Rachel, who had become a good cross-campaign friend – a real-life model of the aspirations of Friendship 2020.

Casey Clemmons, who had been the caucus director for Gillibrand and with earlier presidential cycles under his belt, eventually jumped on with Buttigieg in Iowa. Once things wrapped up with Gillibrand, he had about a month of down time. "I did a lot of walking actually, [which I do] when I'm unemployed in between campaigns." Casey works in a world in which being out of work is a given, and he needed to figure out what he would do. "Whatever city I'm in, I just like to walk … [maybe] 18 miles a day." His Facebook post from October 1, 2019, featuring a head shot of Buttigieg, his new boss, and the news that he was starting as the campaign's political director for Iowa, pulled in lots of enthusiastic comments from an array of friends, political and otherwise. On that same day, the Buttigieg campaign announced that it had raised an impressive amount of money, $19 million in the third quarter, just behind Sanders' staggering $25 million haul.

The race might still have been wide open, but it was increasingly hinting at a four-person contest. Buttigieg appeared to be building an impressive organization, pulling in money and putting concrete resources behind his summer-found celebrity. The stealth campaign of Sanders added an element of uncertainty for those trying to handicap the race, not necessarily seeing visible signs of organizing prowess, but hearing that the campaign had engaged large numbers of young activists. As for Biden, the former vice-president seemed hard-pressed to maintain his front-runner status and build any momentum. But it was Warren who looked to clean up, following a version of the Obama playbook by investing in traditional organizing.

Reinforcing a Ground Game

To veteran observers of caucus politics, Warren seemed to be doing everything right – taking a "methodical approach" (Norvell, 2019) to events and organizing, and because of this looked poised for the sort of Iowa payoff that Obama had received in 2008. Maybe other 2020 campaigns had new twists on organizing, but Warren was scoring on the fundamentals. National polls had shown the senator surge from mid-September to mid-October, and in Iowa she had unseated Biden as the most-preferred candidate among likely caucus-goers by the end of September.[5] The Warren campaign had played up its traditional organizing since early spring, and as the campaign progressed, it followed through on its pledge to prioritize the ground game by adding even more organizers, opening field offices earlier than any other campaign, and even organizing at the precinct level by fall. Precinct-level organizing signals to everyone that the campaign has enough capacity in terms of paid staff and volunteers to start planning the details of the lead-up to the February caucuses – which was especially noteworthy when other campaigns had not even filled out their county organizational structure.

Warren had a disciplined and systematic operation, beginning with the candidate herself, whose rhetoric and events showcased policy. One of her standard lines on the stump was "I've got a plan for that!" Indeed, her field staff would often address policy questions by pointing to any number of expansive Warren white papers on a variety of subjects, usually going into the elaborate funding detail commonplace for a US senator. Warren events – even those with huge crowds – featured her signature selfie line, offering an opportunity for anyone to get a photo with the candidate. This is the twenty-first-century version of a long-standing face-to-face Iowa caucus experience, though in Warren's case administered like clockwork. Staff were dispatched immediately upon an event's conclusion to shape the line, with as many as eight to ten workers helping to move people toward the candidate and the staffer who would ultimately use that person's smartphone to take the photo.[6] The Warren campaign's estimate for the number of selfies by the end of October was 10,000, and her events were drawing crowds that dwarfed those of the other candidates in the field.

The key to the Warren ground game, however, was the field staff whose efforts mobilizing for the candidate constituted just a fraction of their work. In most counties across the state, Warren had more organizers than other candidates. By September 2019, she had 65 staffers in a dozen offices. And while they, like staff for other candidates, cultivated connections with local party organizations, the Warren team articulated a philosophy that was music to the ears of the party. They emphasized that while their short-term goal was to nominate Elizabeth Warren, it was also important to build a stronger Democratic Party. This was not lost on Polk County chair Sean Bagniewski, who judged the Warren organization as "one of the best … if not the best," noting that "[the organizers are] very conscientious and thoughtful on the way they give back to the party and their community" (Norvell, 2019).

A Matrix of Data and People

Organizers juggle a variety of tasks on a daily basis, but by fall the main focus of their work is direct voter contact – that is, reaching out to a large number of Iowans for the purpose of persuasion and/or mobilization. This happens by telephone or face-to-face interactions, using phone banks and door-to-door canvassing. The exchanges typically follow a highly scripted format, meant to equip organizers and volunteers with a consistent message intended to optimize the impact of the contact. Who were the recipients of these calls and front-door contact? Usually, they were individuals whose profiles were in the voter file as presented in the VAN.

Campaigns use the summer to lay the groundwork for the ramped-up direct voter contact that will begin in the fall. Even though data vendors work to clean the products that they sell to campaigns, field operatives typically go through a process of early contact with voters, usually on the phone, with an eye toward updating the voter file. Better to find out seven months early, rather than in the lead up to the caucuses, that a phone number no longer works or a voter has moved – or died. These early interactions also tap into attitudes about the current contest. These data will help craft a refined voter profile in the database, a tangible product of the campaign's work. But that's only an intermediate step toward eventually targeting individuals with direct contact techniques, with the hope of efficiently persuading and mobilizing them.

The path to the fall, however, was paved with more than cleaning data and efficiency. For some campaigns like Warren's, it was also about creating a sense of excitement and solidarity. In doing so, they recruited and trained volunteers in the protocols of the campaign, so that when fall rolled around the efforts could scale up. Events like a weekly Warren phone bank were meant to lure in volunteers and to make them feel part of the cohesive community standing behind the candidate. Emails from a Warren organizer played up the social aspect of the regular summer phone bank in a supporter's garage: "Roll in after work, bring a friend, bring a snack [to this] fun and casual volunteer opportunity! We're getting scrappy…meeting in the … garage and making calls to … registered Democrats. Come join the fun with the Garage Crew!"

The "weekend of action," yet another Obama staple, was widely adopted by 2020 campaigns in Iowa. One Warren weekend of action pitched a theme meant to inspire supporters to tackle canvassing. The canvass would "[honor] women and gender-nonconforming folks … by channelling … energy into canvassing for a woman who is consistently rolling out policies to lift up people of all genders." Billed as a family-friendly and accessible activity, there would be experienced babysitters on hand, even "children's 'canvassing' packets." But the feel-good/hang-out-with-friends/bring-the-kids approach had an underlying purpose in mind: sustain the volunteer base, which would be increasingly important as the campaign progressed to fall.

The activities of the campaign, like the general approach of organizers, relied on an incentive structure tapping into "solidary" motivation. James Q. Wilson distinguishes different types of benefits that guide activists, with solidary invoking rewards derived from things like "socializing, congeniality, the sense of group membership" (Clark & Wilson, 1961, p. 134). Some activists might be motivated by "purposive" benefits – looking toward the issue and policy stances taken by the candidates. But there are painfully few "material" benefits for campaigns to dole out to volunteers, certainly no jobs, no promise of government services or other tangible perks that a party machine in the past might have been able to offer. About the closest an organizer can come to something material is securing a spot for a highly valued volunteer – a "super volunteer" – in "the clutch," a private or small group photo-op with the candidate before or after an event, usually offering the chance for the activist to exchange pleasantries with the candidate, maybe even a few substantive words as well.

On the Phone and At the Door

Door-to-door canvasses and phone banks are fundamentally the same, opportunities for the campaign to connect with eligible caucus-goers. There's nothing novel about engaging at a front door or on the phone; they are campaign practices with long histories. But these days, and as employed by the nomination campaigns like most others,[7] this direct voter engagement is tied to the VAN. It has evolved marginally over the twenty-first-century cycles in response to changes in technology, notably putting more capacity directly in the hand of the organizer.

Organizers "pull lists," using VAN to extract the names and contact information of individuals targeted in phoning and canvassing operations. In doing so, they use selection criteria – "filters" typically specified by the campaign. A filter could be simple conceptually, like targeting likely caucus-goers. Or the filter could be more complex, like filtering on a "second choice" if a given first choice pick just pulled out. To set up canvassing operations, the organizer will also "cut turf," meaning partitioning a list geographically so that canvassers can walk an area and hit the door of each targeted voter with reasonable efficiency. These tasks, pulling lists and cutting turf, are embedded in VAN functionality, but for many organizers they involve as much art as science.[8]

Canvasses are more resource-intensive than phone banks but generally considered worth the work and the effort. Organizers or volunteers calling on the phone can complete a "packet" – perhaps 60–80 names – in a couple of hours, less time if the target doesn't answer or the call quickly ends.[9] Walking turf, on the other hand, takes time, even if voters don't answer the door. Some geographies are clearly better suited to telephoning than door-knocking, including low-density rural areas that might have residences separated by long expanses or gravel roads. It might take an entire afternoon to canvass a packet of, say, 40 names. That said, many organizers and volunteers prefer one modality over the other, feeling more comfortable engaging on the phone or in person. The typical organizer at least tolerates the tasks of voter contact, which is a central part of an organizer's job description. The rare volunteer loves the activity. However, its importance is repeated constantly. Direct voter contact is understood to be a critical component of a successful campaign, and the hope is that volunteers will be reluctant to let down the organizer.

Both organizer and volunteer experiences have changed over the past few cycles due to technological developments. "My Campaign" is a volunteer-management platform within VAN that allows organizers to keep track of volunteers and the activities they engage in. For phone banking, organizers have the ability to set up "virtual phone banks" – with access to call lists and even phoning capacity – for volunteers, even those without direct VAN access. And "Mini-VAN" is a mobile canvassing app that volunteers can download on their phones, supplying information about canvass targets – even a map to tell where a targeted voter resides. Mini-VAN also allows the volunteer to enter data generated in the voter contact directly into VAN.

These VAN bells and whistles, as well as smartphones in the hands of most volunteers, have changed the work experience for organizers and volunteers. No more index cards, a go-to medium as recently as 30 years ago for storing information about voters and sorting into decks for phoning and canvassing. No more tracking down after-hours office spaces with a number of landlines for phone banks, thanks to virtual phone bank software embedded in VAN. And now with Mini-VAN, no more stacks of paper for volunteers to juggle on clipboards as they record information on their canvasses. Not surprisingly, these are more than just technological changes to simplify work, but rather a mix of things that contribute to complex power arrangements in campaigns, including the centrality of the for-profit NGP-VAN to campaign life and the degree of centralized control of the campaign.

... and In the Field Office

Almost all of the campaigns were reaching out to Iowans on the phone and at their doorsteps, but by October some still lacked brick and mortar spaces. In that physical space contest, Buttigieg was leading at 22 field offices, followed closely by Warren at 19 and Biden at 17 (Epstein & Wezerek, 2019).[10] In symbolic terms, having field offices sends the signal that the campaign is active and confident it will be around for the duration. If the office is in a storefront or space highly visible to passers-by, all the better. Studies of formal organizations have traditionally considered a physical presence – an office, a building, a headquarters (HQ) – to be a component of institutionalization, a quality typically associated with productive organizations, ones that can withstand challenges and serve their intended purposes (Huntington, 1968). For party organizations, having a physical space is a sign of capacity and related to electoral success (Cotter et al., 1984). Even more specifically, there's a general election payoff for Democratic campaigns related to the presence of a field office in a county (Masket, 2009; Darr & Levendusky, 2014). But changes since 2012, putting the tools of the trade on the smart phones and laptops of staff and volunteers, give pause to consider whether a field office is as important as it once was. Money spent on renting space – or paying organizers, for that matter – is a drop in the bucket compared to what's spent on other things, like digital or broadcast ads. The commitment in rent for local space usually runs from $500 to $2,500 per month, depending on location. But the challenges of finding multiple spaces and dealing with leases, contracts, and insurance make field offices a significant obligation.[11]

The 2020 campaigns typically set up field offices in the more populous counties in the state, along with those holding particular promise for Democrats – meaning, central and eastern Iowa. The state's western third, especially the northwest, is largely inhospitable territory for Democrats. Lyon and Sioux counties, in the northwest corner bordering South Dakota, are Republican strongholds. In 2016, Trump carried Lyon with 85% of the major party vote, a staggering 87% in Sioux. Republican Party registration is strong there too, in both cases over 70% in October 2019. By contrast, Trump pulled in just 30% of the 2016 vote in Johnson County, and Republican registration in that eastern Iowa Democratic bastion was a paltry 19% in fall 2019.[12]

New York Times data showed just a smattering of field offices in the west and northwest, most of them concentrated in Council Bluffs and Sioux City, the population centers of western Iowa. Buttigieg especially played up his investment in largely rural counties that had flipped from Obama to Trump in 2016.[13] He also touted his field office in highly-diverse Storm Lake, a northwest Iowa city of about 10,000 residents, 36% of whom were Latino. Storm Lake also featured a prominent journalist, Pulitzer Prize-winner Art Cullen of the *Storm Lake Times*, who had a national audience as a frequent opinion contributor to *The Washington Post*. Despite the draw of Cullen and potentially positive demographics, no other Democrat opened an office in Storm Lake.

There's considerable physical variation in field offices, which in former lives might have been a Main Street retail store, strip mall space, or a vacant feedmill. Still, almost all have a gritty feel– peeling wall paint, floors untouched since that last tenant, once-discarded furniture, hopefully an old refrigerator or microwave. Warren's field office in Iowa City, which opened in June 2019, occupied a large space across the street from an expansive brewery/taproom on a heavily traveled street. It was just a little more than a mile from downtown and the University of Iowa, tucked back off the street, hidden from view. The campaign appeared to prioritize ready parking over the sort of foot traffic that graces downtown areas. The Harris office, meanwhile, was close to campus on the lower level of an apartment building that catered to university students. The downside: multiple steps, both to enter and to maneuver once inside, posing an accessibility challenge for any disabled staff or volunteer. That said, the campaign encouraged volunteers with children to bring them along for shifts at that office.

It's handy for a campaign to control its own space, a "coordination point" (Darr & Levendusky, 2014), even with considerable mobility associated with digital tools. A field office frees up organizers from the task of finding venues for volunteer gatherings and campaign activities, especially those that involve "staging locations." It also adds an element of privacy to the work setting, something hard to come by in coffee shops and public spaces where organizers from different campaigns post up, or the shared living space of a supporter housing arrangement. Even such mundane things as faster, more reliable internet and space to store yard signs are attractive to campaign staff, who become accustomed to working with few of the amenities that come with other occupations.

On Campus, Too

The Warren Iowa City field office, despite its relative distance from the University of Iowa campus, seemed well-suited to a younger crowd, with a large back room – a repurposed space that used to be a garage, big enough for heavy volunteer activity. Marc Esler was a Warren campus organizer, a Chicago native who went to Grinnell College in Iowa and then organized for NextGen in the 2018 primary cycle. He was bumped to a regional director position with NextGen for the 2018 general elections. Like others, Marc's network from past political work influenced his 2020 career moves. NextGen's focus on mobilizing students is a logical launching pad for a campus organizer.

Iowa college and university campuses are prime targets for nomination campaigns, with age-eligible participants often concentrated in specific precincts.[14] Of course, campuses vary in the level of political activity and left/right balance of the student body, both influencing the treatment they get from campaigns. Right-leaning Dordt College in northwest Iowa attracts about as much attention in a Democratic contest as left-leaning Grinnell College does in a Republican one: hardly any. But with an open Democratic field for 2020, Grinnell, like many other colleges and universities, was a regular stop on the candidate circuit.[15] Drake University in Des Moines played a role that's become routine over the years, hosting a high-profile debate. And Des Moines Area Community College (DMACC) partnered with the state's public television affiliate to host "conversations" with six of the prominent candidates, and its satellite campuses were frequent candidate stops.

As much as some universities and colleges are hotbeds of caucus-related activity, usually with active involvement of Campus Democrats or Republicans and other campus-specific organizations, mobilizing students can be a hard sell. So, too, can demonstrating that impact empirically. The young adult demographic, including college students, generally has low levels of electoral participation.[16] Even in Iowa's record turnout in the 2018 general election, youth turnout – age 18–24 – at 38% lagged behind every other age group, as well as the overall 61% turnout rate.[17] Estimates of *college student*, as opposed to youth, electoral turnout are more complicated. The National Study of Learning, Voting, and Engagement (NSLVE), conducted by Tufts University, merges voter file data with student information provided by colleges and universities; its findings suggest low turnout among that youth category of college students as well.[18]

Estimating student *caucus* – as opposed to electoral – activity is particularly tricky for scholars and journalists with access to conventional data. Even a good read on caucus turnout overall is a challenge because party registration is fluid. That said, entrance polls help pinpoint the proportion of youth among total caucus-goers. In 2008, 17–29 year olds made up 22% of the Democratic attendees, 18% in 2016, proportions that could very well make a difference in the results.[19] Those same entrance polls showed that Clinton tanked with that youth demographic, picking up support from just 11% in 2008 (to Obama's 57%) and 14% in 2016 (to Sanders' 84%).[20] In fall 2020, the trio of Sanders, Warren, and Yang appeared to be leading the pack in terms of student enthusiasm. The "free college" proposals of all three, ranging from "tuition-free" for Sanders to "debt-free" for Warren and Yang, as well as Yang's UBI proposal, resonated with this demographic (Skelley, 2019). At the same time, on college campuses across the state there was a little enthusiasm for Biden, viewed increasingly as the personification of the Democratic establishment.

Tyranny of Data

It's a safe bet that campaign staff in Iowa have never read – or even heard of – "The diffusion of hybrid seed corn in two Iowa communities" (Ryan

& Gross, 1943). The authors of this academic article, two rural sociologists at Iowa State, explained how innovations are diffused. They focused on hybrid corn, which was new in the 1920s. Even 75 years after publication, this Ryan/Gross understanding of the widespread adoption of something new – a technology, a practice – is still important and highly cited. In fact, the twenty-first-century spread of data and analytics in the campaign world looks a lot like the mid-twentieth-century diffusion of hybrid corn.

Modern campaigns for contests up and down the ballot have become reliant on data and analytics over the past two decades (Hersh, 2015; Issenberg, 2012). At the top of the ticket, including most viable presidential nomination campaigns, this reliance pervades all areas of the organization, but digital and field are especially data-centric. Staff, along with the consultants and vendors they hire, collect and analyze a wide variety of data, from enhanced voter lists, sometimes including synthetic/modeled information about voters (Hersh, 2015; Nickerson & Rogers, 2014), to locational data from cellular devices, to the products of social media mining, which lend insight to both individuals and their social networks. Almost every engagement with a voter gives a campaign the opportunity to collect individual data, whether it's an old-school ask at a candidate event to provide name and contact information on a sign-up sheet or, new-to-2020, a request to scan a QR code to enter a Yang event. For their part, most Iowans – like people everywhere – seem either unaware or unconcerned that campaign politics is, in effect, a large-scale data collection project. Each conversation with a canvasser at a door, click to open a campaign email, or text to sign up for early notification about some important information from the campaign results in data to add to the VAN or some other list. What's different about these data, compared to data that campaigns have used for a very long time,[21] is that they are about *individual* voters, collected, stored, and analyzed with the benefit of digital technology. And just as Ryan and Gross (1943) observed with an early twentieth-century agricultural innovation, products and practices relating to these mostly new data had been adopted at a rapid rate over the last two decades.

In the world of hybrid corn, effective salesmen convinced farmers of the promise of the new seed in increasing crop yield. In campaign politics, the sales teams are vendors and consultants pitching to clients, along with staff who bring a repertoire of data-related skills from past campaigns, or perhaps hired because of those skills. The corn/data connection doesn't stop there, since both offer transparent, though not perfect, measures of effectiveness. Farmers could literally see how their neighbor's crops were growing (Ryan & Gross, 1943) and a basic win/loss indication gives a sense of the promise of the data and the tools. But the widespread adoption of and high value placed on data have a lot to do with the Obama campaigns, which invested in data and analytics, and played up their role in the 2008 and 2012 wins, aided plenty by those observers who were captivated by their practices. To be sure, Obama broke new ground, but in some cases just accelerated existing practices to the extent that even a difference in degree began to resemble a difference in kind.

Goals

For organizers in Iowa tied to the VAN, being data-driven meant exacting direct voter contact campaigns, which shaped – and at times dictated – their day-to-day schedules and activities. These voter contact mandates, typically the product of some combination of strategists/analysts at the state and national level, are implemented by organizers on the ground who themselves are managed by regional field directors. Republican campaigns in Iowa follow a similar model, and so do Democratic organizing efforts across the nation to a great extent, certainly in nomination and general election contests for federal and statewide offices, and even down-ballot in some cases. It's the widely diffused modern data-driven version of a grassroots campaign: grassroots activity, orchestrated and tightly controlled by the top.

In Iowa, the norm for each organizer was to start the week with goals, always expressed in quantitative terms, usually tied to the VAN, and typically ramping up over the course of the campaign. For organizers, these goals became a central organizing device for the work experience. They largely dictated allocation of time and served as a measure of success or failure on the job. They were also a source of considerable anxiety, sometimes patently unachievable, but meeting them conveyed as a must for the success of the collective campaign enterprise. When organizers constructed a volunteer network to share the responsibility of meeting goal, their time spent on direct voter contact diminished, though effort in volunteer management ramped up. But at the most demanding points over the course of a campaign, an organizer herself might spend 8–10 hours/day making calls or walking turf, relieved only by the allowable hours in a day for this work established by the campaign. Depending on the organizer and the campaign, and with day-to-day variation, this work can be exhilarating, or it can be a total drag.

The Obama model emphasized the importance of goals and the utility of a culture structured around them, instilling in staff and volunteers a sense of responsibility and ownership (McKenna & Han, 2015, p. 141). From a management standpoint, goals translate into metrics, and they serve as a useful lever of accountability in an organization. This is hardly breaking news, with a wide variety of organizations long judging the success of employees, students, even athletes, on the extent to which they met a sales quota, surpassed a score on a standardized test, or perhaps reached a certain batting average. But as Muller (2018) points out in *The Tyranny of Metrics,* basing performance judgments on metrics has a downside, problematic tendencies associated with a "metrics fixation." One is the emphasis on things that are readily measurable to the exclusion of things more difficult to measure yet still important. Another problem comes with the reliance on quantitative indicators rather than qualitative (Muller, 2018), for example tracking *that* there was a contact as opposed to the quality of it. Nomination campaigns are quick to acknowledge these concerns, but still remain goal-focused in their voter contact efforts.

Scholarly Reinforcement

Staffers may not have known about the old study on hybrid corn diffusion, but not so for the book *Get out the Vote!* (Green and Gerber 2004, and subsequent editions). This is one of those rare works by scholars that political operatives read. It's a collection of field experiments, an old methodology that experienced a resurgence in the late twentieth and early twenty-first centuries, approximating the sort of randomized controlled experiment (Campbell and Stanley 1963) that marks research in the lab intended to isolate causal mechanisms. The studies included in Gerber and Green's four editions, along with others by academics and practitioners trained in the approach, reinforced the positive potential of direct voter contact. Earlier iterations focused on traditional contact modalities, like telephoning and canvassing, and the most recent editions include digital techniques. The Analyst Institute, based in DC, is a working group of scholars and practitioners, with considerable overlap with the *Get out the Vote* scholars. The world of relational organizing was a major focus of Analyst Institute efforts heading into the 2020 cycle.

Field experimental research serves multiple purposes. Though it directly informs voter contact, it's used as a device to fire up staff and volunteers, motivating them with evidence that what they'll be doing is effective. Many field staff in 2020 were well-versed in the general messages, if not the empirical details, of the studies that validated their traditional and digital contact procedures. Greta Carnes, the national organizing director for the Buttigieg campaign, implied that evidence of effectiveness is a key step in the diffusion of a technique, in this case of relational organizing. Musing about the Buttigieg headway with the practice, Carnes mapped out the next step. "We need to make sure … working with The Analyst Institute or [someone else] to run … experiment[s] or trials so that we can demonstrate strength" (McGowan, 2020). Consultants and vendors routinely cite that experimental research confirms the utility of their techniques and products.[22]

The data-centric approach to modern organizing and digital media campaigns has the distinct advantage of relying on trackable actions. These can be targeted to individuals in a way that uses campaign resources efficiently. Because they're trackable, they also serve an important administrative role in the campaign organization, structuring goals for campaign staff, and serving as an accountability mechanism. And with tracking comes the possibility that impact can be measured, which in turn reinforces the allure of trackable actions. The cottage industry of academics and others with research agendas honing in on impact are part of the caucus bubble, rarely with a physical presence in the state but lending authority to those overseeing field campaigns and even to organizers in their work with volunteers.

Coming Together… or Not

By fall 2019, there was plenty of reason for optimism among Democrats in Iowa – credible candidates backed up by active campaigns, with enthusiastic staff and volunteers. At the same time, there was a growing sense of unease among all, a reflection of both dismay among the left with the policies and actions of the Trump Administration as well as the divisions among the Democratic contenders themselves. Over the span of two days in September, all of that frustration and angst would be in full display. The third weekend of September had been circled by the campaigns for some time. A key for most was the annual Polk County Democrats' Steak Fry, an event modeled after the old "Harkin Steak Fry," a fundraiser sponsored by Senator Harkin when he held office. The new event – in 2019, a cattle call attracting 17 candidates – was also one of the biggest gatherings of the campaign year with a crowd of an estimated 13,000 Democrats. Most bought tickets themselves, though many attended on the dime of campaigns which also purchased tickets. And for groups planning other events, it was an opportunity to piggyback on the likely presence of every candidate in the state.

Steak Fry, held at Des Moines Water Works Park and its 1,500 acres of parkland, was both an organizer's dream come true and a logistical nightmare. The winding roads through the park forced people to park cars in ditches and trek a mile, even two or three, to get to the main venue. Those roads also provided plenty of space for yard signs – thousands of them – lining the roads and marking the spaces designated for each campaign's staging or tailgate area. That's where staff, volunteers and supporters gathered and socialized, ready to flank the candidate as he or she paraded to the stage for an allotted ten-minute speech to the large crowd. Steak Fry is part picnic and part carnival, an organizational feat – and payday – for the Polk County Democrats. It is also a test of the logistical aptitude and ingenuity of campaigns (Pfannenstiel, 2019).

Beto O'Rourke's state political director was State Representative Chris Hall, a young Democratic leader in his mid-thirties, whose first campaign was John Edwards' 2008 presidential bid, a departure from the well-worn "first worked for Obama" model. Steak Fry was an all-hands-on-deck event, and prep activities for the O'Rourke team involved constructing seven-foot tall letters spelling out "We Believe" as well as a do-it-yourself raft to sail an O'Rourke barn sign. The randomly assigned staging area included a pond, and thus a creative inspiration for the O'Rourke team. In this Steak Fry effort, a circular saw and plywood replaced data and analytics as a path to reach likely Democratic caucus-goers.[23] Chris Hall's team had worked for days on prep and was in place at 6:00 am the morning of the event. After the fact, Hall emphasized what Steak Fry did for the organization. "We really tried to do it in a way that gave the team a meaningful project to work on together, [bringing] us together and … showing people that the caucus isn't all millions of dollars spent and raised, that you can do it on a shoestring, [that you can] do it the right way."

The levity of Steak Fry contrasted starkly with a gathering at the same time, less than five miles away at a convention center in downtown Des Moines. Iowa Citizens for Community Improvement (CCI), the progressive group closely aligned with Bernie Sanders, saw a chance to distance itself from the Democratic mainstream. CCI, with a 2020 mission that included "People Before Politics," focused on a broad array of issues that seemed to elicit deep passion. These included the environment, immigration, racial justice, and a $15 minimum wage. CCI leadership was embedded within Sanders' 2020 Iowa campaign team, their close relationship well known to activists and observers. The CCI Forum, down the road from Steak Fry, aimed to elevate progressive issues and to demand action from the candidates.

CCI organizers insisted they didn't intentionally schedule the Forum to directly compete with the local Democratic Party event. Still, the timing and proximity were fortuitous, allowing the invited candidates to shuttle from one venue to the other. Unlike Steak Fry, with an open invitation to candidates in the field, the People's Forum extended invitations based on responses to a questionnaire distributed to candidates, with four candidates – Sanders, Warren, Castro, and Buttigieg – making the cut.[24] There was no frivolity to this event, instead impassioned speeches from the stage, with attendees sitting in rows of chairs lining a large banquet hall, not the casual lawn chairs in the park down the road. At the Forum, Minnesota Congresswoman Ilhan Omar delivered the keynote, and an array of others, including a Central American refugee, a fast-food worker, an affordable housing advocate, and a number of college students, offered moving testimonials.

Busloads of progressives – activists from the Catholic Worker movement, union members, environmentalists, college students from Iowa, Minnesota, and Illinois – listened to repeated messages that corporate power is the enemy. They heard that they were all part of a progressive movement, along with the occasional slam on the IDP and Obamacare. At times, the crowd weighed in, with yells of "that ain't right" upon hearing accounts of challenges facing workers and immigrants. The crowd levelled heavy boos at Buttigieg for not supporting Medicare for All, chanting "Medicare for All, Medicare for All" until organizers stepped in. They went a little easier on Castro, also a Medicare for All holdout but having detailed plans to protect immigrants, which was popular with those attending. Warren, a long-time progressive favorite, elicited a positive reception. But it was Sanders who owned the crowd and the venue.

Steak Fry and the CCI Forum both were held Saturday in Des Moines. But the night before featured a high-profile multi-candidate event in Cedar Rapids, live-streamed nationally. LGBTQ-focused, it was deliberately timed to capitalize on the candidates' presence in the state. Zack Kucharski, executive editor of the *Cedar Rapids Gazette*, explained that One Iowa, the state's prominent LGBTQ organization, had approached the newspaper about partnering to sponsor an event. In time, *The Advocate*, the long-standing LGBTQ magazine, and media-monitoring organization GLADD joined the alliance. Kucharski noted that each partner brought something different, and together they were able to cover all bases – the muscle to get candidates to the table, the local knowledge to deal with the nuts and bolts required to pull off an event like this, and the horsepower to get a national audience. There's always something that poses a challenge for event organizers, and in this case it was that the final line-up wasn't set until the night before the event. Still, Kucharski was pleased with how it all came together. "I think it was a good partnership."

The free tickets were snatched up quickly in the weeks leading up to the event. The crowd of 750 that packed the sweltering Coe College auditorium watched as eight candidates cycled one by one on stage for about 15 minutes, responding to questions posed by representatives of the sponsoring groups. Sanders didn't attend, but there was national star power on stage.[25] At times the forum had a light-hearted feel, Cory Booker greeting his interviewer, *Advocate* editor Zach Stafford, with a bear hug, lifting him off the ground. But Elizabeth Warren, at that point in the campaign riding a wave of good press, set a somber tone, reciting the names of 24 transgender women of color who had been murdered that year. It's difficult to capture the reaction of a crowd as a whole to particular speakers, but Warren's message seemed to resonate broadly. Buttigieg, welcomed as a member of "our community," played up his experience as a gay man in the military and his relief when the Bill Clinton-era "Don't Ask, Don't Tell" policy was repealed, eight years before to the day. The crowd gave him a standing ovation, and quite a few people left immediately after he spoke, presumably there only to see him.

Biden either wasn't told or didn't understand that he wouldn't start with an opening statement. He stumbled somewhat in responding to the first question everyone got about what he would do for the LGBTQ community in his first 100 days in office. Hitting his stride eventually, the former VP shot back with some force against critiques of his positions and sketched out his role as an early advocate of gay marriage. The response of the crowd in the auditorium seemed generally positive, but he took a hit on social media and in news coverage, which focused on a sarcastic comment – "you're a lovely woman" – he made to his *Gazette* questioner after she pushed back on one of his answers. When Biden left the auditorium, he was followed by a phalanx of reporters. The national audience had the chance to check the record themselves if they weren't watching in real time. Kucharski reported the LGBTQ forum had been viewed online 70,000 times over the 24 hours following the event, giving it considerable reach.

Changing Things up

That weekend's three events created a flurry of activity for the campaigns, and they offered candidates very different stages to address distinct audiences. But there's never just one thing happening in a campaign. While Booker joked on stage at Friday night's LGBTQ Forum, and his local staff went through last-minute plans for the next day's Steak Fry event, his campaign was gasping for air.

Booker organizer Jennifer Koppess had been in Des Moines all day Friday, with staffers from across the state working the Steak Fry event. She spent the day at state campaign HQ, making posters, calling people to confirm they were going to show up the next day, "that kind of stuff." The crew at

HQ watched as Twitter blew up in the afternoon when their Booker staff colleagues – and staff from all the campaigns – were given the go-ahead to race out, running with barn signs to secure optimal visibility for the campaign, part of the established Steak Fry routine. Booker's campaign, like others, approached even this task systematically, a spreadsheet to track signs, set roles for staff, the transfer of wisdom from veteran staff to the newcomers.

Once everything was "good to go," the staff from HQ and the park converged on a brew pub, just a mile or so from the park. Jennifer enjoyed spending time with those in from the national campaign in Newark, including advance staff, people she hadn't previously met. She recounts that they were having a good time when one of the team said they all needed to go back to the office. What crossed her mind – and others' – was that this was for a surprise visit by the candidate. "We knew Cory was [in the state], doing something in Cedar Rapids, so just a two hour drive [away]." She said that "all the wheels were spinning," everyone wondering "is Cory going to be there?"

But the candidate wasn't there. Instead, the campaign manager Addisu Demissie called, reporting that they were at mile marker 190 on the interstate, a stretch Jennifer traveled often in organizing work, actually not far from Malcom. She knew then there was no way she'd see Booker crashing through the door to surprise the Iowa staff, since he was more than an hour away. The manager was calling so that the staff wouldn't "be blindsided tomorrow morning" when the news broke that Booker would drop out unless the campaign raised $1.7 million in the next ten days. *LA Times* coverage the following day noted that Booker was languishing at about 3% support in national polls, doing even worse in Iowa, "roughly on par with Rep. Tulsi Gabbard of Hawaii and New York businessman Andrew Yang" (Finnegan & Mason, 2019).

Notes

1 Ia. Stat. § 49.3.
2 See for example Jin (2019) www.politico.com/interactives/2020/iowa-caucus-how-they-work/
3 A variety of IDP-produced material, for example "2020 Precinct Caucus Guide," offers detailed instructions.
4 By October, candidates needed 130,000 unique donors to make it to the debate stage – a figure that jumped to 165,000 in November. "DNC Announces Qualification Criteria for Fifth Presidential Primary Debate" September 23, 2019 (https://democrats.org/news/dnc-announces-qualification-criteria-for-fifth-presidential-primary-debate/).
5 Real Clear Politics Democratic Presidential Polls: https://www.realclearpolitics.com/epolls/2020/president/us/2020_democratic_presidential_nomination-6730.html and https://www.realclearpolitics.com/epolls/2020/president/ia/iowa_democratic_presidential_caucus-6731.html#!
6 Warren didn't own the selfie-line concept; all 2020 candidates used a version of it. Indeed, the photo-with-candidate model has been a mainstay of caucus

politics through all iterations of camera technology. Former Republican governor of Wisconsin Tommy Thompson, vying for his party's open nomination in 2008, offered the functional equivalent of a selfie line. His staff would take photos at the start of an event, then rush to the one-hour photo developer, delivering the prints by the end of the event. Particularly entrepreneurial event attendees in 2020, maybe just in it for the revenue prospect, would submit items – like baseballs and t-shirts – for the former vice-president to sign, his staff having a systematic approach to that: one item to be signed per attendee.

7 Word choice varies across context in US politics, and it's a sometimes-useful clue to political lineage. "Door-knocking" in Iowa is a term employed by local candidates going door-to-door, who are routinely advised by the state party and legislative leaders to "knock every door" in the district. Sometimes the language of nomination activists carries generational distinctions, with canvassing being the preferred term of campaigns and younger/middle-aged volunteers, door-knocking for the older crowd.

8 Organizers have some discretion in crafting their lists, adding an element of art to the mechanical process. Invoking an organizer version of entertainment, Lauren Parker noted that it's possible to pull lists by horoscope, finding the idea "whimsical" – and apparently a common subject in organizer social media banter.

9 In autodial world, with software connecting the caller once the target answers, the measurement might be "minutes on the dialer," as opposed to packets completed.

10 O'Rourke, Klobuchar, Harris, and Sanders all hovered around ten field offices, with Yang, Booker, and Steyer just one or two in the Epstein and Wezerek (2019) count. By mid-October, ten candidates had none. Field offices serve a variety of purposes, both symbolic and practical. But campaigns weigh their utility against the outlay of resources they require – all in that environment of pervasive uncertainty.

11 Typically, a campaign ops department would deal with these tasks. The state party imposes firm expectations for accessibility for the field offices and HQs it funds during general election campaigns. But ADA-compliant accessibility is frequently sacrificed by nomination campaigns, which scramble under significant constraints – and in 2020 competed for space with the large field of candidates.

12 2016 county vote totals at https://sos.iowa.gov/elections/pdf/2016/general/canvsummary.pdf), and October 2019 party registration at https://sos.iowa.gov/elections/pdf/VRStatsArchive/2019/CoOct19.pdf

13 Pete for America press release, October 31, 2019, archived by www.democracyinaction.us/2020/buttigieg/buttigiegiastaff.html

14 Students from bordering states – especially Illinois and Minnesota – expand the geographic reach of the caucus bubble. Those out-of-state students, like those everywhere in the US, can opt to participate politically either where they attend school or in their home state. Voting in Iowa general elections is especially attractive to students from Illinois, given Iowa's tendency to be more competitive. And for many out-of-state students, the prominence of the caucuses makes the choice to participate in Iowa easy to make.

15 From the start of 2019 until the caucuses, ten candidates held events on the 1,600-student campus, some with repeated visits. Another seven appeared nearby, one to three blocks away in downtown Grinnell (pop. 9,100), just about 15 miles down the road from the Malcom Auditorium.

16 See Fraga and Holbein (2020) for a consideration of both the methodological challenges and substantive findings.
17 Age group-specific turnout figures facilitated by the voter file, which includes an age indication for each registered voter. 2018 turnout reported by Iowa Secretary of State: https://sos.iowa.gov/news/2019_01_10.html
18 Campus-specific NSLVE reports are released only to the campus in question, but published news releases paint a picture that college student turnout in Iowa lagged behind the state average especially in the 2016 presidential election, but also in the 2018 midterms.
19 Entrance polls, as opposed to conventional exit polls, are used in caucus settings, since the start time (i.e. 7:00 pm) is known, but caucuses end at different times.
20 From the *New York Times* "Profile of Iowa Caucusgoers" www.nytimes.com/elections/2008/primaries/results/vote-polls/IA.html
21 Malchow (2008), a pioneer of microtargeting, describes various data used to target before campaigns had the capacity to collect and merge data at the individual level, a development circa 2000.
22 See, for example, website blog of peer-to-peer texting platform Outreach Circle (https://blog.outreachcircle.com/)
23 www.youtube.com/watch?v=gQm7Jmx8J54
24 CCI Presidential Candidate Questionnaire and responses (https://drive.google.com/file/d/14Q-E9vfUHh8PbX_uNsF0SlfGFtvQkYrP/view) show that Gabbard and Williamson responded but were not invited to the event. Inslee responded but had dropped out by the event.
25 Country singer Billy Gilman, actress and tech entrepreneur Angelica Ross, and Karamo Brown from *Queer Eye*.

References

Campbell, Donald P. and Julian C. Stanley. 1963. *Experimental and Quasi-Experimental Designs for Research*. Chicago: Rand McNally.

Clark, Peter B. and James Q. Wilson. 1961. "Incentive systems: a theory of organizations." *Administrative Science Quarterly* 6(2): 129–166.

Cotter, Cornelius P., James L. Gibson, John F. Bibby and Robert J. Huckshorn. 1984. *Party Organizations in American Politics*. New York: Praeger.

Darr, Joshua P. and Matthew S. Levendusky. 2014. "Relying on the ground game: the placement and effect of campaign field offices." *American Politics Research* 42(3): 529–548.

Epstein, Reid and Gus Wezerek. 2019. "Which 2020 candidates have the ground game lead in early primary states." *The New York Times* October 12 (www.nytimes.com/interactive/2019/10/12/us/politics/democratic-candidates-campaigns.html).

Finnegan, Michael and Melanie Mason. 2019. "Cory Booker may leave presidential race soon if he doesn't hit fundraising goal." *The Los Angeles Times* September 21 (www.latimes.com/politics/story/2019-09-21/cory-booker-could-soon-quit-the-presidential-race-aide).

Fraga, Bernard and John Holbein. 2020. "Measuring youth and college student voter turnout." *Electoral Studies* 65: 1–7.

Green, Donald P. and Alan S. Gerber. 2004. *Get out the Vote!: How to Increase Voter Turnout*. Washington, DC: Brookings Institution Press.

Hersh, Eitan. 2015. *Hacking the Electorate: How Campaigns Perceive Voters*. New York: Cambridge University Press.

Huntington, Samuel P. 1968. *Political Order in Changing Societies*. New Haven: Yale University Press.

Issenberg, Sasha. 2012. *The Victory Lab: The Secret Science of Winning Campaigns*. New York: Crown Publishers.

Jin, Beatrice. 2020. "An illustrated guide to the Iowa caucuses." *Politico* January 16 (www.politico.com/interactives/2020/iowa-caucus-how-they-work/).

Malchow, Hal. 2008. *The New Political Targeting*. Washington, DC: Predicted Lists.

Masket, Seth. 2009. "Did Obama's ground game matter? The influence of local field offices during the 2008 presidential election." *Public Opinion Quarterly* 73 (5):1023–1039.

McCaskill, Nolan. 2019. "Booker and Castro accuse DNC of excluding minorities." *Politico* December 5 (www.politico.com/news/2019/12/05/cory-booker-julian-castro-dnc-minorities-076432).

McGowan, Tara. 2020. Podcast: "FWIW Episode 11: Campaigning amidst a pandemic." (www.fwiwpodcast.com/fwiw-episode-11-campaigning-amidst-a-pandemic/).

McKenna, Elizabeth and Hahrie Han. 2015. *Groundbreakers: How Obama's 2.2 Million Volunteers Transformed Campaigning in America*. New York: Oxford.

Muller, Jerry Z. 2018. *The Tyranny of Metrics*. Princeton, NJ: Princeton University Press.

Nickerson, David W. and Todd Rogers. 2014. "Political Campaigns and Big Data." *The Journal of Economic Perspectives* 29(2): 51–73.

Norvell, Kim. 2019. "Elizabeth Warren's systematic approach to Iowa – and why she's rising in the polls." *The Des Moines Register* November 11 (www.desmoinesregister.com/story/news/elections/presidential/caucus/2019/11/11/how-elizabeth-warren-iowa-campaign-differs-democratic-rivals-efforts/3977982002/).

Pfannenstiel, Brianne. 2019. "Largest Polk County Steak Fry in history draws 12,000 attendees, 17 presidential candidates." *The Des Moines Register* September 21 (www.desmoinesregister.com/story/news/elections/presidential/caucus/2019/09/21/caucus-iowa-election-largest-polk-county-steak-fry-des-moines-iowa-poll-waen-sanders-biden-democrats/2388106001).

Redlawsk, David P., Caroline J. Tolbert, and Todd Donovan. 2011. *Why Iowa?* Chicago: University of Chicago Press.

Ryan, Bryce and Neal C. Gross. 1943. "The diffusion of hybrid seed corn in two Iowa communities." *Rural Sociology* 8(1):15–24.

Shepsle, Kenneth A. and Mark S. Bonchek. 1996. *Analyzing Politics: Rationality, Behavior, and Institutions*. New York: W.W. Norton.

Skelley, Geoffrey. 2019. "What we know about Andrew Yang's base." *FiveThirtyEight* December 11 (fivethirtyeight.com/features/what-we-know-about-andrew-yangs-base/).

8 Engagement and Economics

There are always tears when a campaign ends, even when the writing is on the wall. For some, it's the product of a strong attachment to what the candidate represents – a revered policy agenda, months of active work on the candidate's behalf, maybe the sense that only *this candidate* can win in the general election. And while optimism can motivate supporters and staff and sustain them in challenging times, it makes it even harder to process a loss like this.[1] A week after Booker had thrown down the fundraising gauntlet, the campaign triumphantly announced that it had smashed through the $1.7 million fundraising goal. The November 1, 2019 tears were from elsewhere.

The Circle of Life

The Liberty and Justice ("LJ") Celebration, the last of the cattle calls and a "must do" for any serious candidate, had itself evaded demise. It was the 2019 iteration of that iconic "JJ" event, the long-standing party fundraiser in Des Moines that had been named for historical figures Thomas Jefferson and Andrew Jackson. By 2015, these men's records on slavery and treatment of Native Americans had given pause to the IDP, which chose to rename the event, feeling that the "JJ" label carried too much baggage. The new LJ name was tough for experienced Iowa Democrats to remember, as the old initials were seared into their shared language. For those inclined to over-analyze, the new "Liberty and Justice" seemed oddly conservative in symbolism.[2]

The JJ/LJ had outlasted its Republican Party counterpart – the "Straw Poll." This had been a mainstay of GOP nomination contests from 1979 to 2011, a huge Republican Party of Iowa (RPI) fundraiser at the end of the summer, with attendees casting a ballot – a straw poll – as a barometer of candidate strength. The straw poll met its demise when it became clear that candidates were buying up tickets and busing in attendees from out of state, offering a flawed measure of candidate support among *Iowa* Republicans (Fry, 2011). But even though there was no polling at the LJ, nor would it likely have been permitted by the DNC, it did offer a test of organizational strength for campaigns. General admission and upper-deck seating – in the 13,000-seat 2019 venue – were cordoned off for each campaign. At the

LJ, a read on the noise and creativity of the crowd was a substitute for an actual vote.

Team Beto – like most other campaigns – had distributed hundreds of tickets to supporters, securing a prime section of the arena for its cadre to cheer on the candidate. With the LJ set to begin at 6:30 pm, the campaign's Iowa political director Chris Hall was tending to last-minute logistics when he was alerted to a 4 pm conference call for campaign leadership. The news: O'Rourke was going to drop out of the race – in an hour. Hall recalled the uncertainty about what was next. "Was the candidate in Des Moines? Would O'Rourke speak at the LJ? Would he visit the small river-front park across the street from the arena where his soon-to-be devastated supporters were gathering to march with him to the dinner en masse?" O'Rourke, in fact, was in the city and did drop by the staging area. His message landed like a bombshell. Supporters had come in that day from all over, driving, even taking flights, to get to the event. Staff had spent weeks leading up to it, trying to make the event a success.

Hall recalled the sadness of it all, noting that "[It] was an unfortunate way for that whole message to get delivered." He also reflected on O'Rourke's missed opportunity to make an "exit that could have been historic and remembered for many years to come." Hall mused, "How wonderful and powerful it would have been for [O'Rourke] to go on stage to speak to the issues that he was a champion for – to speak to the cause and the challenge that lay ahead and to say, 'I'll be with you 100%, but I might not be the one who's going to be the nominee.'" In hindsight, Hall thought, it would have been especially notable, since there weren't any candidate speeches that "tore the roof off" at the LJ that night, "[not] any historic moments made."

While the event went off without O'Rourke, it did include Sanders, who had suffered a minor heart attack a few weeks earlier, increasing doubts about the 78-year-old's physical fitness for office. Still, Sanders marched that afternoon with about 1,500 supporters. His campaign, though, had opted not to buy a block of tickets as it had four years earlier. The event that year still lingered in the memories of Iowa activists as evidence of the bad blood between Clinton and Sanders, moderates and progressives. In 2019, the Sanders campaign made a contribution to the Iowa Democratic Party in lieu of buying tickets. But as such, his remarks – which had traditional applause lines – generated little audible response. Only one time, when Sanders asked if status quo politics that allowed the wealthy to have extraordinary influence should continue, did one person shout "No!" Sanders responded, "'No' is the right answer."

The Caucus Economy

It's hard to attach an absolute dollar figure to them, but clearly the caucuses contributed to the Iowa economy.[3] Consider even some of the things it took to pull off a big party event like the LJ: contracting with a local event planner, subcontracting with sound and lighting engineers, paying the staff who serve the meal. What's more, money generated from fundraising events was circulated back into the state's economy, whether through salaries of staff hired by the state party or a 1/8th page print ad in a local newspaper purchased by a county party to publicize caucus locations. What complicates the task of estimating the economic impact, however, is that not all caucus-related spending passed through Iowa. Spending by the Iowa presidential campaigns – and pre-candidate PACs and Super PACs, for that matter – also had that inside/outside Iowa mix, but this is especially tricky to track, another "in-the-weeds" phenomenon, this one involving available data.[4]

That said, TV ad spending brought extraordinary sums of money into broadcast outlets in Iowa. From January 1, 2019 through late January 2020, right before the caucuses, ad spending in the state would top $44 million, as reported by Wesleyan Media Project.[5] Over 122,000 ads ran over that same time frame, an increase of 65% over 2016. Spending was also up, but only 11% higher than 2016, the ad vs. spending difference likely due to the nuances of ad rates. 2016 cycle broadcast spending in Iowa had been dominated by Super PACs (Pfannenstiel & Kummer, 2015), which unlike candidate committees are not guaranteed the lowest unit rate (LUR) in their ad buys. Campaigns poured money into digital ads too, but while these ads could target Iowans, the money trail rarely went through Iowa. The big social media platforms were also big players in this world, running digital ads purchased by the campaigns. Nationally, at least as of mid-November, candidate spending on Facebook ads dominated social media space, with the Google platform in second place.[6] Advertising on Twitter hadn't been prominent in the cycle, and even ceased to be an option at the end of October when the platform announced it would ban political ads on November 15, 2019.[7,8] Little of this money directed toward digital ads in Iowa would actually go into the state economy, but it translated into the advertising landscape Iowans saw when they went online or sat down to stream a movie.

Some caucus-related spending went directly into the pockets of people and businesses in Iowa, but the residual financial benefits are difficult to quantify. Spending by campaign staff deployed to Iowa – rent, food, other essentials – indirectly contributed to the local economy. Similarly indirect were the dollars spent by the hundreds of national press traversing the state, renting cars, staying in hotels, eating in restaurants. The occasional reporter – or candidate – even "moved in," making Iowa a temporary, permanent home (Ember, 2020). In the week, and especially the weekend, before the caucuses, the deluge of outsiders – press, national campaign staff deployed to Iowa, and others – overwhelmed Des Moines, which benefitted from hotels filled with visitors racking up hefty bar tabs and restaurant bills and socializing with colleagues and old friends in between work duties. The Des Moines Convention and Visitors' Bureau estimated an economic impact of more than $11 million in the week leading up to the caucuses alone.[9]

Perhaps the most elusive factor in calculating economic impact is the promotional value associated with connecting "Iowa" and "the caucuses" – not to mention the enhanced awareness of the state that came with repeated media mentions. Iowans would have to hope its net impact was positive, but realistically it was probably a mixed bag, some factors reflecting positively and others negatively.

In terms of the caucus economy, one thing was clear: the bubble extended its reach well beyond those just in it for the politics. Anyone who watched network or cable television, whether interested or not, got bombarded by ads in the two or three months before the caucuses. In the few weeks before the caucuses, a three-minute commercial break during the 10 pm local news could serve up six 30-second candidate spots, back-to-back. Watching a single newscast start to finish, one saw as many as 15–20 broadcast spots. Targeted digital advertising, along with direct contact techniques relying on voter file data, tends to be more discriminating, focusing on those with a record of political activity or some expressed interest. But data and targeting techniques are far from perfect, likely erring on the side of exposing those who weren't interested rather than missing those who were. For voters, this generated a sense of "can't escape" the caucuses; for others, it was a window of opportunity.

Dave Heller owns the Quad City River Bandits, a Davenport-based triple-A affiliate of the Houston Astros. In 2015, the team was approached by Rand Paul, the Tennessee senator competing for the 2016 GOP nomination. Paul wanted to take batting practice with the team and asked if he could suit up in a River Bandits uniform. Heller obliged. And knowing that Paul would have to shuttle from batting practice to a CNN interview, he stretched out batting practice. Heller writes: "I take the guy throwing to him aside and ask, 'Do me a favor and keep him on the field a little longer? Throw him a few extras. When he's ready to go…throw a few more pitches to him. Challenge him to hit something'" (Austin forthcoming). Heller's stalling tactic worked, and the candidate, with no time to change clothes, did the live Jake Tapper interview in uniform, delivering good national exposure for the River Bandits.

The caucuses offered a sweet payoff for hotels, especially those in downtown Des Moines. Tara McFarling was director of sales at the Renaissance Des Moines Savery Hotel, and she had been in the business for two caucus cycles. Tara's caucus-related planning started about a year and half before the actual event, and she booked blocks of rooms well in advance, both for a five-day period surrounding the caucuses themselves and around major events – like the LJ – spread out over the campaign season. With room rates tied to demand, hotels can charge significantly more at high-traffic times. The contracts Tara wrote were prepaid and non-refundable, offering an element of certainty for the hotel even if a candidate dropped out before the stay that was booked.

Much of Tara's focus was on news organizations, and by mid-winter 2019 she was working with Fox News, which would ultimately book about one-half of the hotel's 209 guest rooms for the five days surrounding the February

3 caucuses. The network would be spread around other downtown hotels as well. Tara conveyed a commitment to making sure that her relationships with campaigns and news operations ran smoothly, and that the caucus-guest experience at the hotel was positive. For her this was fundamentally business, the caucuses a critical source of revenue for the hotel. In sales, Tara loved to sign contracts. "It makes me all warm and fuzzy inside."

Other enterprises offered a mix of politics and business. RAYGUN is a retailer with a strong left-leaning – and pro-Midwest – image, best known for snarky t-shirt designs that it screen-prints. Founder and owner Mike Draper, originally from small-town Iowa, broke into the t-shirt business as a UPenn student, hawking shirts that said "Not Penn State" playing up Penn's disdain when confused with Penn State. RAYGUN pushes its pro-Iowa, pro-Midwest message by poking fun at both, with the underlying message that there's more to life than what's happening on the coasts. The caucuses figured prominently in RAYGUN's designs and business life. In the 2020 cycle, there was a steady stream of candidate-focused t-shirts. "GIVE PETE A CHANCE!" "I'M F★★KING MOVING TO IOWA – KAMALA HARRIS." The flagship store in Des Moines is right down the street from the state capitol, the go-to backdrop visual for national news stand-ups about the caucuses, which helped put RAYGUN on the radar for out-of-town visitors. Commenting on the flow of people into the store, artistic director Jennifer Leatherby used true RAYGUN form. "[Every] campaign year there are tons of people who moved to Iowa to work – and they're probably bored."

Over time, the store became a popular stop for candidates, though the approach taken had evolved. RAYGUN couldn't lure in Obama in its early years, but by 2020 the stores saw an "avalanche" of candidates, which founder Draper attributed to candidate's willingness to be associated with edgier merchandise and the young, progressive demographic as a political target (Ta, 2019). A visit by Clinton in 2016 required some significant "curating" of store displays, making sure the resulting visual was absent anything potentially offensive, according to artistic director Leatherby. But in 2020, Elizabeth Warren just "swung in" with no fanfare or advance notice. As for caucus impact, Draper notes that they were a windfall for business, and that "[it's] hard … to imagine RAYGUN without the caucuses."

The economic calculus is a little more complicated for some. Tony Wilkins is Director of Sales at KGAN/KFXA, a CBS/FOX affiliate in Cedar Rapids. In a caucus year, political ads were a big source of his station's ad revenue, and the ramp-up to the 2020 caucuses looked to be a record one. The station's 2019 political ad sales through the end of October were more than double the same period in 2015, even though both parties were spending in 2015 and only the Democrats were in play in 2019. Wilkins' numbers for the entire eastern Iowa market through September 2019 showed that Steyer was the big spender, at $1.2 million in broadcast ads out of a total of $3.7. But broadcast TV spots – like hotel rooms – are a finite commodity, meaning that big buyers can theoretically close others out of the market. Wilkins was pleased with high-volume ad sales in 2019, yet still concerned about meeting the needs of his regular advertisers, those who buy consistently throughout the year, caucuses or no caucuses. One of the station's big advertisers, a local car dealership, found itself in the caucus bubble because it was vying for the same ad space as the campaigns. Speaking in the fall of 2019, Wilkins focused on something few others seemed to realize – that the caucuses would be held just one day after NFL Super Bowl LIV. Selling local ads as an affiliate of FOX, the network broadcasting the Super Bowl that year, meant a special challenge for Wilkins, who wanted to meet the needs of both his regular and his caucus-related clients in the local ad time he controlled during the February 2 football spectacle.

Commit to Caucus

While the bubble stretched to catch those with no special political interest, the work of the campaign organizers and their volunteers zeroed in on those who were interested. If they could lure a few more into the candidate camp, all the better. But their main task was to ensure that the identified supporters would turn up. The hook to do this: a "commit-to-caucus card." It was a physical card to be signed by the supporter, signaling a promise to caucus for the candidate. Of course, there was more to it than that.

The standard commit-to-caucus card design involved a detachable postcard with a space for the supporter's signature. The campaign kept the signed postcard, and then mailed it back to the supporter as part of the get-out-the-caucus (GOTC) effort in the days leading up to the event.[10] While a signed card warranted a VAN entry, the commit-to-caucus process was decidedly low-tech – paper, pen, and the USPS. It was all backed up by a little cognitive psychology and randomized controlled experiments. The science demonstrated, as Shankar Vedantam said, that when someone makes a commitment like this, "there's ... psychological pressure on [the person] to act in such a way that they keep that commitment" (Keith, 2015). This idea reflects that Obama-era legacy of using social science to inform campaign messages and practices and was inspired by a 2012 "dream team" of behavioral scientists, whose research and understanding of human behavior emphasized the power of invoking a previously made commitment (Carey, 2012).[11]

For organizers, commit-to-caucus cards could take on a life of their own, subject to goals established by the campaign and the source of friendly competition among organizers. For some, they were like a courting ritual. One organizer could easily cite the name of every supporter in her turf who had signed, whether through her efforts or one of her volunteer's. She also knew the lay of the land – who was still up for grabs, which person leaned to a given candidate, even those ripe to be poached from another campaign. But for Gillibrand-turned-Harris organizer Lauren Parker, this was serious work, and she sensed that Iowans only signed when they were truly committed to a candidate.

The Balancing Act

There is a popular image of a campaign organizer logging long hours, subsisting on whatever food happens to be handy, popping outside the field office or HQ to grab a smoke. In reality, there's no singular campaign experience, save perhaps the long hours. But there is a common challenge: arriving at a healthy work-life balance, something that in Iowa became especially difficult as the caucuses approached. In its treatment of its own workers, Democratic parties and campaigns, as well as progressive organizations, had often fallen short of the work environment that they had promoted programmatically (Trish, 2018). But by many accounts, the conditions for workers improved in the 2020 cycle; better pay and benefit packages, guaranteed time off including holidays, and generally more attention to health and wellness were distinctive features of the cycle. In fact, workers in almost every campaign signed union contracts, formally drawing labor unions into the bubble.

Campaign workers – mostly organizers – signed contracts with different unions, most with no particular ties to the political campaign industry. The Sanders campaign was the first presidential campaign ever to organize (Kopp, 2019), and it did so under the United Food and Commercial Workers' Union. Warren and Buttigieg organized with the International Brotherhood of Electrical Workers (IBEW), the union which had supported John Delaney's college education. Biden workers entered into collective bargaining agreements with the Teamsters, while Yang staff organized with the Campaign Workers Guild (CWG), a union with a focus on the campaign industry, making a deliberate attempt to organize that space. The norm was for campaigns to organize with a union local proximate to the campaign's national HQ. Biden's campaign was an exception, organizing with an Iowa Teamsters local. Across all of the campaigns, labor agreements covered organizers, though some treated regionals as management, exempting them from the terms of the collective bargaining agreement. Somewhat ironically, the Delaney campaign had no union ties.

Union contracts are complex legal documents, not readily available to the public, the terms of which are not fully scrutinized by every organizer. Still, many organizers expressed a degree of general comfort at being covered by a union. For Jim Flores, having union representation was something more, a deciding factor in his signing on with NextGen. Beyond the certainty of the Super PAC's promise of staying in Iowa through November 2020, the union contract provided security to Jim and the prospect for better working conditions than he had experienced on past campaigns. With union contracts quickly becoming the norm, Jim felt a degree of "solidarity" that extended across the unionized workers in all campaigns. But union contracts on their own don't eliminate some of the inherent workplace risks of the campaign world.

Consider the process of sending out organizers – or volunteers – for door-to-door canvassing, often alone, sometimes in rural remote areas, even after dark. While staff routinely hear that they should not put themselves at risk, organizers are driven to meet goal and to advance the prospects of the candidate. Having a door slammed in your face or hearing some mildly abusive responses are par for the course for organizers, due to a variety of factors, including data that don't always accurately portray the leanings of voters. But sometimes it was more serious than people who weren't "Iowa nice." One organizer told of a door opening and the person inside trying to pull her into the house. Another was grabbed and assaulted in a public library, out of range of the security cameras. All organizers experience irate responses on the phone, some hearing threats, veiled or explicit. Certainly, incidents like these are game for VAN entries, warning others of the threat. Lauren Parker visualized something more – a mechanism by which this sort of information could be readily transmitted across all 2020 campaigns, or even to campaigns in the future. In other words, it is the kind of shared data that others envision more generally for the party.

Contracts and collective bargaining agreements formalize things like maximum hours per week, personal time off (PTO), and vacation days. Whether reality comports with the formal terms is something else. Like workers in many other industries, staff are faced with work pressures that make it difficult to take advantage of the terms of the contract. Even so, there was a pervasive sense in the 2020 cycle – among both organizers and those who would be considered "management" – that protecting the personal safety of staff and supporting reasonable work-life balance was a noble goal. One area in which the goal generally succeeded was in protecting Thanksgiving and religious holidays in December, allowing staff the time and enough advance notice to travel.

In other respects, as well, the work environment appeared to be better in 2020 than in the past. Campaigns relied less on unpaid interns and "fellows," with most campaigns committing to an hourly wage for those workers – mostly students – who filled these positions. The organizers operated marginally less under the tyranny of metrics and goals, appearing to have a reasonable degree of control over their own work, even the ability to take on tasks beyond the direct voter contact that had largely monopolized the days of organizers under the Obama model. When Booker announced his "do-or-die" fundraising goal, staff from all units of the campaign turned to that task, hitting up anyone in their work or personal networks for money. As such, regional organizing director Hamblin became – in effect – a finance team member, in his case texting the ask, using as bait his hope for a tattoo if he could "break $1000" in total contributions. "[If] you would like to help me get this Iowa tattoo, anything would help." Campaign insiders talk a lot about "breaking down silos," the willingness to move traditional jurisdictional boundaries. The 2020 campaign was marked by a movement in that direction and, at times, what might be called a distributed organizing mindset.

Campaigns, however, still exercise tight control over the ability of staff to speak to the media and to scholars. Many organizers feel bound by the confidentiality agreements they sign, some even encouraged by campaigns to consider them "in effect" after the campaign folds. At the same time, staff in leadership positions appear to speak freely about their experiences, even to the point of writing about them or heading out on a lecture circuit. This would seem to be a double standard. It's true that comms departments will, at their discretion, allow reporters access to staff, with the resulting products – maybe print pieces, podcasts – offering a window into organizing. But it remains that comms teams are responsible for curating a particular message about a campaign, and decisions about access undoubtedly reflect that motive.

Campaign work requires a bit of a balancing act for staff, who are expected to control their own emotions in order to get the job done. Sociologist Arlie Hochschild (2012) first coined the term "emotional labor" in 1983, noting that workers in some professions need to regulate their emotions in the interest of creating "a proper state of mind" in others (p. 7). Many service workers are emotional laborers, with workplace success requiring that they take on a disposition that projects – whether accurately or not – their own satisfaction to the customer. Hochschild asks her readers to consider a flight attendant, with "smiles … a part of [the] work, a part that requires [coordination of] self and feeling so that the work seems to be effortless" (2012, p. 8). The campaign organizer labors under similar demands, expected to convey a consistent face of "can-do" optimism and enjoyment of the work to the volunteers and supporters. Service workers manipulate their own emotions for a commercial purpose; the organizer does it for a political one. But the practical impact is the same: added stress and exhaustion for the worker, whether with a campaign on the upswing or in freefall.

The Democratic field narrowed considerably in November and December 2019, with some campaigns closing down completely and others just closing their Iowa operations. Kamala Harris had doubled down in Iowa earlier in the fall, shoring up the field staff, the candidate taking the risky move of stating her goal of a top-three finish. She hovered at 5% in the polls, having seen her Iowa support plunge by double digits in September, compared to mid-summer when she had picked up support after clashing with Biden on issues of race in the first debate (Korecki, 2019). In late October, in a proverbial Hail Mary pass, the campaign reported it was closing shop in New Hampshire and some other early states, laying-off some Baltimore HQ staff and redeploying others to Iowa, signaling a do-or-die situation (Scherer, 2019). When a campaign is teetering on the brink, it's not unusual for word to leak of operational discord or staff discontent. In the case of the Harris campaign, it came in what the *New York Times* (Martin et al., 2019) called a "blistering resignation letter" by the campaign's national operations director, Kelly Mehlenbacher. In the letter posted by *The Times* dated November 11, presidential campaign veteran Mehlenbacher honed in on issues relating to campaign staff, noting that she had "never seen an organization treat its staff so poorly."

122 *Engagement and Economics*

Neither Lauren Parker nor Rachel Salas, sharing a turf as Harris organizers, expressed any discontent with their campaign or the way they were treated. And personally, Lauren didn't feel like the campaign was struggling at all, though she was puzzled by the media's insistence on portraying the campaign in a negative light. She wondered if there was something that organizers could possibly do to counter what she considered persistent negative coverage. Reflecting on the way the contest had played out, she expressed dismay that the Democratic Party had set up debate rules – especially the polling component – that served as effective barriers to underdog candidates, though noted that Harris was unaffected by this. At the same time, Lauren wasn't thrilled that the party did little to stop the self-funded candidates from swooping in.

Harris withdrew from the Democratic field on December 3. Staff had been alerted that the candidate would be joining them on a conference call that morning, one of those tell-tale signs. Among the messages delivered was the go-ahead to reach out to friends and family, giving them the news personally so they didn't have to hear it from the media. But even before the call ended, staff saw the Twitter post by *Atlantic* reporter Edward-Isaac Dovere: "Kamala Harris is dropping out of the presidential election today, I'm told reliably. She's informing staff now." When Lauren got off the line, she reached out to one of the high schoolers who had been committed to the campaign, breaking the news to him that the campaign had folded.

For staff out of work in December, it was no less of a seller's market than it had been earlier in the season; open season on Harris staff started immediately. That angered Harris endorser and former Iowa Democratic chair Sue Dvorsky, who tweeted later the day that Harris had withdrawn: "Stay the f*** away from the Harris field. Of course you want them to work for you. They're … amazing, … sad, [a]nd grieving." Lauren, who turned to Harris after Gillibrand dropped out, didn't sign on with another presidential campaign. She had been sad for personal reasons when Gillibrand withdrew, but it was more than that with Harris, feeling that something was wrong with a system that hadn't allowed the candidate a fair shot. For her, a *New Yorker* article about a committed volunteer making 13,000 phone calls for the candidate said it well: The story with the positive tone about how the candidate could inspire (Lach, 2019) came out only *after* Harris had withdrawn.

Starting the Home Stretch

As 2019 drew to a close, the race for the Democratic nomination gained some surprising clarity. And that set the stage for what was to be a frenetic final month before Caucus Day. The billionaire former mayor of New York, Michael Bloomberg, had entered the race – promising to skip Iowa and focus on California and Super Tuesday states. Harris' failure to gain traction and ensuing withdrawal was seen by some as the result of a late investment in Iowa. Elizabeth Warren, who had vaulted to the top of many Iowa and national polls earlier in the fall, slipped in the face of attacks from other candidates, including targeted assaults on her proposed Medicare for All plan. Pete Buttigieg continued to gain, as his organization and fundraising prowess expanded. Joe Biden maintained his lead in most national polls, but his Iowa operation struggled to find footing. And Bernie Sanders, whose early October heart attack had prompted harsh scrutiny of his physical condition, had done well in ensuing debates and was suddenly surging. Sanders also enjoyed high-profile endorsements from congressional "Gang of Four" members Alexandria Ocasio-Cortez and Ilhan Omar. It appeared that the progressive wing of the party was throwing its arms around Sanders in a bid to help carry him to the nomination.

Along rural Iowa gravel roads were the campaign corpses of many should-have-been-strong contenders: Harris, fellow senator Gillibrand of New York, Montana Governor Steve Bullock, former Colorado governor John Hickenlooper, and former Texas congressman Beto O'Rourke had all seemed viable at one point in time. So, too, had a number of remaining candidates, like Senators Booker of New Jersey and Bennet of Colorado and former HUD secretary Julián Castro. Minnesota's Amy Klobuchar was hanging in, visiting her 99th – out of 99 – Iowa county. But her Iowa poll numbers continued to lag.

Then there was Andrew Yang, the 44-year-old American-born son of Taiwanese immigrants who had staked his campaign on his tech-based entrepreneurship background and his commitment to the $1,000 monthly UBI payment to every American adult. Yang had a young base, one unfazed by social media or the use of QR codes. By late 2019, he had qualified for each of the six debates to that point and was even with Klobuchar in national tracking poll averages.

Yang supporters were noticeably distinctive, skewing young and male. Of his supporters, 74% were between the ages of 18 and 44. They wore hats that simply read "MATH," short for *Make America Think Harder*. Perhaps they had been lured in by his willingness to embrace memes and social media. Maybe they were attracted by his knowledge of new technology. Or his willingness to draw attention to the job losses created by automation – a by-product of technological development. Regardless, there were legions of young men working and volunteering in Yang's campaign – enough to allow him to keep his candidacy alive, but not enough to push him out of the single-digits (Skelley, 2019).

Still, it was the two billionaires – Steyer and Bloomberg – who added new plot lines to the final sprint to caucus night. Steyer spent tens of millions on TV ads – dating back to pre-candidacy spots calling for President Trump's impeachment. He also built a ground game in Iowa and made an attempt at retail politics. Bloomberg, meanwhile, got in late and never intended to engage in Iowa. But his presence was felt by the candidates on several fronts. Bloomberg was an easy target because of his personal wealth and a long, highly visible public career. He opened his vast campaign war chest to hire staff, pay them well, and equip them. His campaign immediately began reaching out to the former staff of candidates who had left the race.

It's hard to imagine two billionaires more out-of-place than in this Democratic field. Sanders, Warren, and their progressive forces railed against the 1% on an almost-nightly basis. Biden's blue-collar upbringing and Buttigieg's Midwestern roots and military service also painted stark contrasts. But soon there would be a new plot line in January, once 2019 rolled over to 2020 – and a focus on the rules and procedures and what would happen after Iowa.

Notes

1 The campaign world is replete with political actors at all levels – candidates, staff, volunteers – who display the sort of "optimism bias" described by behavioral psychologist Daniel Kahneman (2013), viewing goals "as more achievable than they are likely to be" (p. 255), contributing to inability to judge prospects accurately.
2 "Fall Gala" used in 2018 was too elitist for some ears. That year, Cory Booker was the keynote speaker, the event considered to be his effective entre to the 2020 caucus contest. Eschewing the "Jefferson/Jackson" name for events has marked many state and local Democratic parties across the nation over the past decade.
3 In earlier eras in which nomination campaigns opted into the public financing system, tracking candidate spending in a state was straightforward, since reporting expenditures in states was a condition of the public finance. Rice and Kenney (1984) using those FEC data found that nomination campaigns brought significant sums into state economies, but more so in primary than caucus states.
4 Some expenditures are pretty clear in FEC reports, like payments to local printers, which can be tracked to an Iowa address in the data. But not so with payroll directed to Iowa campaign staff, since the FEC entries reflect the address offered up by the staff member, sometimes an Iowa address, sometimes one in another state. FEC reports also don't help much in tracking broadcast advertising in Iowa, a significant outlay for some campaigns, because ad flights are typically purchased through a third party, usually a media consulting firm in the DC Beltway. Notably, the 2020 Warren campaign was an exception, handling its ad buys in-house (Korecki, 2020) out of the national campaign, not Iowa. Better estimates of broadcast advertising come from public inspection files, which document the contracts for the ad sales, a requirement updated in 2012 to make data available on the web for TV stations, though still only in the physical files of radio stations. Better yet, commercial firms track TV and radio broadcast buys. Kantar/CMAG is the major player in tracking TV advertising.
5 Wesleyan Media Project Release "$44 million on presidential ads in Iowa," January 29, 2020: http://mediaproject.wesleyan.edu/releases-012920/
6 Both TV and digital ad spending addressed in Wesleyan Media Project Release "TV Ad Volume Way Up Over 2016," November 20, 2019: http://mediaproject.wesleyan.edu/releases-112019/
7 At about the same time, Google made news by announcing that it shut down some of its options for targeted political advertising, including the use of the voter file for targeting. A significant move on many counts, this would limit campaigns' ability to reach an identifiable pool of *unregistered* voters, useful for bringing new participants into politics (Farinella, 2019). Open Secrets reports show that only Buttigieg dabbled in Snapchat advertising.

8   Other digital forms targeted Iowans for the caucuses, like "programmatic" and "OTT/CTV" ads. Programmatic ads show up on websites, sometimes purchased in real time in a way that builds from a unique user's web history – for example, the repeated ad in news sites for the pair of shoes that a person eyed but didn't buy. "Over the Top" (OTT) and "Connected TV" (CTV) advertising are two ways to place ads in front of viewers when they stream TV shows and movies (Adgate, 2019).
9   Catch Des Moines release "For Des Moines, Iowa Caucuses Equal Big Economic Impact, but Exposure is Priceless." www.prnewswire.com/news-releases/for-des-moines-iowa-caucuses-equal-big-economic-impact-but-exposure-is-priceless-300976427.html, December 17.
10 The more familiar term "GOTV" frequently substitutes for "GOTC," and while the tasks of mobilizing to a daylong election and vote are fundamentally different, most in the bubble didn't care much about the semantic slip.
11 GOTV campaigns used in primaries and general elections routinely employ the same logic as a commit to caucus card, invoking an "implementation intention" that increases the likelihood of voter follow-through (Nickerson & Rogers, 2010). The Obama campaign innovation of asking "Do you have a plan to vote?" in GOTV canvasses, phone banks and digital communications are now diffused widely in campaign practices.

References

Adgate, Brad. 2019. "The 2020 elections will set (another) ad spending record." *Fortune* September 3 (www.forbes.com/sites/bradadgate/2019/09/03/the-2020-elections-will-set-another-ad-spending-record/#1845df6f1836).

Austin, Jerry. Forthcoming. *True Tales from the Campaign Trail, volume 2*. Akron, OH: University of Akron Press.

Carey, Benedict. 2012. "Academic 'Dream Team' helped Obama's effort." *The New York Times* November 12 (www.nytimes.com/2012/11/13/health/dream-team-of-behavioral-scientists-advised-obama-campaign.html).

Ember, Sydney. 2020. "I wanted to understand Iowa. So I moved there." *The New York Times* February 3 (www.nytimes.com/2020/02/03/reader-center/iowa-caucus.html).

Farinella, Marc. 2019. "Where are the platform policy changes taking us?" *Campaigns and Elections* December 18 (www.campaignsandelections.com/campaign-insider/where-are-the-platform-policy-changes-taking-us).

Fry, Erika. 2011. "Straw dogs: Why the press can't quit Ames, Iowa." *Columbia Journalism Review* August 10 (https://archives.cjr.org/campaign_desk/straw_dogs.php).

Hochschild, Arlie R. 2012. *The Managed Heart: Commercialization of Human Feeling, 3rd edition*. Berkeley: University of California Press.

Kahneman, Daniel. 2013. *Thinking, Fast and Slow*. New York: Farrar, Straus and Giroux.

Kopp, Emily 2019. "Bernie 2020 becomes first unionized presidential campaign in history." *Roll Call*, May 8 (www.rollcall.com/2019/05/08/bernie-2020-becomes-first-unionized-presidential-campaign-in-history/).

Keith, Tamara. 2015. "Democrats Clinton and Sanders use postcards to organize support in Iowa." *NPR* November 12 (www.npr.org/2015/11/12/455717401/democrats-clinton-and-sanders-use-postcards-to-organize-support-in-iowa).

Korecki, Natasha. 2019. "New poll finds Harris' support has plunged 13 points in Iowa." *Politico* September 18 (www.politico.com/story/2019/09/18/kamala-harris-iowa-poll-support-plunged-1501812).

Korecki, Natasha. 2020. "Did Warren get her ad campaign wrong in Iowa?" *Politico* January 31 (www.politico.com/news/magazine/2020/01/31/iowa-caucus-2020-warren-buttigieg-ads-109153).

Lach, Eric 2019. "After making thirteen thousand calls for Kamala Harris, a volunteer reacts to the end of the campaign." *The New Yorker* December 4 (www.newyorker.com/news/as-told-to/a-kamala-harris-volunteer-reacts-to-the-end-of-the-presidential-campaign).

Martin, Jonathan, Anstead W. Herndon, and Alexander Burns. 2019. "How Kamala Harris's campaign unraveled." *The New York Times* November 29 (www.nytimes.com/2019/11/29/us/politics/kamala-harris-2020.html).

Nickerson, David W. and Todd Rogers. 2010. "Do you have a voting plan?: Implementation intentions, voter turnout, and organic plan making." *Psychological Science* 21(2):194–199.

Pfannenstiel, Brianne and Jacob C. Kummer. 2015. "Super PAC millions show little return in Iowa so far." *The Des Moines Register* December 27 (www.desmoinesregister.com/story/news/elections/presidential/caucus/2015/12/27/super-pac-cash-shows-little-return-in-iowa/77746152/).

Rice, Tom W. and Patrick J. Kenney. 1984. "Boosting state economies: the caucus-convention vs. the primary." *Presidential Studies Quarterly* 14(3): 357–360.

Scherer, Michael. 2019. "Kamala D. Harris lays off staff, shutters offices in New Hampshire." *The Washington Post* November 1 (www.washingtonpost.com/politics/kamala-d-harris-lays-off-staff-shutters-offices-in-new-hampshire/2019/11/01/cb2ed9ae-fce5-11e9-8190-6be4deb56e01_story.html).

Skelley, Geoffrey. 2019 "What we know about Andrew Yang's base." *FiveThirtyEight* December 11 (https://fivethirtyeight.com/features/what-we-know-about-andrew-yangs-base).

Ta, Linh 2019. "As Iowa caucuses approach, RAYGUN is a 'slightly hipper bale of hay' for presidential candidates." *The Des Moines Register* October 11 (www.desmoinesregister.com/story/news/elections/presidential/caucus/2019/10/11/iowa-caucus-2020-raygun-shirts-des-moines-elizabeth-warren-bernie-sanders-candidates-pizza-ranch/3910742002/).

Trish, Barbara. 2018. "Congress isn't paying its interns enough." *The Washington Post* September 2 (www.washingtonpost.com/opinions/congress-isnt-paying-its-interns-enough/2018/08/31/bc8c3e78-ad40-11e8-8a0c-70b618c98d3c_story.html).

9 The Final Stretch

In a competitive year, the month prior to the caucuses had always been a blur of frantic activity for candidates and staff, and increased engagement for that subset of Iowans drawn in. In 2020, there was extra high anxiety thanks to the drama of the impeachment and the trial of President Trump.[1] It's never possible to fully compartmentalize the local from the national, but still those in the bubble hunkered down on those activities that would have a direct effect on how the caucuses would transpire. The party put the finishing touches on the events themselves, the venues – both figurative and literal – in which the formal competition for delegates would begin. For their part, those campaigns still alive honed in on getting supporters to show up and to know what to do at the caucuses themselves, fully aware that effective participation comes with an understanding of the process. And the presence of reporters from all over the world, fixtures of the Iowa landscape, was never more apparent.

A Media Event

What transpired in the Iowa caucus campaigns and the caucuses themselves was politically important in a variety of ways. Some were concrete and obvious, like the selection of precinct delegates. Others were less apparent to the casual observer, like campaign activities as trial runs, venues for testing procedures and tools that would be refined in subsequent contests. At the same time, since 1976 there had been a symbolic role played by Iowa in the larger, sequential process of presidential nominations, one that had real-world consequences. This was the sense in which the caucuses became "media events," with their importance constructed by the national mass media through the way it chose to cover the contests. That coverage, according to Winebrenner and Goldford (2010) "obscure[s] the basic ... functions of the caucuses" (p. 7). As such, the caucuses took on a significance well beyond their role as party gatherings to begin the process of delegate selection in Iowa. Rather, they had become – for better or worse – mile-markers in the longer race to nomination. This role cast on the state came about because of the horserace approach that the national media took in its coverage. But it was quite different for the local press.

Local and National

In Iowa, much of the small-town media – almost 300 newspapers and more than 230 radio stations – didn't cover the caucus campaigns at all. Some local outlets avoided coverage of politics in general (Guth, 2015; Darr, 2019), since it wasn't a money-maker like high-school athletics, which is a big revenue stream for small-town outlets. Even more, covering 2020's Democratic avalanche of campaigns would have been a good way to alienate Republican and conservative listeners and subscribers. Many of the local outlets which did cover the campaign relied on statewide networks, such as the Associated Press (Darr, 2019) or Radio Iowa. But even the presence of high-profile, national political figures on the ground locally wasn't the draw one might expect.

At the same time, some local media do cover the caucuses, devoting considerable resources to them, in part out of a sense of civic responsibility. The 2020 field was a challenge for even the larger urban-based papers. Executive Editor Zack Kucharski of the *Cedar Rapids Gazette*, the paper with the state's second-largest circulation, pointed out the obvious. "[T]here are more of them [i.e., the candidates] than there are of us." *The Gazette's* coverage gravitated toward issues. Still, according to Kucharski, it was not a money-maker for the paper like college football – or like the caucuses were for local TV. With tight newspaper budgets, even the costs accrued in mileage for the paper's main political reporter, traversing routinely the 120 miles from Cedar Rapids to Des Moines, added up. Kucharski acknowledged that the campaign ads running on the paper's digital platform brought in very little revenue, mostly sold through a third-party vendor.

The *Des Moines Register*, with the state's highest circulation, stretched its staff to cover the campaigns. Kathie Obradovich, then the *Register's* opinion-page editor, noted that when the race was wide open "pretty much every reporter on the staff except the sports reporters [were] covering at least one presidential candidate," juggling caucus coverage with their normal beats. Like the *Gazette*, the *Register* acknowledged what amounted to a sense of civic responsibility to its readers, emphasizing that with its access to candidates came the responsibility to provide voters information to help them make up their minds. The *Register* editorial board had unparalleled access to the candidates, interviewing 18 Democratic contenders over the course of the campaign (Grundmeier, 2020).

The *Register's* reach extended beyond its own coverage. The Iowa Poll, which the *Register* commissions, garners considerable national attention as a window on the competitive state of the contest at critical junctures. In past cycles, it was a key preview of results – the final poll traditionally coming the Saturday before the caucuses. What's more, the caucuses have been a launching pad over the years for political reporters, just as they have for campaign staff. Jeff Zeleny of CNN and Jennifer Jacobs of *Bloomberg* both covered the caucuses for *The Register* before moving on to national outlets. And it's fair to say that Ann Selzer, who runs the Iowa Poll, has become a star in her own right (Malone, 2016).

In 2020, two new-media operations were favorites of local Democrats: *The Bleeding Heartland* and *Iowa Starting Line*. The Bleeding Heartland calls itself a community blog. Around since 2007, its primary author and editor was Laura Belin, whose caucus coverage focuses on the progressive left. *Iowa Starting Line* was newer, in place since 2015. It was founded by former Democratic staffer Pat Rynard, whose campaign work started in 2008 as a Hillary Clinton organizer in Iowa. To the extent that fine distinctions can be drawn, the *Starting Line* leans left, but not quite so far as *The Bleeding Heartland*. Together, though, they represent the sort of agile coverage offered by new media. Caucus politics is a focus during nomination seasons, and these two outlets are commonly read by those in the bubble. *Starting Line*, especially, drew national attention. According to the *New York Times*, "Elite reporters follow it. Candidates care about it" (Grynbaum, 2020).

Reporters from national print and broadcast outlets blanketed Iowa in 2019 and 2020 like they had in recent cycles, often juggling time in Iowa with stops in other early states. Some reporters, like candidates, even moved in, setting up shop in the state. Sydney Ember with the *New York Times* moved to Iowa in November 2019 (Ember, 2020), and from August through caucus date, Ember's byline appeared in close to 50 *Times* articles on Iowa. There is no ready measure of national coverage in the 2020 cycle, but in print alone there were at a minimum 11,000 caucus-related articles in the year preceding the February 3, 2020 event.[2] The sheer volume of coverage sent an implicit message that the caucuses were significant national political events, with meaning well beyond what they held for Iowa delegate selection and party business. The nature of the coverage, with a heavy focus on the competitive situation in the state – that is, the horserace – reinforced that same message.

The Horserace, Momentum, and Electability

Horserace coverage, a focus on who's up and who's down, has characterized the news media's approach to nomination campaigns in the post-reform era (Bartels, 1988). It's derided as trivializing the contest as simply a race to the finish line at the expense of a more substantive consideration of issues. The rare voice will argue that this approach might serve a useful purpose; Marx (2011) for example believes that horserace coverage makes the conversation among insiders "more transparent" for average voters, equipping them with better information and the possibility of more effective participation. Regardless, in Iowa the horserace can take on a life of its own.

The coverage doesn't just report on the competitive situation; it *affects* the competition as well. It delivers signals picked up by a variety of political actors, whose decisions – in turn – contribute to the state of the race. When a candidate is on the upswing – has momentum – she'll pull in more media coverage. She'll attract more donors (Mutz, 1995) and pique the interest of activists, drawing them into her camp, thereby reinforcing her position of strength. That people will jump on the bandwagon – be drawn to a potential winner – may seem superficial, but it's more complicated in nomination politics. Signs of strength are interpreted as evidence that the candidate is electable, able to prevail not just in the nomination race but in November as well.

Concerns with candidate electability had been a thread running through the entire caucus campaign, with Iowa Democrats highly focused on beating President Trump, trying hard to discern who among the field had the upper hand. CNN's Jeff Zeleny, the veteran caucus reporter who after the *Register* went to the *New York Times* before moving to CNN, commented in October on Iowan's fixation on electability. It was so much on voters' minds, according to Zeleny, that those he interviewed would ask – in a reversal of roles – *who he thought* was electable.

Each candidate in the field pushed some sort of blatant or subtle message that he or she was the candidate who could win. Biden would point to the national polls, which showed his strength in capturing the support of Democrats nationwide. His supporters and those of others labeled as moderates – like Senators Amy Klobuchar and Michael Bennet – touted their candidate's ability to draw in independents, or even Republicans, in November. But candidates on the progressive left were in no mood to concede the electability card, emphasizing that their bold plans and grassroots campaigns would draw in enough new and enthusiastic supporters to tip the balance in November. The Sanders campaign tackled it head on, equipping volunteers with printed talking points emphasizing that "Bernie is the most electable candidate." The campaign advised volunteers of the utility of that message. "You may have more success talking about electability than talking about any issue or even sharing your own personal story."

The media had willing partners in their bid to portray the caucuses as events with significance for the broader nomination race. In part, that was because candidates and their supporters knew that their actions would be interpreted in the horserace context, carrying meaning beyond their basic utility for the campaign. So when Pete Buttigieg made a fourth quarter haul of $25 million, it infused his campaign with cash, but also showed the political world the once-unknown had arrived politically. The Sanders fundraising total for the fourth quarter, $35 million, was a record. But in his case, the volume of 1.8 million contributors who gave an average of $18 conveyed the enthusiasm of a large grassroots supporter base spread across the nation (Almukhtar et al., 2020). Formerly obscure candidate Andrew Yang, suddenly a December/January draw, raced around the state firing up the college-age demographic, triggering memories in the bubble of Obama's 2008 prowess. In Yang's case, it was also the camera crews packing the event venues, announcing to the world that this quirky candidate who pitched MATH might be taking off.

The first-in-the-nation role that Iowa enjoyed brought with it complications, best characterized as yet another media event. In the same way that horserace coverage ascribes meaning to what transpires during a campaign, news coverage ascribes meaning to the outcomes, with ramifications well beyond Iowa. Of course, the media had ready partners through all of this, especially the campaigns and the state party. What's remarkable is that over the years they pulled it off – convincingly telling Americans what the results meant in the absence of an intuitively-meaningful measure of the outcome. That was set to change in 2020.

Expectations and Outcomes

Success or failure in politics is often judged in relative terms. In campaign debates, for example, a candidate who does better than expected, though perhaps not great in absolute terms or compared to his competitors, might still be judged a "winner." Strangely enough, even in general elections there can be a sense in which a candidate who just ekes by is hampered by the results, unable to claim a mandate. But in presidential nomination, expectations take on added significance (Bartels, 1987, 1988; Aldrich, 1980) because of the sequential nature of the delegate-selection contests, spread out over a six-month period. Presidential nomination is a collective enterprise, with no single state alone – even the biggest, California – able to determine the outcome of the nomination. Add to this, the Democratic Party's reliance on proportional rules, which made it likely that delegates would be split among candidates in a competitive race. Even when there is a clear winner or loser by an objective delegate count, how candidates fare compared to expectations will have important consequences, factoring into the competitive environment marking the next contest.

Expectations have been especially important in interpreting the caucus results, starting back in 1976 when Jimmy Carter "won" the caucuses, far exceeding expectations even though he came in second, behind "uncommitted." But in 2020 there would be a new twist – an additional objective measure of the outcome, straightforward yet still complicating the expectation game. Since 1972, the state party had reported the caucus outcome exclusively in terms of those state delegate equivalents (SDEs). When the IDP projected how many state convention delegates each candidate would amass, it was in part a nod to the caucuses as the first step in Iowa's caucus/convention process. Among other factors in the calculation, there was a weighting component in the projection, since the number of delegates up for grabs in any precinct was, in part, a function of the local party's decision regarding county convention size.

Even to many firmly entrenched in the bubble, the SDE metric was confusing, a bit of smoke and mirrors that the state party injected into caucus numbers. More to the point, the delegate equivalents reflected the same biases inherent in the caucus rules. Support for a candidate could only be expressed if it reached the 15% caucus viability threshold. The weight of a single person's vote depended on the turnout at a given caucus. And in very small, rural precincts, with just one or two delegates to allocate, proportionality gave way to something more like a winner-take-all result. Those same qualities that may have seemed rational when conceptualizing the caucuses as party events were perverse if caucuses were, in fact, media events with the expectation that they conveyed clear messages about candidate support.

The 2016 Sanders faction in Iowa had stressed that the delegate-equivalent projections were part of the rigged system. And its voice prevailed in the process of reworking the rules for 2020, which provided for that recorded expression of preference on a presidential preference card to be debuted at the caucuses. It would be, in loose terms, a plain old vote, to be aggregated across precincts statewide and reported by the party, along with SDEs. A seemingly straightforward addition to the process, more consistent with norms of democracy and transparency, the prospect of raw votes added some complexity to the expectation game. It also introduced the very real possibility that different metrics would point to different winners.

The Caucus Process Reconsidered

Caucuses themselves are unusual events, certainly unlike elections and even unlike most public meetings in the US. They are highly scripted by the formal, written rules established by the state party, leaving little room for discretion in terms of procedure. At the same time, caucuses vary dramatically across the state and across individual precincts – in size, mood, and even outcome. What's more, the experience of individual attendees can be quite different, even those in the same caucus location. Some who attend are alive to the complexity and strategic opportunities, perhaps taking on leadership positions, while others just do their best to figure out what they should be doing. They may follow the lead of friends or family, possibly other attendees who support the same candidate.

At a caucus, the delegate-selection process commands the most attention and almost always takes up the most time. Attendees tackle other aspects of party business, namely starting the process of state party platform construction and selecting a representative to the county party central committee. Both are key to party organizational life, though for most precinct attendees they're a distant second to the presidential nomination work – if on their radar at all. For that matter, how the presidential nomination portion of the caucuses works is a mystery to many. The rules are – if anything – arcane. But they're not arbitrary; they are in place for some reason, even though that reason may have been sound decades ago.

Public Displays of Support

When caucus participants align into preference groups by walking to a designated area of the caucus venue – a corner of the room, a section of bleachers, or whatever suitable spaces are available – they are offering a public demonstration of their support for a candidate, on display for all to see. To some, the idea that neighbors, co-workers, teachers, and students know each other's political dispositions is unnerving, at a minimum a surprise if they're not forewarned. It strikes some as downright undemocratic, so engrained are Americans to secrecy in voting. But norms are different in party politics, and for many under the party umbrella, requiring a public expression of support isn't so much a barrier to participation as a signal of partisan commitment.

This first alignment is an easy call for some attendees, whose support for a candidate is firm, perhaps with volunteer activity under their belts. Well-organized campaigns typically have put in place precinct chairs[3] tasked with keeping supporters together and persuading those at the caucus who are undecided. Heading into the 2020 caucuses, the *LA Times* summarized what polls had found: with just three weeks to go "[a]bout 60% of Iowa voters [were saying] they may change their minds" (Mason and Mehta, 2020). But caucus rules provided for those undecided or wavering attendees, carving out space at the outset for short speeches made by attendees on behalf of the candidates. And with 15–30 minutes allocated for participants to assemble into candidate or "uncommitted" preference groups, there's even a little time for discussion and persuasion should attendees want to engage in that.

Viability and Realignment

The determination of viability that follows is a core component of the caucus process, with that 15% viability threshold for preference groups ingrained in the minds of organizers and activists. However, the logic employed when viability was initially adopted is different than the purpose it serves now. In 1971, Richard Bender, now retired but a longtime aide to Senator Tom Harkin, had been one of a four-person band of Democratic operatives tasked with writing the party's new post-reform rules for 1972. Bender turned to the anti-war group Students for a Democratic Society (SDS) for inspiration about proportional procedures (Schier, 1980). Having a threshold was intended to limit fractionalization of the party on divisive issues, ones that might carry over to the general election to the detriment of the party.[4]

From the earliest post-reform caucuses, attendees were aligned based on candidate support, and the viability call was interpreted as an indication of which candidates were politically viable. The realignment phase was an opportunity for supporters of non-viable candidates to still have their voices heard. The underlying logic of realignment is the same as a ranked-choice-vote (RCV), used in some US local elections and recently adopted in Maine for statewide elections. It gives voters a second chance to express their support for a candidate if their most-preferred candidate isn't competitive. The 2020 move to a single realignment phase, as opposed to the possibility of many in the past, was coupled with the provision that only attendees in non-viable groups could realign. In limiting opportunities for strategic behavior, it reflected more fully the principle of giving attendees who need it a second chance.[5]

Counting and Reporting

The move by the IDP to have attendees report their candidate preference in writing was a significant departure from past practice. It facilitated a true count of candidate support among attendees, not one filtered by the precinct viability threshold or mysteriously translated into SDEs by the party. But in a strange way, it was more than a nod to transparency – or even acceding to the demands of the Sanders voices in the party. Using a card was a practical move, recognizing that a seemingly simple task of counting people at a caucus or in preference groups is difficult – more than you might imagine – with hundreds of people, perhaps as many as one thousand at play. Collecting and counting cards is doable, and a paper trail can come in handy.

Satellite Caucuses

The IDP had been vexed by the lack of inclusiveness in the caucus system, and since early 2019 had been trying to settle on a plan for the 2020 cycle. The ultimate solution arrived after the DNC shot down the virtual caucus plan. It involved holding a number of "satellite caucuses," additional caucuses in locations that would remove some of the barriers to participation. There would be 87 satellite caucus locations: 60 in Iowa, 24 elsewhere in the US, and 3 in international locations.[6] The satellite caucuses would follow the same rules and procedures as the regular ones, with one exception: while the expression of candidate preference would be tallied, no delegates would be allocated at the caucuses. Unlike the regular precinct caucuses, where numbers of delegates assigned to the caucus are known in advance and not sensitive to 2020 caucus turnout, turnout at the satellites would ultimately factor into the satellite delegate calculus.[7] The satellite caucuses offered more venues for participation, but they didn't fully resolve the mobility problems faced by some Iowa Democrats or the time constraints limiting participation on Caucus Day. Some were scheduled for earlier on Caucus Day, but they were all to be held on February 3.

Wrangling Uncertainty

The final days of the caucus campaign kicked off amid the usual chaos and uncertainty of nomination politics, plus a heavy dose of angst unique to 2020. There was a lot at stake, both for candidates fighting to stay alive and for Iowa Democrats, needing to prove that they had resolved the problems highlighted by the 2016 contest. As usual, the press was on hand, but it was dealing with a decidedly unusual situation: the peripheral drama of the impeachment trial of President Trump. It played out in the US Senate, competing for the attention of the American public and tethering the senators in the race to the nation's capital. But as the candidates, the party and the president fought for their survival, so too did the approximately 700–800 staff who were on the ground in Iowa, most unsure about what February 4, the day *after* the caucuses, would hold for them.

Doubling Down on the Ground … and on the Spectacle

Traditionally, every field operation kicked it up a notch in the days preceding the caucuses. For those campaigns that had invested heavily in a ground game and were true contenders, the final GOTC push resembled a highly sophisticated operation and not just a mad flurry of calls, texts, and knocks on the door. Instead, it was an elaborate deployment of resources, especially during the weekend before the caucuses and extending straight through to the start of the main show at 7 pm on Monday. This was the endgame for organizers, the conclusion they'd been laboring toward for months as they cultivated teams of volunteers and trained them in the protocol of GOTC and the caucuses themselves.

A division of labor prevailed in all of this, with volunteers taking on leadership positions, even the VAN entries – "tags" – documenting the roles. Some would run staging locations, pop-up field offices ideally in the precinct itself. These were venues for last-minute training, phone banking, or shift changes for canvassers. Others organized food for the staging location, a role attractive to those activists who despised the world of phone banking and canvassing. Others were slated to be precinct chairs for the campaign, ready to shepherd supporters at the caucuses through the ins and outs of the mysterious process, implementing the campaign's strategic directives during the evening. In some campaigns, workers would have to report in from the caucus site so the campaign could track its performance in real time, equipping it with information to craft the narrative in whatever way necessary to create an image of success.

About the same time that the field operation reached a fever pitch, the candidates and a bevy of surrogates blanketed Iowa, hoping to build enthusiasm and perhaps grab some new supporters. They also might inspire volunteers, many weary by the last few days of the campaign. The well-financed campaigns shuttled the candidates on leased private jets, along with a small entourage that included select members of the press corps, since there was no time for ground travel.[8] Surrogates were more important than ever for the campaigns of the sitting senators, who found their time in Iowa limited because of obligations in DC related to the Senate's impeachment proceedings.

Surrogates are more than fill-ins for the candidates; they fuel the frenzy. High-profile surrogates, sometimes A-list celebrities and their equivalent from the political space, would appear at rallies and other events scattered across the state. Obama in 2008 had taken the game to a different level, bringing in surrogates with star power, like Oprah Winfrey, dwarfing the efforts of his opponents (Johnson & Crowley, 2007). In 2016, Clinton tapped her share of celebrities as well, but the actions of two towering figures are reminders that surrogates can serve the campaign in multiple ways. One such Clinton surrogate, Madeline Albright, the nation's first female Secretary of State who served under President Bill Clinton, was in the state when she saw a *New York Times* article mentioning an undecided Iowan. Grabbing contact information from the VAN, she called that voter and made a pitch for Hillary. Civil rights icon Congressman John Lewis paired his public events in the days before the 2016 caucuses with a stop at a field office for a canvas launch, picking up some bananas at a gas station along the way. He reasoned that organizers could stand some healthy food in their lives at that juncture.

When surrogates trek through Iowa, they imply a not-so-subtle message about campaign strategy, hinting at a play for supporters more national in scope. The Black vote in Iowa, while likely not large enough to tip the balance in the caucuses, was especially important for 2020 candidates who sought to send a message to Democrats nationally: that they could resurrect the coalition Barack Obama had built in 2008. In 2020, Biden was thought to have strong support among Black voters nationally, with an early January Washington Post/Ipsos poll confirming that. He dominated the field, with support of Black Democrats at 48%, with only Sanders among the others registering much support at all. Warren was at 9%, and Buttigieg just 2%. The polling confirmed that the mayor had "a Black problem" (Trudo, 2019).

Buttigieg's surrogate cast represented a wide array of state and national African American leaders, a rejoinder to the doubts plaguing the campaign. Mayor Quentin Hart of Waterloo, greeted by Buttigieg at the summer labor event in Waterloo, was fully on board, endorsing the candidate in January 2020 and stumping with him. But Mayor Hart emphasized that it had been important to him to be a "gracious host" for all the candidates, getting them to Waterloo to communicate with residents. Hart admitted that he'd even do that for President Trump. In the end, Hart liked the idea of a "mayor's touch" in the White House and thought that Buttigieg had probably "the most aggressive plan for Black America" (Bryant, 2020).

Sanders' surrogate strategy, on the other hand, targeted the broader Obama coalition of Black Iowans and youth, showcasing charismatic African American voices like that of Nina Turner who had stumped in Iowa for the campaign all along, even back at the Malcom Auditorium in April, 2019. The campaign also brought in the erudite voice of Dr. Cornel West. But undoubtedly Sanders' primary surrogate pitch was to young progressives; in this, he was aided by those celebrity-status surrogates who would resonate with the left: members of The Squad, filmmaker Michael Moore, as well as musical artists running the gamut, from bands like Las Cafeteras to hipsters Vampire Weekend. *The Starting Line* labeled a Cedar Rapids event right before Caucus Day, featuring Vampire Weekend and the lead singer of Grammy-winning Bon Iver, the "biggest of the entire caucus cycle."

Tending to Detail

As the campaigns made a final push to turn out supporters, the Democratic Party was in the closing event-planning stage, mired in the sort of rules, procedures and details that occupy the minds of the party apparatus. No change from the past, the caucuses would still run on a lot of paper, printed packets of material to be distributed to each of the some 1,700 precinct caucus chairs. They'd be routed through the county parties, which would be swamped with storage boxes filled with materials. One key printed document would be the Caucus Voter Roll, which is the list of registered Democrats in each precinct, used for attendees to sign in at the caucuses. It's drawn from the Secretary of State's voter file, but because of a several-week lag between printing and caucus night, the roll was always incomplete. It missed those people the campaigns had registered during the final few weeks before the caucus, and certainly those who would register on caucus night as well.

Even something as mundane as settling on details of a process for signing in at the caucuses held potential drama for party people, factoring into the final touches. The party wanted to be sure that things ran smoothly, from determining the optimal arrangement of sign-in tables to ensuring that precincts had enough registration forms on hand, both of which had contributed to problems in 2016. There are hosts of other things that occupy the party's precinct leadership, like knowing who to call if the caucus site is locked or how to handle an attendee who showed up in the wrong precinct, too late to make it to the right one. But some fixes new to 2020 weighed heavily on those tasked with running the caucuses. Would limiting realignment to just one round effectively simplify and shorten the process as the IDP had assured? What would happen if an attendee lost or asked to void a preference card? For that matter, who exactly would assume responsibility of keeping the cards in their custody? The training sessions and mock caucuses that Iowa Democrats held in 2020 as the real caucuses inched closer took on more significance than usual. With fierce competition and the possibility of small margins separating the candidates, there was lot at stake. And the nation was watching.

A Pre-Caucus Read

Part of the late pre-caucus routine in Iowa had historically been the Saturday release of the final Iowa Poll, offering a smidgeon of clarity about the state of competition. The poll had a good track record, notably predicting high turnout and an Obama caucus win in 2008. And in the 2016 general election, pollster Ann Selzer was spot on with her final pre-election poll, predicting a large-margin win in Iowa for Donald Trump, when other state and national polls seemed to be signaling a resounding Clinton win.

The Iowa Poll wouldn't just satisfy curiosity; it could fuel last-minute enthusiasm – or dash the hopes of staff and activists. Since a high percentage of caucus attendees had not yet settled on a candidate, the poll results could factor into eleventh-hour decisions about candidate support. And the poll could have legs once the caucus results were in, a benchmark against which to judge the final results, indicating which candidates were riding a late surge – or a decline. This could be key for judgments about momentum the candidates were carrying into New Hampshire.

The Iowa Poll had become a media event in its own right, and CNN – the *Register's* national partner on the poll – scheduled an 8 pm Saturday night CNN Special Event to release the final poll results. But as broadcast time approached, news spread that there would be no Special Event, no release of the results. At 8:46 pm, the *Register* posted a cryptic explanation: "Nothing is more important to the *Register* and its polling partners than the integrity of the Iowa Poll. Today, a respondent raised an issue with the way the survey was administered, which could have compromised the results of the poll. It appears a candidate's name was omitted in at least one interview in which the respondent was asked to name their preferred candidate" (Hunter 2020).

It turned out that Buttigieg was the omitted name. But conspiracy theorists reasoned that more was going on, that the poll was yanked to obscure results pointing to insurgent candidate success – that some "candidates [Yang and Sanders] were more successful than the public had been led to believe" (Collins, 2020). Axios poured water on the conspiracy take, reporting that a CNN source had revealed the backstory: "An interviewer at the poll's call center increased the font size of the questionnaire on their screen so much that the bottom choice (which rotated between calls) wasn't visible" (Falconer & Allen, 2020). In short, a minor technology-glitch felled the Iowa Poll.

Hanging by a Thread

Of the approximately 750 paid staff in Iowa by caucus time, most were field operatives, a few had been in place for a year or longer. Others parachuted in for the final push. Some were Iowa natives; most weren't. Some had grown fond of their life in the state, forging close connections with co-workers and the volunteers they cultivated; they felt strong attachment to the state and the little things that define place – the spaces where they had posted up, the gas station pizza, the Midwest pace of life. Others relished the thought of leaving ASAP.

Despite these differences, many staff shared one thing as February 3 approached: pervasive uncertainty about what would come next. It applied to staff working on those campaigns seemingly poised for success, not knowing where they would be deployed. And it applied to those whose campaigns couldn't possibly continue. If staff knew what plans the campaigns had for them, they didn't let on. Unionized campaigns might have shaved off a little uncertainty, but not enough to fill in all the blanks about life after February 3. Jonathan Williams, a spokesperson for UFCW Local 400, the union under which the Sanders campaign had organized, put it in clear-cut terms: "[Y]ou are [either] out of a job ... or you get relocated."

Winning Iowa doesn't necessarily bring clarity for the staff, even for those who work for the eventual nominee. Carlo Makarechi was that Clinton staffer who in the summer of 2015 had approached mental-health advocate Leslie Carpenter in Iowa City. Five months later, the day after the 2016 caucuses, Carlo started down his itinerant path of serial deployments to Nevada, Washington State and then back to Iowa. In Iowa, he worked on delegate protection after the county conventions – ensuring that Clinton maintained her delegate strength in subsequent contests in the caucus-convention system. Eventually the campaign gave him a general election assignment. There was no question of Carlo's commitment to Clinton as the candidate or to the Democratic Party.[9] He understood that the decision-making process for the campaigns was complicated: "[Real] time decisions about where to deploy staff [are] based on constantly changing data and uncertainty." Still Carlo was frustrated by the process after Iowa. He noted that he and his co-workers felt unappreciated during the deployment process. "My questions were rarely answered honestly and my requests about where I'd like to be [sent] were ignored."

Despite his concerns, Carlo kept it all in perspective, knowing that the frustration and uncertainty are just part of the deal when working in this field. Kurt Meyer has observed presidential campaign staff who've come to Iowa for decades, and he had hosted many of them in his home, noting that most are accustomed to uncertainty. It's just the trade-off "for being where the action is, for helping determine the course of our country," according to Meyer.

As the 2020 caucuses drew near, the only staff with some semblance of clarity were those whose candidates had already dropped out. After Kamala Harris had withdrawn in December, Lauren Parker took two weeks to close down the campaign and say goodbye to her colleagues and volunteers. Before moving to Iowa, she had lived briefly in a large city in a southern state, and while she couldn't picture herself working for another presidential candidate, she felt drawn to the idea of working in campaign politics in that state. It seemed primed for a Democratic win after years of Republican dominance. In November 2019, Lauren had totaled the rusted, gold car she had bought on her first day in Iowa, the result of another driver blowing through a stop sign and crashing into her. The insurance settlement covered the rental she used to drive herself to her new base and a position she would maintain even after the November 2020 election.

Rachel Salas, Lauren's friend and fellow Harris organizer, signed on with another Iowa campaign; she eventually wound up working the general election as a regional organizer in a high-profile Senate contest in a different state. Casey Clemmons had moved from Gillibrand to Buttigieg, leveraging his caucus experience into a prominent role as Iowa deputy state director. After Iowa, he moved on to become Virginia's state director for Buttigieg. Jim Flores had been drawn to the protection offered by a union contract and NextGen's commitment to stay in Iowa through November 2020. By mid-spring 2020, he would be out of a job, seeing no option but to resign his position in exchange for a small severance package offered by the Super PAC. Jim's apartment lease ran through the general election.

Jacob Hamblin had been one of the first Booker staffers to plant himself down in Iowa. He stayed around for a couple of weeks after Booker withdrew in mid-January, making a final good-bye tour of Iowa co-workers and friends. Jacob then made his way to New York City, where on the Saturday before the caucuses, while politics in Iowa was reaching a fever pitch, he sat in a bar with friends. At that point, the US had begun to take notice of the outbreak in China of what was then labeled the "novel coronavirus." By then, eight cases had been reported in the US. Just one day earlier, President Trump had issued a travel ban that restricted access of non-US citizens from China to the US.[10] Jacob was relieved to be sitting at the bar with his friend, a middle school classmate who had just flown in from China.

February 3

On February 3, Iowa Democrats attended caucuses in 99 domestic and three international satellite locations, many of them held before 7 pm CST (Lynch, 2020). Early reports suggested that this new caucus form went smoothly. Taylor Beckwith-Ferguson, a 28-year-old Iowan who worked as a ski instructor in the Republic of Georgia, caucused in Tbilisi. He recalled that his satellite caucus consisted of "three Iowans, hanging out and drinking wine." Beckwith-Ferguson said that the actual caucus itself lasted about five minutes, since with a group of three there were "no issues with viability and no difficult math." He added, "The result was 100% Bernie."

But the main event that Monday night would be the 1,678 caucuses in precincts across the state. Those recruited to set up and preside over the individual caucus sites would arrive early, arranging the space if it wasn't already set up. Same, too, for campaign organizers and precinct chairs who would be on hand. The Malcom Auditorium hadn't seen much action since the Sanders event in April 2019, nine months prior. It had been a full ten months since Jacob Hamblin had walked into the auditorium to introduce himself to the county party activists, one of his first stops after landing in Iowa. On caucus night, it was a completely different set of participants: those who lived in that precinct. But there was someone new – an out-of-state volunteer with the Sanders campaign. Andrew Cook, a young lawyer from St. Louis, had been in Iowa since that Saturday, crashing three nights with three different sets of Sanders supporters and staff, including a "sweet, retired couple." Like other out-of-state supporters who dropped in for the last days of the campaign, Andrew was now part of the caucus bubble. He wouldn't be able to participate – he couldn't even be seated with the supporters at the caucus – but he kept an eye on the proceedings, checked the math and reported the counts to the Sanders campaign. Andrew wasn't the only new face. None of the 30 participants who showed up to caucus had been there on the Saturday morning in March 2019 for the county's odd-year caucuses.

The Malcom precinct – which controlled three delegates – was small, but not the smallest in the county. At the caucus, three preference groups passed the five-person viability threshold: Sanders, Biden, and Buttigieg. And after realignment, the math was clear-cut, revealing that each of those three candidates would be allocated one delegate. The state party's intent to streamline the caucus process seemed to work well in Malcom. It was about 8 pm when the caucus chair started calling the IDP reporting line; she left the auditorium after several tries and continued trying once she arrived at home.

Notes

1 On September 24, 2019, the US House Speaker Nancy Pelosi announced an impeachment inquiry against President Trump. Over the next three months, Congress would investigate allegations that Trump used the power of his office to solicit interference from Ukraine in the 2020 election. Majority Democrats in the House approved two articles of impeachment against Trump on December 18: one for abuse of power and one for obstruction of Congress. It named impeachment managers on January 15, 2020, and voted to send the articles to the Senate. There, a trial began on January 16, and members of the Republican-controlled Senate voted on February 5 to acquit the president (Stevens et al., 2020).
2 LexisNexis search on "Iowa Caucus" or "Caucuses," with duplicates removed, yielded 11,728 "hits" – certainly an underestimate of even print, since not all outlets are archived with the search tool.
3 The "caucus chair," on the other hand, is selected at the caucus to preside over it.
4 Bender anticipated that caucus attendees would be divided by issue positions, not candidate preference; the party was wracked with contentious factionalization, especially over the Vietnam War. The 15% value was the result of a simple calculation intended to keep the caucuses from fracturing into "insignificantly small issue groups," though not completely arbitrary, according to Bender. "The congressional districts that year were going to elect seven national delegates in most of the districts. One-seventh is 14.28%. [After rounding] … the minimum level of 15% was born" ("Caucus Iowa: Journey to the Presidency," Iowa PBS, 2016).
5 The initial virtual caucus plan had specified RCV procedures, coupled with a 15% threshold, thereby approximating the in-person viability and realignment processes.
6 These caucuses would be held in a variety of sites. Some were scheduled for worksites or elder care facilities, both with potential caucus attendees who would be unable to leave the site to attend a regular caucus. Others were on college campuses or foreign-language sites. Many out-of-state satellite sites were in places where retired Iowans winter. (Iowa Democratic Party document "2020 Iowa Democratic Party Caucus: Satellite Caucuses" www.thecaucuses.org/satellite-caucuses.)
7 Results from satellites across Iowa would be aggregated to a special "satellite-caucus county" in each congressional district, while results from out-of-state caucuses added at the state convention. Delegates ultimately assigned to satellite caucuses could constitute a maximum of 10% of delegates awarded across the state, the share originally envisioned for the virtual caucuses.
8 News organizations pay for their reporters to travel with a candidate. Reimbursement options are covered by FEC guidelines. (www.fec.gov/regulations/100-93/2020-annual-100#100-93-b-3)

9 In the 2020 cycle, Carlo worked for the DCCC as a regional field director, having directed community mobilization for a DC-based non-profit over the 2018 cycle.
10 January 31, 2020, "Proclamation on Suspension of Entry as Immigrants and Nonimmigrants of Persons who Pose a Risk of Transmitting 2019 Novel Coronavirus" (www.whitehouse.gov/presidential-actions/proclamation-suspension-entry-immigrants-nonimmigrants-persons-pose-risk-transmitting-2019-novel-coronavirus/)

References

Aldrich, John H. 1980. *Before the Convention: Strategies and Choices in Presidential Nomination Campaigns.* Chicago: University of Chicago Press.

Almukhtar, Sarah, Thomas Kaplan, and Rachel Shorey. 2020. "2020 Democrats went on a spending spree in the final months of 2019." *The New York Times* February 1 (www.nytimes.com/interactive/2020/02/01/us/elections/democratic-q4-fundraising.html).

Bartels, Larry M. 1987. "Candidate choice and the dynamics of the presidential nomination process." *American Journal of Political Science* 31 (1): 1–30.

Bartels, Larry M. 1988. *Presidential Primaries and the Dynamics of Public Choice.* Princeton, NJ: Princeton University Press.

Bryant, Christa Case. 2020. "Why the black mayor of this Iowa city endorsed Buttigieg." *The Christian Science Monitor* January 31 (www.csmonitor.com/USA/Politics/2020/0131/Why-the-black-mayor-of-this-Iowa-city-endorsed-Buttigieg).

Collins, Ben. 2020. "Conspiracy theories swirl over canceled Iowa poll, pushed by Sanders and Yang supporters." *NBC News* February 3 (www.nbcnews.com/tech/social-media/conspiracy-theories-swirl-over-canceled-iowa-poll-pushed-sanders-yang-n1128621).

Darr, Joshua P. 2019. "Earning Iowa: local newspapers and the invisible primary." *Social Science Quarterly* 100 (1): 320–327.

Ember, Sydney. 2020. "I wanted to understand Iowa. So I moved there." *The New York Times* February 3 (www.nytimes.com/2020/02/03/reader-center/iowa-caucus.html).

Falconer, Rebecca and Mike Allen. 2020. "Font fiasco tanks climactic Iowa poll." *Axios* February 2 (www.axios.com/iowa-2020-poll-not-released-des-moines-register-caeea162-0861-47d9-a4d9-107725c81dfc.html).

Grundmeier, Lucas. 2020. "Register editorial board has announced caucus endorsement." *The Des Moines Register* January 21 (www.desmoinesregister.com/story/opinion/editorials/caucus/2020/01/21/des-moines-register-editorial-board-announce-iowa-caucus-endorsement-saturday/4530929002).

Grynbaum, Michael. 2020. "A scrappy Iowa start-up is the 'It' read for political insiders." *The New York Times.* January 31 (www.nytimes.com/2020/01/31/business/media/iowa-caucus-media-starting-line.html).

Guth, David. 2015. "Amber waves of change: rural community journalism in areas of declining population." *Journal of Applied Journalism and Media Studies* 4(2): 259–275.

Hunter, Carol. 2020. "Register, partners cancel release of Iowa Poll after respondent raises concerns." *The Des Moines Register* February 1 (www.desmoinesregister.com/story/news/2020/02/01/des-moines-register-cnn-cancels-release-iowa-poll-over-respondent-concerns/4637168002/).

Johnson, Sasha and Candy Crowley. 2007. "Winfrey tells Iowa crowd: Barack Obama is 'the one.'" *CNN* December 8 (www.cnn.com/2007/POLITICS/12/08/oprah.obama/).

Lynch, James. 2020. "Democrats approve 99 satellite caucus locations in Iowa, US, overseas." *The Cedar Rapids Gazette* December 18 (www.thegazette.com/subject/news/iowa-democratic-party-presidential-caucus-satellite-voting-locations-20191218).

Malone, Clare. 2016. "Ann Selzer is the best pollster in politics." *FiveThirtyEight* January 16 (https://fivethirtyeight.com/features/selzer/).

Marx, Greg. 2011. "In defense of (the right kind of) horse race journalism." *Columbia Journalism Review* September 6 (https://archives.cjr.org/campaign_desk/in_defense_of_the_right_kind_o.php).

Mason, Melanie and Seema Mehta. 2020. "Many Iowa Democrats, desperate to pick a candidate to beat Trump, are undecided and under pressure." *Los Angeles Times* January 16 (www.latimes.com/politics/story/2020-01-16/iowa-caucus-nears-undecided-voters-feel-the-pressure).

Mutz, Diana. C. 1995. "Effects of horse-race coverage on campaign coffers: Strategic contributing in presidential primaries." *The Journal of Politics* 57(4): 1015–1042.

Schier, Steven E. 1980. *The Rules and the Game: Democratic National Convention Delegate Selection in Iowa and Wisconsin*. Washington, DC: University Press of America.

Stevens, Harry, Dan Keating, Kevin Uhrmacherand, Chris Alcantara. 2020. "How President Trump's impeachment unfolded in the House and Senate." *The Washington Post* February 26 (www.washingtonpost.com/graphics/2019/politics/impeachment-calendar/).

Trudo, Hanna. 2019. "'Pete has a black problem': top Black leaders say Buttigieg is naive on race." *Daily Beast* June 24 (www.thedailybeast.com/pete-buttigieg-has-a-black-problem-top-african-american-leaders-say-he-is-naive-on-race).

Winebrenner, Hugh and Dennis J. Goldford. 2010. *The Iowa Precinct Caucuses: The Making of a Media Event*. Iowa City: University of Iowa Press.

10 Caucuses, Chaos, and Coronavirus

In many respects, the 2020 caucus cycle had gone smoothly, shoring up the caucus bubble that had seemed vulnerable to puncture after 2016. Iowa Democrats – including new progressive voices of Sanders supporters within the party's decision-making structure – had agreed to new rules to limit the advantage of party insiders, compliant with the guidelines established by the national party. The leading candidates, with the exception of Bloomberg, treated Iowa as if it were important, most devoting considerable resources to a ground game and many to an air war as well. And when the candidates showed up in the state, the media did as well. Even the close to 1,700 precinct caucuses themselves, operating under the most significant rules changes since 1972, had transpired without some of the problems that had marked past cycles.

Until about 9 pm on caucus night, it looked as if everything had gone according to plan. From that point onward, all hell broke loose.

The Elusive Caucus Results

Given the new streamlined rules, most caucuses had wrapped up by 9 pm. Analysts on network television, aided by live shots from correspondents at various caucus sites, chewed on entrance poll data, exit interviews with caucus-goers, and pundit speculation. They were waiting for the IDP to report the official caucus results. Shortly before 10 pm, the official word came from the IDP spokeswoman: results were delayed so the party could conduct quality checks. "The integrity of the results is paramount," Mandy McClure said in her statement. "What we know right now is that around 25% of precincts have reported, and early data indicates turnout is on pace for 2016" (Becker, 2020).

Meanwhile, observers began to question what was going on. *The Wall Street Journal* reminded its readers that by 10 pm on caucus night in 2016, more than 90% of the Democratic precincts had reported and Ted Cruz had already been declared the Republican victor.[1] Social media had gone nuclear. Conspiracy theories abounded – from allegations that the caucuses were rigged to assertions that Russia played a role (Graham, 2020). Posts derided Iowa and Iowans. Democrats grumbled and Republicans crowed, looking past their own 2012 caucus problems when some precinct results had been temporarily lost. At the same time, posts from actual 2020 caucus-goers celebrated the orderliness of their meetings and their success at managing large crowds. After all, more than 176,000 Iowa Democrats had turned out for the caucuses – better than in 2016 but below the 2008 record of close to 240,000 (Richardson, 2020).

There was also a sense that the hard-fought campaign had not embittered neighbors who came together that evening. But another storyline took shape as well, based on reports from the chairs who presided over the precinct caucuses. They told of difficulties downloading the reporting app that the IDP had asked them to use. At the same time, they couldn't get through to the party on the phone, the fallback plan for reporting. Repeated tries all ended in a busy signal.

If the caucuses were just party events kicking off Iowa delegate selection, a delay in the results would be no big deal. But their role as a media event – with national relevance – had been well-established for decades. With no results to report publicly, it would be as if the caucuses hadn't happened at all. It would be even a bigger loss this year, when – for the first time ever – the raw vote total, documented on the new preferences cards, would be available. These would offer a more intuitive measure of candidate success than cryptic SDEs. Using the app was supposed to help with efficiency in processing the expanded cache of results each precinct would be conveying. The party's counting drama, however, didn't stop the campaigns from jockeying for control of the narrative, in much the same way they might have on a typical caucus night. It turns out that the campaigns had been doing some counting too.

The party's caucus chairs were supposed to relay results to the IDP once their caucus adjourned. But campaigns had also set up real-time reporting systems, elaborate networks of caucus participants or observers tasked with passing along to the campaign reports of the counts at each caucus site. Sanders' experienced network of volunteers – methodical and efficient – had a sophisticated system with precinct leaders responsible for reporting back to the headquarters. Warren, who had invested significantly in a broad-based team of local organizers, also had a well-organized caucus night structure working with an app created in-house (Edelman, 2020).

The early buzz from these crowdsourced results, even while caucus action was still ongoing, indicated that Sanders and Buttigieg were especially strong, Warren was solid, but Biden was fading. At one urban precinct in a diverse Des Moines neighborhood, one that should have been full of his allies, Biden failed to meet the viability threshold. Across the state, early word emerged that the caucuses had become a two-man contest. Those two leaders – and the other candidates as well – took different post-caucus paths.

The Momentum Grab

Polls from New Hampshire before the Iowa caucuses had pointed to Sanders' strength, with Biden on his heels. Back-to-back wins for Sanders in Iowa and New Hampshire could establish his strength, maybe even crown him the front-runner nationally. Buttigieg wasn't out of the running in New Hampshire but had faltered in recent polls, meaning momentum coming out of Iowa could be especially important to sustain his promising candidacy. In Iowa, he had come from nowhere, leveraging big fundraising numbers and an expansive organization to go toe-to-toe with both Sanders and Warren. He coupled a classic underdog story with some traditionally astute political moves.

Buttigieg would eventually make the early grab for the win, staking out a different path than the other candidates took. Before 11 pm and with not even partial results, Klobuchar had told her supporters "we're punching above our weight." She would be the first to land in New Hampshire, greeted by a cheering crowd there. Biden's campaign wrote to the IDP complaining of "considerable flaws" in the reporting system and stressing the need for unity. Warren acknowledged that the race was "too close to call," while Sanders told his cheering supporters that he had "a good feeling we're going to be doing very, very well here" (Coltrain, 2020a). Buttigieg, on the other hand, claimed more than a good feeling. By 11:30 pm he had declared victory. "So we don't know all the results. But we know by the time it's all said and done, Iowa you have shocked the nation. By all indications, we are going onto New Hampshire victorious." Mayor Pete added, "Tonight Iowa chose a new path."

Within the hour, the Sanders campaign shot back in the post-caucus skirmish, releasing its numbers from "nearly 40 percent of precincts" and justifying that release by appealing to the candidate's supporters. "[Our] supporters worked too hard for too long to have the results of that work delayed."[2] The campaign's count for that fraction of precincts had Sanders leading the pack, both in the raw vote and in SDEs. In the first expression of preference, he had about a seven percentage-point lead over Buttigieg, but it dropped to a one-point lead in the adjusted world of SDEs. On both counts, Warren was in third place, Biden fourth and Klobuchar fifth. Fifth place may have supported Klobuchar's assertion that she punched about her weight, but the only credible interpretation for Biden's fourth place was that he had tanked.

The Party Counts

Like any Tuesday morning after the caucuses, the non-stop flight to DC was packed with Beltway media types, while still others took connecting flights to their next nomination destination. But unlike other cycles, this Tuesday-morning-after had a state party which hadn't even started to release results. Instead, it bought a little more time by announcing that it would begin releasing results later in the day. When the results did start coming in that evening, 62% of the reporting precincts showed Buttigieg with a slight lead over Sanders, with almost 27% of the SDEs to Sanders' 25%. Warren was third with 18% and Biden was three points behind her. That initial report also showed that Sanders had an almost 1,200 vote lead in the popular vote count (Watson & Becket, 2020). By the end of the day, 75% of the precincts had been counted, but the Democratic Party had imploded into a full-blown finger-pointing frenzy about the delays in the count. When IDP Chairman Troy Price and DNC Chairman Tom Perez were both accused of bumbling the caucuses, each pointed the other's way. In the meantime, it was becoming clear that technology – namely the app for reporting the results to the IDP – had been at the root of the problem. 2020 wasn't the first time that the IDP had provided an app to local party leaders, but never before one for reporting, only for assisting with the sometimes-cumbersome calculations at the caucuses themselves (Lapowsky, 2016).

Local party leaders in Iowa are no different than people anywhere – some technologically sophisticated, willing to try out new gadgets, and others opting to stay old school if given the choice. But the app remained a mystery to many, even those willing to give it a try. The IDP sent out the final app instructions just hours before the start of the caucuses (Ember & Epstein, 2020). Chairs who planned to phone in their results, the traditional method of reporting, found lines busy when they called in. No surprise, given the number of precincts and the multiple metrics to report, but in short order rumors began to circulate that trolls on the internet conspiracy forum *4chan* had posted the phone number for the IDP's dedicated reporting line. Eventually the party confirmed that Trump supporters had flooded the lines (Pager & Epstein, 2020).

It took almost four full weeks to get a final, official vote count from the Iowa Democrats verified by the state central committee. The initial days of the counting slog captured the attention of the media, a new twist to the horserace, but one enhanced with the storyline of a state party under siege. The release of the full results, from 100% of the precincts, three days after the caucuses on Thursday, showed in the raw vote – the first expression of preference – a three-point lead for Sanders over Buttigieg. But in projected state delegates, the order was reversed, with a very narrow lead for Buttigieg over Sanders – 564 to 562 SDEs, amounting to a mere .2 percentage-point margin. Sanders had narrowed the gap in SDEs when the results from the satellite caucuses came in.[3]

In the initial full count, Warren, Biden, and Klobuchar landed third, fourth, and fifth places in both metrics, Warren trailing second-place Buttigieg in the raw count by less than three points, with Biden languishing at fourth in both counts (Stieb et al., 2020). Earlier that week, Biden had called the result a "gut punch" but also came out swinging, warning Democrats that Sanders' Democratic-Socialism would be a target for President Trump and that Buttigieg lacked the experience to make him electable.[4]

The Sanders and Buttigieg campaigns waged their battle over the results, both calling for a recanvass of selected precincts, essentially a check on the calculations. Later they called for a partial recount, which started with the preference cards themselves. Each modified report showed Sanders and Buttigieg holding their metric-dependent leads. The count that the party certified on February 29 showed a .04 percentage-point lead for Buttigieg in SDEs. Sanders maintained a 6,100 (four percentage-point) vote lead in the raw vote and 2,500 in the second expression of preference (Rynard, 2020). By then, the Democratic race had moved on, already past the New Hampshire primary and the Nevada caucuses.

A New Media Event: An "Epic Fiasco"

The count chaos didn't completely obscure the obvious caucus outcomes – that both Sanders and Buttigieg were credible candidates and Biden might be in trouble. But while the delay in counting had made it more difficult to ascribe meaning to the results, it brought into focus even more problems with the caucuses.

Despite weeks devoted to counting, there were lingering concerns about the validity of the results. Some mistakes in the count are relatively easy to catch, like delegate calculation errors. But there is no way to correct for an error in a viability calculation, which sets in motion the rest of the process. The Associated Press, which routinely declares the winner in the caucuses as it does other nomination and general election contests nationally, took the unusual step of not declaring a winner. It noted likely irregularities in the count, coupled with the slim margin separating the candidates.[5] The most obvious problem in the count was the app, the product of Shadow Inc., a Washington DC-based firm by then the subject of deep investigations. The ultimate issue had been in the code used by the app to relay the results to the IDP. But adding to the intrigue was the revelation that Shadow was co-founded by two former Hillary Clinton campaign staffers, a fact that the IDP had not previously disclosed (Clayworth, 2020). And what's more, Shadow was tied to other high-level Democratic players, digital organizing firm ACRONYM and its related Super PAC PACRONYM, well financed by large donors (Stewart, 2020). On the one hand, this sort of nexus is the stuff of a modern extended party network (Koger et al, 2009). On the other hand, the suggestion of ties to the Clinton campaign and big donors gave legs to the story.

But the problems extended beyond – or started before – the app. Caucus procedures are complex, made even more difficult by the pressure of time that hangs over a regimented meeting and the sometimes-chaotic nature of the events. Whether on the app or on the phone, the caucus leaders under the new procedures were expected to submit 36 different figures, as well as two six-digit security verification numbers (Epstein et al., 2020). That's a big ask for a volunteer precinct chair. And even though Democrats are rules-oriented, there was little appetite at the local level to disenfranchise Democrats who wanted to participate. So minor violations of the rules could slip by at the caucuses – like attendees filling out ballots incorrectly or not turning them in – revealed only as problems in recanvasses or recounts (Rynard, 2020).

The conflict within the party added even more drama. The tension between the DNC and the IDP had been simmering for some time. After 2016, when other states bowed to DNC pressure and substituted primaries for their caucuses, Iowa held firm. And only six months had passed since the DNC had vetoed Iowa's virtual caucus plan. National chairman Perez said that he was "mad as hell" about what had happened in the Iowa count (Beavers, 2020). Nine days after the caucuses, while the counting controversy lingered, IDP chairman Troy Price resigned, apologizing and accepting responsibility for the failures in the caucuses. But he noted that the IDP worked collaboratively with the DNC and said that the IDP "is not the only party to blame" (Korecki & Montellaro, 2020).

Shortly after Price's resignation, but well before the final, final count, the *New York Times* published a scathing investigative report that found the IDP was ill-prepared for the caucuses, underscoring a series of failures – some its fault and others not – that combined to create a firestorm that may have doomed Iowa's first-in-the-nation status once and for all. "As disastrous as the 2020 Iowa caucuses have appeared to the public, the failure runs deeper and wider than has previously been known." Calling the caucuses an "epic fiasco," the paper offered a laundry list of shortcomings. It concluded that the caucuses "crumbled under the weight of technology flops, lapses in planning, failed oversight by party officials, poor training, and a breakdown in communication between paid party leaders and volunteers out in the field, who had devoted themselves for months to the nation's first nominating contest." (Epstein et al., 2020).

Foot On – and Off – the Pedal

The caucuses were just the start of a nomination season that didn't proceed as planned. Even though the first reported cases in the US of the novel coronavirus had been recorded by February 3, the precinct caucuses – like the next few contests in the nomination calendar – proceeded largely untouched by the onset of what would eventually upend politics and life around the world. But by early March, the Democratic race, which had appeared open until then, settled informally on a nominee just as the COVID-19 pandemic spread across the US. The Democrats would work their way through the remaining contests and the final stages of the nomination season under a modified calendar and terms dictated by the crisis.

More Early Contests

The 2020 Democratic race had been marked early on by extraordinary uncertainty due to the expansive field of candidates, as well as Democratic Party state and national rules changes. To a large extent, uncertainty translated into the expectation of a contest that would drag on, possibly even making it to the summer with no clear nominee. That could put the pick in the hands of national delegates and superdelegates in a brokered convention. Such an occurrence had last been seen in 1952, when both parties failed to select a candidate on their convention's first ballot (Kamarck, 2020). It was easy to picture a long contest with no single leader, candidates each with pockets of strength and weakness, and state contests apportioning delegates proportionately to keep candidacies alive. California figured heavily in the calculus, primed to be a player in 2020 like never before, since it had moved its primary from its usual June date to March 3, adding to a "Super Tuesday" collection of states which would command 1,344 delegates, about one third of the total at stake (Prokop, 2020).

The Iowa debacle was a bit of a mixed bag. Despite the drawn-out counting process and the lingering questions about the validity of the outcome, there was a clear message that Biden had flopped, feeding questions about his strength and whether other presumed pockets of support would materialize. The new system relying on two different reported outcomes had resulted in a split decision, giving both Sanders and Buttigieg hope, but depriving each of them of a clear win. But even in years with a clear winner, Iowa's role in the larger nomination process, despite the attention devoted to it, had never been all that certain. Sometimes it had helped to jump start an ultimate nomination as with Jimmy Carter and Barack Obama, and other times it had merely winnowed the field. In 2020, the inability to gain footing in Iowa certainly contributed to the withdrawal of candidates – from Gillibrand to O'Rourke to Harris (Bernstein, 2019). Still, not a single remaining candidate withdrew in the immediate aftermath of Iowa. The winnowing process would resume with a trickle after New Hampshire and then turn into a deluge after South Carolina's primary.

For different reasons, New Hampshire would be a critical test for several Democratic candidates. Sanders had scored a big win against Clinton there in 2016 and was hoping for the same. New Hampshire was especially important for Buttigieg because his prospects in the contests that followed – Nevada and South Carolina – were slim. Warren, who was in a state neighboring her own, needed to bounce back from Iowa. And Klobuchar, for her part, also needed a good performance to stay alive. New Hampshire was her best bet, with its historical affinity for middle-of-the-road moderates and the fact that the primary would be open to independents. Even better, polls showed that a sizable proportion of New Hampshire voters remained up for grabs even days before the primary (Kranish, 2020).

As for Biden, although the former vice-president had never counted on an Iowa win, observers were beginning to wonder whether he could demonstrate support anywhere, including South Carolina. The presumed support of African American voters there had been envisioned as a firewall, a last-ditch layer of protection between his candidacy and failure. But even the South Carolina firewall was harder and harder to picture, given varied poll results. Biden's lead was at times only in single-digits, and Steyer in the new year had been coming on strong, a potential wild card with deep pockets.[6] What's more, Biden was like many of the other remaining candidates, running short of cash and lacking Sanders' seemingly endless reservoir of small-dollar donors (Severns, 2020).

There was no delay in finding out the results from the New Hampshire primary. Sanders edged Buttigieg 25% to 24%, while Klobuchar carried a stunning 19% of the vote, enough to catapult her into the national limelight. At the same time, Warren got 9% of the vote, a stunning failure given that she had led the field in several national polls as late as October (Cummings, 2019). But Biden's fifth-place 8% finish, on top of the poor performance in Iowa, seemed to confirm that the vice-president was in trouble. Momentum for Sanders and Buttigieg prompted other candidates to reflect, and on New Hampshire primary night both Michael Bennet and Andrew Yang suspended their campaigns, acknowledging the reality that their chances were non-existent. Former Massachusetts governor Deval Patrick, rarely mentioned among the Democratic contenders, also called it quits. Only eight Democrats were left.

The COVID situation had worsened across the globe over the 11 days leading up to the Nevada caucuses, the next Democratic nomination contest on Saturday, February 22. But while numbers approached 78,000 cases worldwide, the vast majority were in China.[7] The outbreak was still modest in the US with just 15 total reported cases, none yet in Nevada.[8]

Nevada would offer a second 2020 test of a state party's ability to run a caucus effectively, and there was reason to be concerned. In 2016, the Nevada caucuses had been marked by the same sort of problems, maybe worse, that Iowa had suffered, including bad blood between the Clinton and Sanders camps. Like Iowa, Nevada had revamped its rules going into 2020, adopting many of the same changes as Iowa, including a proposed virtual-caucus model that the DNC also struck down (Messerly, 2019). However, Nevada had one distinct advantage over Iowa: the ability to drop its plans to use the Shadow app for counting its results, adjusting its plans to avoid its own caucus chaos. Plenty of concern, however, remained about the technology Nevada Democrats would use, including Google Forms on iPads. There was also a lack of training provided to volunteers. (Barron-Lopez, 2020)

In the end, Democrats in Nevada were spared the drama that had marked the Iowa caucuses, and they gave Sanders a resounding win, measured in both raw votes and delegate totals.[9] The state also handed Biden his first credible finish, a distant second to Sanders. Buttigieg was third, and Warren came in fourth. The Massachusetts senator had elevated her supporters' hopes when she hammered Bloomberg in the days before the contest for, among other things, his past treatment of women (Chiu, 2020). With the results from Nevada included, Sanders emerged as the front-runner, but those first three high-profile contests constituted less than 3% of the total pledged delegates that would be awarded.[10]

The South Carolina primary was the Saturday following Nevada. With 54 pledged national convention delegates up for grabs, it was the biggest haul to date and was increasingly seen as a must-win for Biden, who had a long history in South Carolina, with close ties to its Democratic infrastructure and Black leaders. The Columbia newspaper *The State* described Biden's relationship with Blacks in South Carolina as more like that of a "family member than a politician swooping in and asking for their vote" (Sele & Schechter, 2020). Biden promoted that relationship at every stop. At the same time, Sanders had built a strong organization in South Carolina since 2016 and was polling a credible second behind Biden.[11] The Sanders threat, along with billionaire Tom Steyer's decision to spend money right and left in a last-ditch effort to gain traction, worried Biden supporters. The candidate himself acknowledged that there were only two outcomes for him in South Carolina: "Win big or lose big!"

South Carolina indeed delivered Biden his first outright win of the primary season. The vice-president commanded a full 48% of the vote in what was still a seven-way contest, a 28 percentage-point margin separating him from Sanders in second place. He had won big, but it required a tremendous boost from South Carolina Congressman Jim Clyburn, the Democratic House Whip and highest-ranking Black member of Congress. Clyburn and Biden had a long-standing relationship, going back to their days as congressional colleagues. Clyburn's support of Biden had been a given, but a week out he hadn't made a formal endorsement. Then, as the congressman recounted, he attended a funeral service eight days before the primary when a constituent asked him who he would be voting for. When he told her "Joe Biden," she urged him to speak out. "[She said] I needed to hear that, and the people in this community need to hear from you."

Clyburn endorsed Biden three days before the primary, and it appeared to be transformational. Exit polls showed 47% of Democrats said that endorsement affected their vote. And the carry-over effect from Biden's South Carolina win would prove to be momentous. First, it would prompt billionaire Tom Steyer to end his campaign, bringing to a close a multi-year spending spree that started with national TV ads calling for the impeachment of President Trump, followed by his July 2019 entry into the race. Steyer spent $24 million in a final push in South Carolina, on top of the projected $200 million he spent after announcing his candidacy. After his withdrawal, Steyer vowed to spend millions more to help the Democrats unseat Trump. Second, that surge would come just three days before Super Tuesday, with its line-up of Southern state primaries plus newly-added California. Those states, like Alabama, Arkansas, North Carolina, Tennessee, Texas, and Virginia, would have large African American blocs within Democratic electorates, thought to be a plus for Biden.

But the South Carolina primary date would mark another milestone: COVID cases worldwide hit 100,000 and, according to CDC reports, there were 26 reported US cases of the virus that day.[12] That number would increase three-fold – to 81 – by Super Tuesday, just three days later.

The results of the Super Tuesday contests confirmed that the Biden momentum from South Carolina was real. He won 10 of the 15 contests that day, most by wide margins. He even held his own in California, where Sanders' organization was highly effective and broadly established, coming in second place, within eight points of the Vermont senator. Sanders had hoped to rack up delegates in California, but the Biden surge limited that haul. The AP tracking by March 9, which included the Super Tuesday results, showed that with 36% of the pledged delegates already determined, the Democratic race, which at one time boasted a field of 27 candidates, with considerable diversity on lines of gender and race, had become a two-person contest – between two white men, both in their 70s. Biden, the establishment figure, led Sanders in the pledged national delegate count, 670 to 574.

Winnowing to One

The first few days of March had witnessed a dramatic acceleration of winnowing and a remarkable degree of coalescence around Biden, with the candidate's Super Tuesday success empowered by a flurry of activity. Two days before Super Tuesday, the day after South Carolina, Mayor Pete Buttigieg ended his bid for the presidency. The next day, Minnesota Senator Amy Klobuchar suspended her campaign. And on the night before Super Tuesday, Klobuchar, Buttigieg and Beto O'Rourke would collectively endorse Biden at a rally in Dallas, taken as a message from the party's moderate middle that it was lining up behind the former vice-president. Klobuchar's words at the Dallas rally revealed the same motivation to unseat President Trump and concern with electability that had animated Iowa Democrats from the outset of the caucus contest. "If we spend the next four months dividing our party and going at each other, we will spend the next four years watching Donald Trump tear apart this country." The senator added, "We want to win big, and Joe Biden can do that" (Schneider, 2020). Bloomberg pulled out the next day, endorsing Biden. And the day after that, Elizabeth Warren announced that she was ending her campaign, though she made no endorsement. Two days after Super Tuesday, only the two front-runners and Tulsi Gabbard remained in the race. And Biden had the momentum.

The Democratic Party coalesced around Joe Biden as the nation was coming to terms with the prospect that it would experience a pandemic of extraordinary proportions. Over the week following Super Tuesday, the number of cases in the nation surged ten-fold, from fewer than 100 to close to 1,000. The next spate of contests would come on March 10, including key states Michigan and Washington, both with strong Sanders organizations. Biden won both, building on the trajectory started in South Carolina. But the course of the Democratic nomination contest – and the general election for that matter – would change in ways no one could have anticipated.

On March 13, 2020 – Friday the 13th – President Trump declared a national emergency. As the nation became familiar with the concept of "flattening the curve" and how social distancing could limit the spread of the virus, offices emptied in favor of work-from-home. Schools began transitioning to remote learning. Grocery stores saw a run on toilet paper, canned goods and hand sanitizer. And campaign politics – in the presidential nomination contest as well as the other sub-presidential nomination races that would be contested in 2020 spring and summer primaries – took a 180-degree turn. The well-laid plans and extensive training of staff and volunteers were abandoned for remote interaction and socially-distanced voter outreach efforts. Candidates cancelled in-person campaign events.

The scheduled Arizona, Florida and Illinois Democratic primaries took place on March 17 as planned, after which Gabbard withdrew. But Ohio, next on the schedule, postponed its contest, followed by a number of states – Georgia, Alaska, Hawaii, Louisiana, and Wyoming, as well as Puerto Rico. In fact, the party had put the brakes on the nomination contest in late March. April 7 was the date of the next contest – in Wisconsin, but its primary was shrouded in controversy. The state's Democratic governor tried to extend absentee voting, and then even postpone the primary, due to the virus. But Wisconsin Republicans objected and won favor with a conservative state supreme court and then the US Supreme Court. Voters would stand in long lines on primary Election Day, "forced to choose between their health and civic duty" as the global pandemic swirled around them (Herndon et al., 2020).

As it turned out, every remaining 2020 nomination contest after Wisconsin – and the general election itself – would be altered. With 63% of the primary vote, Biden logged a decisive win in Wisconsin, a state Sanders had won handily in 2016. The next day, the Vermont senator waved the white flag, effectively ceding to Biden the nomination. Biden was still short by almost 800 of the 1,991 national delegates needed for nomination. And though theoretically Sanders could still reach that majority figure with wins in the remaining contests, that prospect looked unlikely. The pandemic had infected more than 42,000 Americans, with new cases each day in the tens of thousands and total deaths approaching 15,000. COVID, Sanders acknowledged to his supporters when he withdrew, was too great a threat for him to continue. "I cannot in good conscience continue to mount a campaign that cannot win and which would interfere with the important work required of all of us in this difficult hour." The next week Sanders sealed the deal by endorsing Biden, asking "all Americans … to come together… to make certain that we defeat somebody who I believe is the most dangerous president in the modern history of this country" (Caputo & Otterbein, 2020). Sanders' endorsement of Clinton in 2016 had come only in July, just two weeks before the national convention. In 2020, Warren's endorsement of Biden followed Sanders' by two days, signaling that the progressive wing of the party had closed ranks around the presumptive establishment-backed nominee.

Crisis Politics

The US had not seen a pandemic like COVID in a century. And as hospitals filled to capacity and people died at accelerating rates, the virus became a political hot-potato. Donald Trump initially called it a hoax (Egan, 2020) and rejected public health recommendations intended to lessen its transmission

(Romano, 2020). But he quickly signed a gargantuan $3 trillion aid package intended to protect businesses and individuals. That plan came with a direct payment to households – a concept not unlike the Universal Basic Income plan Andrew Yang had touted during the Iowa caucus campaign (Albertson, 2019), though the COVID relief plan was just a one-time check, not a monthly one. Other policies like Medicare for All, front and center in the Sanders and Warren caucus campaigns, gained traction when millions of Americans lost their jobs, and along with it their health insurance. April unemployment exploded to almost 15%.[13] It didn't take all that much scrutiny to see that nomination politics – even caucus politics – were being resurrected in the COVID setting.

Then on May 25, in the midst of the pandemic, the nation exploded for a different reason. Four Minneapolis police officers, responding to a call about counterfeit currency, subdued suspect George Floyd. One White officer handcuffed the 46-year-old Black man and pinned him to the ground, using his knee on Floyd's neck. Bystander-filmed video showed Floyd saying repeatedly "I can't breathe." Floyd died in police custody, and the video went viral the next day, prompting both peaceful demonstrations and violent, night-time rioting, first in Minneapolis and then in cities across the country.

The fury prompted by Floyd's murder was widespread. So, too, was the partisan response. At issue was another in a decades-long series of murders of Black Americans by White police officers. Cries of "systemic racism" went out under the Black Lives Matter banner, and protesters voiced demands to cut funding for police departments. Joe Biden's immediate response was to voice his support for the protestors and his sympathy for George Floyd's family. At the same time, the former vice-president expressed his opposition to de-funding police (Garrison, 2020). Meanwhile, President Trump, faced with growing protests in the streets outside the White House, brought in extra federal law enforcement and ordered controversial measures to clamp down on the demonstrators. He also started voicing a "law and order" message, not unlike that of Richard Nixon in the months after the 1968 Democratic national convention in Chicago.

The shadow of past politics – and even the recent nomination contest – spread into the summer crisis in very visible ways, from the basic income-like payment to the new law and order debate. It entered in less obvious ways as well, like the ongoing tension between New York's Mayor de Blasio and the city's police union. It might as well have been a different world, but it was just one year earlier that the Police Benevolent Association (PBA) sponsored a little-noticed digital truck ad at a campaign event in Cedar Rapids, targeting Mayor and then-candidate de Blasio.[14]

A Technological Fix

There is a theory conveyed in any number of different ways, from the colloquial "necessity is the mother of invention" to the more complex notion that a crisis will not necessarily change but accelerate the course of events (Haass,

2020). The pandemic catalyzed the widespread adoption of the digital tool chests that had been developed in the pre-COVID era, and it also inspired some monumental turns to new technologies to formalize the Democratic nomination.

While the Iowa caucuses had set in motion a sequence of delegation-selection contests across states, they also fed into the next stage of Iowa's tiered system of conventions that would ultimately result in the selection of the state's national convention delegates. The caucus-night failure of technology may have dominated the February 2020 caucus narrative, but technology came to the rescue for Democrats in the later stages of the process. It helped Iowa Democrats formalize their picks, aided by one of the post-2016 reforms that turned out to be a bit of a silver lining.

Those delegates selected at the precinct caucuses were scheduled to convene in county conventions across the state on Saturday, March 21, less than seven weeks after the caucuses. On that infamous Friday March 13, the state party announced that it would be postponing the county conventions because of COVID. The conventions were moved to April in a remote format with voting – online, phone or mail – extending over a nine-day period. This foray into remote voting was a significant development in the party's delegate-selection process, just nine months after the DNC had nixed the IDP's plans for virtual caucuses due to what it saw as a security threat of the remote world.

In the past, county conventions could be hotly contested affairs, filled with the same sort of politicking that marked the precinct caucuses. One of the rules changes intended to cut down on insider control – and gamesmanship – was to lock in the delegates chosen in the precincts. This meant that the distribution of delegates who would move on after the county conventions was, in fact, largely predetermined by the precinct caucus outcomes. This provision, in turn, eliminated much of the "delegate chase" and potential for maneuvering at the conventions. In short, a much more circumscribed county convention seemed tailor-made for a pandemic-racked world.

Iowa Democrats also shifted to remote formats for both the district conventions at the end of May and the state conventions at the beginning of June. Long before those conventions, the field had already winnowed to just Biden, with his competitors voicing support for the presumptive nominee. The distribution of pledged national delegates in Iowa selected in the district and the state conventions looked different than both aggregate raw votes from the caucuses and the projected delegate equivalents. In total, 20 of the state's pledged delegates went to Biden, 12 to Buttigieg, 9 to Sanders, 5 to Warren, and 1 to Klobuchar.[15] But there was no mischief going on, just the ability of delegates whose candidates had withdrawn to shift their candidate support.

As those results were announced, it was clear that strategic decisions made months earlier had impacted the caucus outcomes, no matter the impact of failed technology. Pete Buttigieg had made significant investments in time and talent in rural and suburban precincts, and they paid off for him on caucus night. He was viable in more precincts than other candidates, lost relatively little support than others during the realignment phase, and won 21 of the so-called "flip" counties that had voted for Obama and then Trump. Buttigieg, however, did not fare well in the urban areas with a more diverse electorate (Rodriguez, 2020). Bernie Sanders and his time-tested Iowa team came close to Buttigieg in delegates. Where he won, Sanders tended to win with big margins in places with lots of delegates – urban counties like Johnson, Story, Black Hawk, Linn, and Woodbury.

By the time Iowa had selected its national convention delegates, the US had logged more than two million COVID cases and 115,000 deaths. Early pandemic projections that the spread would slow in warm weather had not been borne out, and the reality began to sink in that the battle with the disease might extend beyond the summer. The party's national convention was scheduled for mid-July in Milwaukee. But by early April, it was clear that a monumental gathering of tens of thousands of people – not just the delegates, but press, activists, and convention organizers – in an enclosed space would spell disaster. After first postponing the national convention, the party then rescheduled it to August and turned to a remote format. Not one to miss a chance to slam the caucuses, national Chairman Perez made news in Iowa on the first day of the convention, when he said that he would push for reform of the next cycle's nomination process, laying down the gauntlet with this statement: "I think by 2024 we ought to have everyone being a primary state." (Murphy, 2020).

Iowa Democrats saw a familiar face at the convention when former vice-president Biden finally picked his running mate: Kamala Harris, the California senator who had built a devoted Iowa team, confronted candidate Biden in the first debate, and boasted a RAYGUN t-shirt about moving to Iowa. Harris was well known to Iowa Democrats. The *Des Moines Register's* "Candidate Tracker" found that she had held 87 events in the state between October 2018 and her December 2019 withdrawal. She became the first woman of color on a major party presidential ticket.

The convention itself went smoothly under the terms set by the pandemic, with the national party producing a reasonable approximation of a traditional in-person convention – maybe even a little more entertaining for an at-home audience. When each state delegation patched in to announce its balloting in the presidential contest on night three of convention, former Democratic Governor Tom Vilsack and his wife Christie delivered the state party's vote from a cornfield. Initially planning to plug biofuels, one of those topics dear to the state, Vilsack changed direction after the state was pummeled in August by high winds in a storm known as "derecho." Hard-hit communities across the state were still in a clean-up mode, prompting a less-economic message during the Vilsacks' 20-second spotlight during the roll call of states (Coltrain, 2020b). Still, the convention did what it was meant to do. It nominated Joe Biden and sent him on to the general election as the party's chosen candidate (Glauber et al., 2020).

Iowa national convention delegates had cast 38 votes for Biden and 11 for Sanders. While 2020 Iowa rules locked in the caucus outcomes at subsequent stages in the Iowa contest, national party rules permitted delegates to change their candidate support at the national convention. The delegates may be "pledged" to a candidate, but not necessarily legally bound to support. Sanders' delegates stuck with the candidate, while delegates pledged to the others all cast ballots for Biden. Scott Brennan on Iowa's state central committee cast no vote as an unpledged delegate in 2020, since that new 2020 rule had superdelegates voting only if no candidate received a majority on the first ballot. Altogether, Biden won a first-ballot majority with 3,558 of the 4,714 national convention delegates,[16] a decidedly ordinary ending to a cycle that had been marked by extraordinary circumstances. The outcome, despite the bumpy road there, seemed consistent with what *The Party Decides* (Cohen et al., 2008) might have predicted: Biden, the establishment figure and consummate party insider, got the nod.

The pandemic that dictated new terms of life in the US – including masks and social distancing – left the political camps divided over their merits. Across the nation, Democratic campaigns took dramatic precautions to slow the spread of the virus. Biden drastically limited his contact with voters – in effect, campaigning in a "bubble." (Weigel, 2020) But just as technology had permitted the state and national parties to wrap up the formal nomination process, tools of campaigning, many refined in the months leading up to the caucuses, allowed the campaigns to campaign in a pandemic (Trish, 2020). The same relational organizing approach, with a heavy focus on texting and outreach starting with friends and family, took on added value when door-to-door canvassing ceased to be an option. Even more, relational organizing techniques – which appear to the voter to be personalized in a genuine way – seemed well-suited to an era in which wide segments of the American population struggled under the heavy weight of public health and financial crises (Weigel, 2020).

For Democrats, the fall campaign became an exercise in rapid deployment of new and refined technologies. The cyclical world of campaign politics has always been amenable to learning from past contests, but the usual two- or four-year lag gave way in 2020 to almost a real-time adoption and refinement. Mobilize, the go-to event platform of the left that had been widely adopted for the nomination, shifted to support virtual, remote events when the pandemic hit. And by the fall, Mobilize had added a new feature, one which could automatically invite engaged volunteers to host their own virtual event for a campaign (Miller, 2020). For those activities with no obvious digital solution, like registering voters in many states, the fix was a version of the world Americans had grown to know well under the pandemic. Temperature checks were required for volunteers and elaborate low-contact procedures developed, the very same protocols and technologies that would be used widely on Election Day (Mervosh & Smith, 2020).

Notes

1. *Wall Street Journal* live caucus coverage: www.wsj.com/livecoverage/2020-election-democratic-iowa-caucuses/card/IXUTaqjEHiTmFi3PJ2IA
2. Sanders release embedded in Stone (2020).
3. The satellite SDE calculations were sensitive to 2020 turnout in a way that the regular precinct caucuses weren't. Sanders cleaned up there (Rakich, 2020), reportedly alone among the candidates in targeting the satellite caucuses (Grim, 2020). But it wasn't enough to overtake Buttigieg in the tight SDE count.
4. www.youtube.com/watch?v=m5fl7i5n2-0
5. "AP Explains: Why there isn't a winner of Iowa's Dem caucuses": https://apnews.com/article/77484bf5d16361ce51088ad191c864ce
6. *Real Clear Politics* South Carolina Polling Data: www.realclearpolitics.com/epolls/2020/president/sc/south_carolina_democratic_presidential_primary-6824.html#polls
7. World Health Organization February 2020 COVID Situation Report: www.who.int/docs/default-source/coronaviruse/situation-reports/20200222-sitrep-33-covid-19.pdf?sfvrsn=c9585c8f_4
8. CDC COVID Tracker: https://covid.cdc.gov/covid-data-tracker/#trends_totalandratecases
9. Nevada results at www.reviewjournal.com/nevada-caucus-results-2020/
10. *AP Delegate Tracker*: https://interactives.ap.org/delegate-tracker/
11. *Real Clear Politics* South Carolina Polling Data: www.realclearpolitics.com/epolls/2020/president/sc/south_carolina_democratic_presidential_primary-6824.html#polls
12. CDC COVID Data Tracker: https://covid.cdc.gov/covid-data-tracker/#trends_totalandratecase
13. US Bureau of Labor Statistics April 2020 Unemployment Report. www.bls.gov/opub/ted/2020/unemployment-rate-rises-to-record-high-14-point-7-percent-in-april-2020.htm#:~:text=Unemployment%20rate%20rises%20to%20record%20high%2014.7%20percent%20in%20April%202020&text=The%20unemployment%20rate%20in%20April,available%20back%20to%20January%201948
14. The union, which hadn't endorsed a presidential candidate in decades, would eventually endorse President Trump in the general election. (www.nytimes.com/2020/09/14/nyregion/ny-police-unions-racial-disparity-trump.html)
15. IDP Release "Iowa Democratic Party Announces Delegation to National Convention" (https://iowademocrats.org/iowa-democratic-party-announces-delegation-national-convention/)
16. Democratic presidential state-by-state roll call results: https://ballotpedia.org/Democratic_National_Convention,_2020

References

Albertson, Teresa Kay. 2019. "Meet the Iowa Falls family Andrew Yang is pledging to give $1,000 a month for the next 12 months." *The Des Moines Register* June 11 (www.desmoinesregister.com/story/news/elections/presidential/caucus/2019/06/11/2020-andrew-yang-universal-basic-income-iowa-family-kyle-pam-christiansen-president-iowa-caucus/1413666001/).

Barron-Lopez, Laura. 2020. "'A complete disaster.' Fears grow over potential Nevada caucus malfunction." *Politico* February 16 (www.politico.com/news/2020/02/16/nevada-avoid-iowa-caucus-mess-115437).

Beavers, David. 2020. "DNC Chairman: we can't force Iowa to change." *Politico* February 9 (www.politico.com/news/2020/02/09/iowa-caucuses-dnc-chairman-perez-112748).

Becker, Amanda. 2020. "Iowa Democratic presidential caucus results delayed over 'quality checks.'" *Reuters* February 3 (www.reuters.com/article/us-usa-election-delay/iowa-democratic-presidential-caucus-results-delayed-over-quality-checks-idUSKBN1ZY0C0).

Bernstein, Jonathan. 2019. "Kamala Harris's withdrawal shows that winnowing works." *Bloomberg* December 4 (www.bloombergquint.com/gadfly/kamala-harris-withdrawal-shows-that-winnowing-works).

Caputo, Marc and Holly Otterbein. 2020. "Bernie makes it official: It's Biden or bust." *Politico* April 13 (www.politico.com/news/2020/04/13/sanders-endorses-biden-183961).

Chiu, Allyson. 2020. "Titanic, meet iceberg. Warren's devastating takedown of Bloomberg goes viral." *The Washington Post* February 20 (www.washingtonpost.com/nation/2020/02/20/bloomberg-warren-debate/).

Clayworth, Jason. 2020. "Clinton campaign veterans linked with app that contributed to caucus chaos." *The Des Moines Register* February 4 (www.desmoinesregister.com/story/news/elections/presidential/caucus/2020/02/04/iowa-caucus-app-problems-shadow-inc-clinton-campaign/4653989002).

Cohen, Martin, David Karol, Hans Noel and John Zaller. 2008. *The Party Decides: Presidential Nominations Before and After Reform*. Chicago: University of Chicago Press.

Coltrain, Nick. 2020a." "Bernie Sanders trails in delegates but claims a measure of victory, with most precincts tallied." *The Des Moines Register* February 4 (www.desmoinesregister.com/story/news/elections/presidential/caucus/2020/02/04/bernie-sanders-disappointed-iowa-democrats-havent-released-caucus-results/4656451002/).

Coltrain, Nick. 2020b. "An Iowa cornfield for Democratic convention roll call votes for Joe Biden, Bernie Sanders? Of course!" *The Des Moines Register* August 19 (www.desmoinesregister.com/story/news/politics/2020/08/19/tom-vilsack-iowa-dnc-biden-sanders-votes-highlight-derecho-storm-damage/3400650001/).

Cummings, William. 2019. "Elizabeth Warren jumps to 7-point lead over Joe Biden in latest Quinnipiac poll." *USA Today* October 24 (www.usatoday.com/story/news/politics/elections/2019/10/24/elizabeth-warren-leads-joe-biden-quinnipiac-poll/4082017002).

Edelman, Gilad. 2020. "The Warren is gone – but its tech may live on." *Wired* March 2 (www.wired.com/story/elizabeth-warren-campaign-open-source-tech/).

Egan, Lauren. 2020. "Trump calls coronavirus Democrats 'new hoax.'" *NBC News* February 28 (www.nbcnews.com/politics/donald-trump/trump-calls-coronavirus-democrats-new-hoax-n1145721).

Ember, Sydney and Reid Epstein. 2020. "The 1,600 volunteers who were supposed to make the Iowa caucuses run smoothly." *The New York Times* February 6 (www.nytimes.com/2020/02/04/us/politics/iowa-caucus-problems.html).

Epstein, Reid, Sydney Ember, Trip Gabriel and Mike Baker. 2020. "How the Iowa caucuses became an epic fiasco for Democrats." *The New York Times* February 9 (www.nytimes.com/2020/02/09/us/politics/iowa-democratic-caucuses.html).

Garrison, Joey. 2020. "Joe Biden comes out against 'defund the police' push amid mounting attacks from Trump after George Floyd protests." *USA Today* June 8 (www.usatoday.com/story/news/politics/elections/2020/06/08/joe-biden-against-defund-police-push-after-death-george-floyd/5319717002/).

Glauber, Bill, Patrick Marley, Mary Spicuza and Alison Dirr. 2020. "'With bravery. With unwavering faith.' Jill Biden lauds husband Joe Biden as he claims Democratic presidential nomination." *Milwaukee Journal Sentinel* August 18 (www.jsonline.com/story/news/politics/elections/2020/08/18/dnc-joe-biden-claims-democratic-nomination-virtual-convention/3394305001).

Graham, David A. 2020. "Why the Iowa caucus birthed a thousand conspiracy theories." *The Atlantic* February 4 (www.theatlantic.com/ideas/archive/2020/02/iowa-caucus-conspiracy-theories/606055/).

Grim, Ryan. 2020. "Nontraditional voters at Iowa satellite caucuses could tip the balance to Bernie Sanders." *The Intercept* February 5 (https://theintercept.com/2020/02/05/bernie-sanders-iowa-satelllite-caucuses/).

Haass, Richard. 2020. "The Pandemic will accelerate history rather than reshape it." *Foreign Affairs* April 7 (www.foreignaffairs.com/articles/united-states/2020-04-07/pandemic-will-accelerate-history-rather-reshape-it).

Herndon, Astead W., Nick Corasaniti, Stephanie Saul and Reid Epstein. 2020. "Voters forced to choose between their health and their civic duty." *The New York Times* April 7 (www.nytimes.com/2020/04/07/us/politics/wisconsin-primary-election.html).

Kamarck, Elaine. 2020. "What is a brokered convention? What is a contested convention?" *Policy 2020 Brookings* February 22 (www.brookings.edu/policy2020/votervital/what-is-a-brokered-convention-what-is-a-contested-convention/).

Koger, Gregory, Seth Masket, and Hans Noel. 2009. "Partisan webs: information exchange and party networks." *British Journal of Political Science* 39(July): 633–653.

Korecki, Natasha and Zach Montellaro. 2020. "Iowa Democratic Party chairman resigns over caucus debacle." *Politico* February 12 (www.politico.com/news/2020/02/12/iowa-democratic-party-chairman-resigns-over-caucus-debacle-114689).

Kranish, Michael. 2020. "Undecided New Hampshire prepares for key first primary role after Iowa caucuses." *The Washington Post* February 3 (www.washingtonpost.com/politics/undecided-new-hampshire-prepares-for-key-first-primary-role-after-iowa-caucuses/2020/02/03/abad7c68-45f4-11ea-8124-0ca81effcdfb_story.html).

Lapowsky, Issie. 2016. "Clinton camp gives the Iowa caucus a silicon valley upgrade." *Wired* January 31 (www.wired.com/2016/01/clinton-camp-gives-the-iowa-caucus-a-silicon-valley-upgrade/).

Mervosh, Sarah and Mitch Smith. 2020. "The coronavirus, raging in battleground states, looms over election day." *The New York Times* November 3 (www.nytimes.com/2020/11/03/us/coronavirus-cases-election-day.html).

Messerly, Megan. 2019. "After bitter 2016 cycle, Nevada Democrats overhaul caucus process to build a bigger tent." *The Nevada Independent* March 19 (https://thenevadaindependent.com/article/after-bitter-2016-cycle-nevada-democrats-overhaul-caucus-process-to-build-a-bigger-tent).

Miller, Sean J. 2020. "Democratic organizing platform adds automation while empowering volunteers." *Campaigns and Elections* September 17 (www.campaignsandelections.com/campaign-insider/democratic-organizing-platform-adds-automation-while-empowering-volunteers).

Murphy, Erin. 2020. "Iowa caucuses again come under fire." *The Cedar Rapids Gazette* August 18 (www.thegazette.com/subject/news/government/democratic-convention-iowa-caucuses-20200818).

Pager, Tyler and Jennifer Epstein. 2020. "Trump fans flooded Iowa caucus hotline, Democrats say." *Bloomberg* February 5 (www.bloomberg.com/news/articles/2020-02-06/trump-fans-flooded-iowa-caucus-hotline-top-democrat-says).

Prokop, Andrew. 2020. "Super Tuesday, explained." *Vox* March 3 (www.vox.com/2020/3/2/21142609/super-tuesday-2020-polls-delegates-contested-convention).

Rakich, Nathaniel. 2020. "Satellite caucuses give a surprise boost to Sanders in Iowa." *FiveThirtyEight* February 6 (https://fivethirtyeight.com/features/satellite-caucuses-give-a-surprise-boost-to-sanders-in-iowa/).

Richardson, Ian. 2020. "Iowa caucus turnout surpassed 2016 but fell far short of 2008 record" *The Des Moines Register* February 7 (www.desmoinesregister.com/story/news/elections/presidential/caucus/2020/02/07/election-2020-democratic-iowa-caucuses-turnout-eclipsed-2016-fell-short-2008/4691004002/).

Rodriguez, Barbara. 2020. "How Pete Buttigieg climbed to the top (for now) in Iowa: he showed strength across Iowa counties." *The Des Moines Register* December 13 (www.desmoinesregister.com/story/news/elections/presidential/caucus/2020/02/13/iowa-caucuses-pete-buttigieg-performed-well-across-iowa-counties-alignment-process-delegates/4729180002/)

Romano, Aja. 2020. "A new investigation reveals Trump ignored experts on COVID-19 for months." *Vox* April 12 (www.vox.com/2020/4/12/21218305/trump-ignored-coronavirus-warnings).

Rynard, Pat. 2020. "Final Iowa caucus results: Pete Buttigieg wins!" *Iowa Starting Line* February 27 (https://iowastartingline.com/2020/02/27/final-iowa-caucus-results-pete-buttigieg-wins/).

Schneider, Gabe. 2020. "Klobuchar endorses Joe Biden for president." *MinnPost* March 3 (www.minnpost.com/national/2020/03/klobuchar-endorses-joe-biden-for-president).

Sele, Jamie and Maayan Schechter. 2020. "Joe Biden's firewall held in South Carolina. Here's how he won." *The State* March 1 (www.thestate.com/news/politics-government/election/article240751596.htm).

Severns, Maggie. 2020. "Biden gets a late burst of cash at a key moment." *Politico* February 29 (www.politico.com/news/2020/02/29/biden-donors-2020-118280).

Stewart, Emily. 2020. "Acronym, the dark money group behind the Iowa caucuses app meltdown, explained." *Vox* February 8 (www.vox.com/recode/2020/2/5/21123009/acronym-tara-mcgowan-shadow-app-iowa-caucus-results).

Stieb, Matt, Benjamin Hart and Chas Danner. 2020. "Iowa results 2020: live updates." *New York Magazine* February 10 (https://nymag.com/intelligencer/2020/02/iowa-results-2020-live-updates.htm).

Stone, Zach. 2020. "Sanders campaign releases internal caucus results." *News 7 KWWL* November 4 (https://kwwl.com/2020/02/04/sanders-campaign-releases-internal-caucus-results/).

Trish, Barbara. 2020. "From recording videos in a closet to Zoom meditating, 2020's political campaigns adjust to the pandemic." *The Conversation* October 7 (https://theconversation.com/from-recording-videos-in-a-closet-to-zoom-meditating-2020s-political-campaigns-adjust-to-the-pandemic-145788).

Watson, Kathryn and Stefan Becket. 2020. "Buttigieg and Sanders lead in first Iowa caucus results." *CBS News* February 4 (www.cbsnews.com/live-updates/pete-buttigieg-bernie-sanders-lead-iowa-caucuses-updates-today-2020-02-06/).

Weigel, David. 2020. "Goodbye, basement campaign. Hello, bubble campaign." *The Washington Post* September 10 (www.washingtonpost.com/politics/2020/09/10/trailer-goodbye-basement-campaign-hello-bubble-campaign/).

11 The Shadow of 2020

Shortly after Sanders' withdrawal in April 2020, which assured Biden's nomination, the *New York Times* ran a piece titled "Iowa Was Meaningless." *Times* reporter Reid Epstein, who had logged time in the state covering the caucuses, observed that there was a disconnect between what happened in Iowa and the outcome of the 2020 nomination race. "The things that mattered in Iowa – excitement, organization, money spent on TV ads, crowd sizes for town hall meetings – had next to no bearing on who eventually won the Democratic presidential nomination" (Epstein, 2020).

It's a bold claim, but it has some logic, given that the Democratic contest forged ahead regardless of the delayed caucus results. Plus, the "gut punch" that Biden took in Iowa – or for that matter in New Hampshire – didn't ultimately derail his presidential aspirations. Still, it's not breaking news that Iowa doesn't crown the winner. And for that matter, it's not clear to what extent the factors Epstein cited even matter for *Iowa* outcomes. Consider Elizabeth Warren, who built a juggernaut of an organization but finished third in Iowa. Or Tom Steyer, who if TV ad spending had done the trick would have cleaned up. Caucuses – like elections more generally – are complex phenomena with outcomes driven by a combination of factors that are hard to pinpoint.

The impact of the caucuses on the nomination is also tough to determine. Arguably, Sanders' lead in the Iowa raw vote, despite the weeks required to validate, contributed to the broader message that his progressive ideas resonated widely. Even though Biden was the presumptive nominee by early April 2020, Democrats couldn't ignore Sanders' supporters or delegates. The "Unity Task Forces" appointed by Biden were the summer 2020 equivalents of the 2019 Unity Commission. Just as the Commission, with progressive and establishment voices, had hammered out the rules for the 2020 nomination contest, the task forces brought Sanders and Biden voices together to talk policy, a sign of Sanders' continued strength. As for Buttigieg, who shared the top spot in the caucus results and performed well in New Hampshire, Iowa was a critical element in his ascension to the national stage. He became a prominent, respected voice of the party, eventually a member of President Biden's cabinet.

The future of the caucuses, however, doesn't hang much on whether or not they matter. As the calendar turned to 2021, with a pandemic still waging and a new administration just taking shape, Iowans – Democratic and Republican – as well as their national parties turned their gaze to 2024. At the time, the role of the Iowa caucuses – or even *whether* there would be Iowa caucuses – was unclear. Change, though, seemed highly likely. Iowa Democrats may have stumbled into a privileged and prominent position after 1968, but after 2020 they seemed to be tumbling out of it.

The Democratic Party was no stranger to internal party discord, whether factional or structural. As Democrats began looking to 2024, the caucus bubble appeared squeezed between both, the lingering progressive vs. establishment divide and an ongoing standoff between the IDP and DNC. A November 2020 IDP internal audit of the caucuses assigned blame to both the state and the national parties for the counting problems, a report that did little to smooth the rough edges marking the IDP/DNC relationship.[1]

Moving forward, both the national and the state Democratic parties had notable challenges to resolve. For all its flaws, giving Iowa a prominent role in the nomination process still offered a point of access to a nationwide audience for those without the traditional resources to compete nationally. Proposals for a single national Democratic primary seemed likely to shut out the candidates without deep pockets. Some sort of a hybrid system, like the one described by Redlawsk et al. (2011, pp. 248–250), seemed increasingly attractive. That plan would retain a role for a limited number of states that would test the field of candidates and provide cues to inform decisions made by voters in a broader national primary.

Iowa Democrats had a hefty challenge to resolve as well. Even though the caucuses had engaged small percentages of Iowans, they were woven into the fabric of the state and into state code. Any move away from the caucus model would require deft maneuvering, since the fate of Iowa Democratic caucuses is to some extent in the hands of Iowa Republicans. In 2021, the GOP held the governor's office and controlled both chambers of the legislature. Still, it was hard to imagine how Democrats could retain the caucus model as it stood without addressing elements flagged as undemocratic. At a minimum, the Democrats' COVID-era adjustments, including pivoting to remote technology, demonstrated their ability to evolve and improve accessibility.

One thing that united Iowa Democrats with the national party was their shared rural problem. Donald Trump carried rural America by a significant margin in 2020, just as he did in 2016. In Iowa Trump won resoundingly in both elections, dominating in all but eight of the state's counties in 2020. Whether a function of differences over social issues, agriculture, or civil rights, the divide between small town and big city had never been bigger. Clearly, the caucus system – despite the disproportionate voice it gave to rural precincts in Iowa and the injection of rural issues into the national process – did not resolve the Democrats' small-town woes.

The 2020 election brought heavy losses for Iowa Democrats in the US House and Senate contests as well as in the state legislature. Pat Rynard (2021), founder of the left-leaning news outlet *Iowa Starting Line*, wrote about the "demoralizing" political situation in the state, a feeling that seemed to capture the view of many Iowa Democrats. After the losses in 2016, Democrats seemed set to compete, and then were buoyed by some key victories in the 2018 midterm. While they took solace in the Biden November 2020 win and the party's eventual US Senate majority, the local losses in Iowa weighed heavily.

It's impossible to know how much of the 2020 general election hit was attributable to COVID and the pandemic-era campaigning limits that were honored by Democrats to a greater extent than Republicans. Democratic campaigns did embrace new tools like P2P texting; yet it's possible that the absence of candidate events, inspirational surrogates, as well as traditional organizing protocols ultimately hurt the party.

The caucus system – with its heavy demands on person-to-person relationships – incentivized campaigns to staff up in ways that brought campaign organizers and activists together. A version of this strategy is found in primary states, and even to some extent in general election campaigns. And while it may or may not be a blueprint for success, it does make an important contribution to campaigns and to the party. Staff on the ground – whether deployed to Iowa, New Hampshire, or elsewhere – get to see first-hand life in places that may well be unfamiliar to them. They get a feel for what politics, and in particular candidates, can mean to individuals. And they learn what those local voters and activists want from the party and from government. Those campaign staffers leave with a better understanding of democracy and the democratic process.

National staff may swing into the state for an occasional event or to staff the candidate. Strategists may spend their days modeling data and the comms departments cultivating press relationships. But it's the organizers who are on the ground, seeing up-close what life is like for average voters, urban or rural, wealthy or poor. And when the organizer leaves, whether for a next campaign, a new career or a stint on unemployment, she takes with her a set of skills, a network of colleagues and friends, and a better understanding of a place and a people. At the same time, the relationships Iowans build with those campaign staffers can extend far into the future, perhaps paving the way for average people to achieve their political goals.

This may be a romanticized view of the merits of the caucuses. It doesn't only apply in Iowa; a version of it could play out in any number of states. But as the political parties weigh their options for the future of presidential nomination politics, they should toss into the mix the value that comes from those working for campaigns understanding voters better, not just from the data they collect but from the personal interactions they share.

If 2020 turns out to have been the end of the road for the caucuses, then the greatest loss for Iowa may not be its role in the selection of a presidential nominee but the luxury of partnering with enthusiastic young campaign workers who show up to work for a candidate or cause, but who contribute to the civic life of the state while there.

Note

1 "Internal Review Report for the Iowa Democratic Party: 2020 Iowa Caucuses," dated November 10, 2020.

References

Epstein, Reid J. 2020. "Iowa was meaningless." *The New York Times* April 9 (www.nytimes.com/2020/04/09/us/poitics/iowa-caucuses-meaning.html).

Redlawsk, David P., Caroline J. Tolbert, and Todd Donovan. 2011. *Why Iowa?* Chicago: University of Chicago Press.

Rynard, Pat. 2021. Starting line on hiatus as we consider future. Iowa Staring Line January 4 (https://iowastartingline.com/2021/01/04/starting-line-on-hiatus-as-we-consider-future/).

Index

Act Blue 67
Affordable Care Act 80, 107; *see also* Obamacare
Alaska 154
Albright, Madeline 136
Analyst Institute 105
Appleman, Eric 30n8
Arizona 154

Bagniewski, Sean 44–45, 97
Beckwith-Ferguson, Taylor 140
Belin, Laura 129
Bender, Richard 133, 141n4
Bennet, Michael 48, 57, 130, 151
"Bernie Bros" 44
Biden, Beau 19
Biden, Joe 19–20, 39, 79–80, 84, 100, 123, 146, 150–154, 156, 158
Biden, Hunter 79
Birkestrand, Carl 28, 89
Bleeding Heartland, The 45n6, 129
Bloomberg, Michael 48, 122–123, 153
Booker, Cory 1–2, 21–22, 33, 40, 44, 48, 73, 95, 108–109, 110n10, 123, 124n2
Bradley, Bill 43
Brennan, Scott 33, 37, 88, 158
Brown, Sherrod 44
Bullock, Steve 48
Buttigieg, Pete 20–21, 39, 48, 59, 68, 71, 100, 107, 117, 123, 130, 136, 139, 146–148, 151, 153, 156–157

California 122, 131, 150, 152–153
Call for Convention 34
Campaign Workers Guild (CWG) 119
Carnes, Greta 68, 105
Carpenter, Leslie 24, 71–73, 139
Carter, Jimmy 7–8, 20, 83, 131, 150
Castro, Julián 26, 89, 95, 107, 123

caucuses: basics of 93–94; as "bubble" 11, 22–27; criticism of 9–11; history of 6–9; new rules for 95–96; organizing 81–82; realignments in 94–95, 133; results 144–149; satellite 134; students 102; turnout in 23; virtual 37–38, 62n1, 87–89, 134, 141n5, 141n7, 149, 151, 156
CCI *see* Citizens for Community Improvement (CCI)
Cedar Rapids Gazette 107, 128
China 49, 140
Citizens for Community Improvement (CCI) 106–107
Clemmons, Casey 61, 74–75, 95–96
climate change 49–51, 53; *see also* environmentalism
Clinton, Bill 8, 19, 108, 136
Clinton, Hillary 83; in 2008 primary 8; 2016 loss by 2; in 2016 primary 9–10, 36; surrogates and 135–136; Sanders and 9, 36, 44; Shadow, Inc. and 148
Cloud, Melanie 52
Clyburn, Jim 152
Coe College 108
Colbert, Steven 19
commit-to-caucus card 118
contributions 58, 62n14, 66, 85–86, 90n9, 120; *see also* "unique donors"
convention(s): 1952 Democratic 150; 1952 Republican 150; 1968 Democratic 4–5, 82, 155; 1972 Democratic 6; 1984 Democratic 90n6; 2020 Democratic 34, 83, 90n6, 156; county 45n6, 80, 89n1, 93–94, 139, 156; first Democratic 3–4
Cook, Andrew 140
Corn Feed 59–60
COVID-19 pandemic 149, 151, 153–158, 166

Cruz, Ted 9, 61, 144
Cullen, Art 101
CWG *see* Campaign Workers Guild (CWG)

D'Alessandro, Pete 13
Daley, Richard J. 5
data 54–55, 86–87, 97–106, 120, 166; *see also* VAN; voter files
Dean, Howard 67, 71, 87
debates 13, 65–67, 74, 75n1, 95, 121, 123, 157
de Blasio, Bill 39, 48, 57, 60, 62n13, 155
DeJear, Deidre 27
Delaney, John 1, 18–19, 57, 119
delegate apportionment 34–35, 83–84, 88, 89n2, 94, 150, 156; *see also* state delegate equivalents (SDEs); superdelegates
Demissie, Addisu 109
Democratic National Committee (DNC) 87–89; 2016 primary and 10; 2020 caucus results and 149; 2020 primary and 11, 34, 36, 83, 134; debates and 65–66, 74, 95; Iowa Democratic Party and 149, 156, 165; Rule 10A and 7; rule changes and 34; Sanders and 10; Unity Reform Commission 36–37, 83, 88; VAN and 55
Democratic Party: 2016 primary 9; in 2018 midterms 12; data technology and 86–89; *see also* convention; Democratic National Committee (DNC); Iowa Democratic Party (IDP); primaries
Dillon, Lauren 27
Des Moines Register 12, 17, 50, 128; *see also* Iowa Poll
distributed organizing 71, 120
door-to-door canvases 98–100, 110n7
Drake, Marge 69
Draper, Mike 117
Dvorsky, Sue 122

Eadon, Derek 11, 14n10, 37
Edwards, John 106
Electoral College 3
Ember, Sydney 129
Emily's List 41
endorsements 26, 84–85, 90n8, 123, 152–154
environmentalism 12, 51, 107; *see also* climate change
Epstein, Reid 164
Ernst, Joni 15n15
Esler, Marc 101
Exley, Zack 71

Flores, Jim 53, 139–140
Florida 154
Floyd, George 155
Ford, Gerald 7, 14n4
Franken, Al 74
"Friendship 2020" 44–45, 61, 95
fundraising 30n13, 55, 58–59, 66–67, 76n3, 85, 95, 113, 130; *see also* contributions; "unique donors"

Gabbard, Tulsi 153–154
"Gang of Four" 12–13
Ganz, Marshall 67
Geiken, Kevin 81–82, 90n5
Georgia (Republic of) 140
Georgia (state) 154
Get Out the Caucus (GOTC) 118, 135
Gillibrand, Kirsten 33–34, 61, 69, 74–75, 95, 118, 122, 150
Gingrich, Newt 65
Gore, Al 43
Gross, Mitch 52
ground game 96–97, 123, 135

hacking 37–38, 88
Hall, Chris 106, 114
Hamblin, Jacob 1, 11, 21–22, 24–25, 40, 73–74, 80, 140
Harkin, Tom 55, 106, 133
Harris, Kamala 42, 95, 110n10, 117, 121–123, 139, 157
Hart, Quentin 57, 136
Hart, Thomas 52
Hawaii 154
health care 49–51, 80, 107
Heller, Dave 116
Hickenlooper, John 58, 74, 123
Hochschild, Arlie 121
Holland, Bill 51
housing, supporter 51–53, 75, 95
Howard, Dick 46n12
Humphrey, Hubert 5–6
Hustle 70, 76n6

IBEW *see* International Brotherhood of Electrical Workers (IBEW)
IDP *see* Iowa Democratic Party (IDP)
Illinois 154
Inslee, Jay, 59, 74
International Brotherhood of Electrical Workers (IBEW) 119
Iowa Democratic Party (IDP) 6, 10–11, 33–35, 37–38, 55–56, 80, 88–89, 94, 107, 113, 131, 134, 137, 141, 144–149, 156, 165

170   Index

Iowa Poll 12, 15n12, 128, 137–138
Iowa Starting Line 129, 166

Jackson, Andrew 113
Jacobs, Jennifer 128
Jefferson, Thomas 113
Jefferson-Jackson Dinner (JJ) 43–44, 113
Johanssen, Monica 61
Johnson, Alfred 87
Johnson, Lyndon 4
Johnson County, Iowa 21–22, 100

Kamarck, Elaine 90n6
Kavanaugh, Brett 12
Kennedy, John F. 4
Kennedy, Robert F. 4
King, Martin Luther, Jr. 4
Klapper, Matt 73–74
Klobuchar, Amy 20, 27, 57–58, 68, 110n10, 123, 130, 146–147, 151, 153, 156
Koppess, Jennifer 40, 108–109
Kucharski, Zack 107, 128

labor 56–57, 82, 85, 119
Lewis, John 136
LGBTQ Forum 107–108
Liberty and Justice Celebration (LJ) 113–114
Link, Jeff 19, 41
LJ *see* Liberty and Justice Celebration (LJ)
Louisiana 8, 154

Malcom Auditorium 1, 3, 27–29, 110n15, 136, 140
Makarechi, Carlo 24, 71, 139, 142n9
McCarthy, Eugene 5
McClure, Mandy 144
McFarling, Tara 116–117
McGovern, George 7, 83
McGovern-Fraser Commission 5, 83
McGowan, Tara 76n4
McGuire, Andy 10
Medicare for All 80, 155
Mehlenbacher, Kelly 121
Meskwaki Pow Wow 60–61
Messem, Wayne 55
Meyer, Kurt 139
Minnesota 23, 107
Mobilize (events platform) 87, 158
MobLab 71
Moulton, Seth 39, 74
Muskie, Edmund 7

National Study of Learning, Voting, and Engagement (NSLVE) 102

NGP-VAN 54–55, 67
Nagle, Dave 81
Nevada 23, 88, 150–151
New Hampshire 4, 7, 14n7, 37, 121, 145–146, 150
NextGen 46n9, 53, 85–86, 101, 119, 140
Nixon, Richard 5–7, 83, 155
North Iowa Wing Ding 72–73; *see also* Wing Ding

Obama, Barack 8, 14n10, 15n11, 27, 67–68, 70, 79–80, 83–84, 86, 136, 150
Obamacare 80, 107; *see also* Affordable Care Act
Obradovich, Kathie 128
Ocasio-Cortez, Alexandria 13, 123
Ohio 154
O'Malley, Martin 44, 94
O'Malley Dillon, Jen 27
Omar, Ilhan 107, 123
One Iowa 82 107
one-on-ones 42–43
Oregon 4
O'Rourke, Beto 21, 27, 61, 106, 110n10, 114, 123, 150, 153

PACs *see* political action committees (PACs)
Parker, Lauren 33–34, 69, 74–75, 95, 118, 122, 139
party registration 35, 54, 100, 102, 110n12
Patrick, Deval 151
Paul, Rand 116
peer-to-peer (P2P) texting 69–70, 76n5
Pelosi, Nancy 13, 141n1
Perez, Tom 87–88, 147, 149
Perry, Rick 65
phone canvases 98–100
Plouffe, David 41
Police Benevolent Association 60, 155
political action committees (PACs) 53, 85–87, 90n9, 115, 119, 140
Polk County Democrats' Steak Fry 106–109
Price, Troy 37, 82, 147, 149
primaries: 1952 150; 1968 4–5, 82; 1972 6; 2008 8; 2012 8; 2016 9–10; 2018 101; 2020 11, 34, 36, 83, 134, 150; California 150; debates 65, 75n1; direct 4; first, as designation 37; indirect 4; New Hampshire 151; Rule 10A and 7; rules for 34–38; single national 165; South Carolina 150–152
Progressives 4

Quad City River Bandits 116

RAYGUN 117, 157
Reagan, Ronald 83
Rebik, Misty 27
relational organizing 67–69, 105
Republican Party: 2012 primary of 8–9; 2016 primary of 9; data technology and 87; *see also* convention; Trump, Donald
Republican Party of Iowa (RPI) 9, 113
Riffe, Verne 58
Romney, Mitt 9
Rottenberg, Janice 27
RPI *see* Republican Party of Iowa (RPI),
Rule 10A 7
Ryan, Tim 39, 57, 60
Rynard, Pat 129, 166

Sabato, Larry 46n12
Salas, Rachel 41–43, 122, 139
Sanders, Bernie 9–10, 13, 27–29, 36, 41, 44, 60–61, 70–73, 79–80, 89, 94, 106–108, 110n10, 136, 145–148, 150–154, 156–158, 164
Sanford, Mark 90n4
Santorum, Rick 9
Sasse, Ben 18
Schaffner, Brian 10
SDEs *see* state delegate equivalents (SDEs)
Sebian-Lander, Cynthia 26–27
selfie-line 109n6
Selzer, Ann 128, 137
Sestak, Joe 39, 48, 57
Shadow, Inc. 148
Shelton, Danny 53
Silberman, Michael 71
Silver, Nate 10
Skelley, Geoffrey 23
"snowflake model" 67–68
South Carolina 150–152
Squad *see* "Gang of Four"
Stafford, Zach 108
state campaign directors 26–27
state delegate equivalents (SDEs) 36, 95, 131–132, 145–146, 148; *see also* delegate apportionment
Steak Fry 106–109
Steyer, Tom 48, 85, 110n10, 123, 164
superdelegates 83–84, 158
Super Tuesday 122, 150, 152–153
Swalwell, Eric 39, 67

tariffs 49
"team model" 67–68
technology 69–71, 86–89, 155–158; *see also* data; VAN

texting, peer-to-peer 69–70, 76n5
third-party votes 10
Trump, Donald 2; in 2016 primary 9, 100; 2020 nomination of 90n4; COVID-19 pandemic and 154–155; Delaney and 18; Floyd protests and 155; impeachment of 134, 141n1; rural voters and 165; Sanders supporters and 10; tariffs and 49
Turner, Nina 29, 136

UBI *see* Universal Basic Income (UBI)
Ukraine 141n1
"unique donors" 66–67, 74, 95, 109n4
United Auto Workers (UAW) 56–57
Unity Reform Commission 36–37, 83, 88, 164
Universal Basic Income (UBI) 19, 102, 155
University of Iowa 101–102

VAN 54–55, 67, 70, 86, 97–100, 104, 120, 135
Vedantam, Shankar 118
Vietnam War 4–5, 141n4
Vilsack, Tom 55, 84, 157
Virginia 46n12
virtual caucuses 37–38, 62n1, 87–89, 134, 141n5, 141n7, 149, 151, 156
voter files 54–55, 86, 116; *see also* VAN

Wahls, Zach 58–59, 84
Walsh, Joe 90n4
Warren, Elizabeth 21, 26–27, 44, 48, 79–80, 95–98, 100, 102, 107–108, 109n6, 122–123, 124n4, 146–147, 151, 156, 164
"weekend of action" 98
Weld, Bill 90n4
West, Cornel 136
Wilkins, Tony 117–118
Williams, Jonathan 138–139
Williamson, Marianne 38, 66
Wilson, James Q. 98
Winebrenner, Hugh 29n2
Winfrey, Oprah 38, 135
Wing Ding 72–73; *see also* North Iowa Wing Ding
Wisconsin 4, 154
Wyoming 154

Yang, Andrew 19–20, 102–103, 109, 110n10, 123, 140, 151, 155

Zeleny, Jeff 128, 130

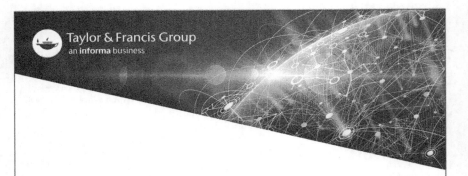